Critical ISSUES in EDUCATION

For Meg Kaeper
a small token of my appreciation
for the many kindnesses you and Richard
showed to an awkward young man
many years ago

Critical Issues in Education

An Anthology of Readings

Edited by
Eugene F. PROVENZO, Jr.
University of Miami

For information:

Sage Publications, Inc.
2455 Teller Road
Thousand Oaks, California 91320
E-mail: order@sagepub.com

Sage Publications Ltd.
1 Oliver's Yard
55 City Road
London EC1Y 1SP
United Kingdom

Sage Publications India Pvt. Ltd.
B-42, Panchsheel Enclave
Post Box 4109
New Delhi 110 017 India

Printed in the United States of America

Library of Congress Cataloging-in-Publication Data

Critical issues in education : an anthology of readings / Eugene F. Provenzo, editor.
p. cm.
Includes bibliographical references and index.
ISBN 1-4129-3655-1 (cloth : alk. paper) — ISBN 1-4129-0477-3 (pbk. : alk. paper) 1. Education—United States—History. 2. Educational law and legislation—United States—History. I. Provenzo, Eugene F.

LA212.C75 2006
370.973—dc22

2005033475

This book is printed on acid-free paper.

06 07 08 09 10 9 8 7 6 5 4 3 2 1

Acquisitions Editor: Diane McDaniel
Editorial Assistant: Erica Carroll
Production Editor: Denise Santoyo
Typesetter: C&M Digitals (P) Ltd.
Indexer: Jeanne Busemeyer

Contents

Acknowledgments ix
Credit Lines ix

Preface xi
Educational Thought in Western Culture xi

Introduction xiii

PROLOGUE: MODERN AND POSTMODERN THOUGHT 1

1. "Orientation" Editorial for *The Social Frontier* (1934) 7
George S. Counts

2. "The Need for Transcendence in the Postmodern World" (1994) 12
Vaclav Havel

PART I: THE AIMS OF EDUCATION 19

3. "My Pedagogic Creed" (1897) 22
John Dewey

4. *Cardinal Principles of Secondary Education* (1918) 32
National Education Association

5. "A Morally Defensible Mission for Schools in the 21st Century" (1997) 39
Nel Noddings

PART II: SOCIETY AND EDUCATION 49

6. Selection From *Notes on the State of Virginia* (1781) 53
Thomas Jefferson

7. "Thoughts Upon the Mode of Education Proper in a Republic" (1786) 58
Benjamin Rush

8. Selections From *Report No. 12 of the Massachusetts School Board* (1848) 62
Horace Mann

9. Selection From *Dare the Schools Build a New Social Order?* (1932) 76
George S. Counts

PART III: COMPULSORY SCHOOLING, EDUCATION, AND THE TRANSMISSION OF CULTURE **81**

10. Massachusetts Compulsory School Law (1852) 84
General Court of Massachusetts

11. Selection From *Compulsory Mis-Education* (1964) 88
Paul Goodman

12. "Vulnerability and Education" (1966) 92
Jules Henry

13. "The Banking Model of Education" (1970) 106
Paulo Freire

14. "Why We Must Disestablish School" (1970) 120
Ivan Illich

PART IV: SEXUALITY AND EDUCATION **135**

15. Selection From *A Vindication of the Rights of Woman* (1792) 138
Mary Wollstonecraft

16. Seneca Falls Declaration (1848) 142
Elizabeth Cady Stanton

17. Equal Rights Amendment (1921) 146
Alice Paul

18. Title IX (1972) 148
Congress of the United States of America

19. "The Absent Presence: Patriarchy, Capitalism, and the Nature of Teacher Work" (1987) 154
Patti Lather

20. "A Queer Youth" (1996) 168
Paul H. Cottell Jr.

21. "How and Why Boys Under-Achieve" (2000) 174
Wendy Bradford and Colin Noble

PART V: RACE, MULTICULTURALISM, AND EDUCATION **181**

22. Laws Prohibiting the Education of Slaves (1830–1832) 184
General Assembly of the State of North Carolina; General Assembly of the Commonwealth of Virginia; and the General Assembly of Alabama

23. "Industrial Education for the Negro" (1903) 188
Booker T. Washington

24. "The Talented Tenth" (1903) 192
W. E. B. Du Bois

25. "A Talk to Teachers" (1963) 198
James Baldwin

26. Education for All Handicapped Children Act (1975) 206
Congress of the United States of America

27. "Border Pedagogy in the Age of Postmodernism" (1988) 210
Henry Giroux

28. "Multicultural Education and School Reform" (2001) 228
Sonia Nieto

PART VI: SOCIAL CLASS AND EDUCATION **245**

29. Selection From *Pygmalion in the Classroom* (1968) 248
Robert Rosenthal and Lenore Jacobson

30. "Social Class and the Hidden Curriculum of Work" (1980) 254
Jean Anyon

31. "Crossing Class Boundaries" (2000) 272
bell hooks

PART VII: TECHNOLOGY AND EDUCATION **283**

32. *Augmenting Human Intellect* (1962) 286
Douglas Engelbart

33. "How Computers Contribute to the Ecological Crisis" (1990) 289
C. A. Bowers

34. "The Field: Knowledge in Computerized Societies" (1979) 297
Jean-François Lyotard

Author Index **303**

Subject Index **305**

About the Editor **313**

Acknowledgments

This book was completed as part of a sabbatical from the University of Miami in the spring of 2005. Thanks go to Dean Sam Yarger and Jeanne Schumm for supporting my scholarship and teaching. Special thanks go to my wife Asterie Baker Provenzo, as always my best editor and critic, and to my editor at Sage, Diane McDaniel, who saw to it that this book was shorter and better, and to her assistant Erica Carroll, who made sure that it fit together and that all its Is were dotted and its Ts were crossed.

Finally, I would like to thank the reviewers whose feedback helped me shape this book so that it will best serve the needs of students and instructors:

Wendy H. Atwell-Vasey, University of Mary Washington

Thomas S. Dickinson, DePauw University

Anne DiPardo, University of Iowa

Kathy Hytten, Southern Illinois University

Patrick A. Roberts, National-Louis University

Credit Lines

Chapter 11: From Goodman, P., *Compulsory Mis-Education and the Community of Schools*, copyright ©1962, 1964 by Paul Goodman. Used by permission of Random House.

Chapter 12: From Henry, J., "Vulnerability and Education," from *Teachers College Record*, vol. 68, no. 2, copyright © 1966. Used with permission of Teachers College Record.

Chapter 13: From Freire, Paulo, *Pedagogy of the Oppressed*, copyright © 1970. Reprinted with permission of Continuum Publishing Company via Copyright Clearance Center.

Chapter 14: From Illich, I., "Why We Must Disestablish School," in *Deschooling Society* (New York: Harper and Row, 1970). Reprinted with permission from the estate of Ivan Illich.

Chapter 19: From Lather, P., "The Absent Presence: Patriarchy, Capitalism, and the Nature of Teacher Work," *Teacher Education Quarterly*, 1987, 14(2): 25–38. Reprinted with permission.

Chapter 20: From Cottell, Jr. P. H., "A Queer Youth," *Harvard Educational Review, 66*(2), Summer 1996, pp. 185–188. Reprinted with permission of Harvard Business School.

Chapter 21: From Bradford, W., "How and Why Boys Under-Achieve," Bradford, W. Noble, C. & Wragg, T. (Eds.) *Getting It Right for Boys—and Girls.* Copyright © 2000. Reprinted with permission from Taylor & Francis.

Chapter 25: "A Talk to Teachers." Originally published in *Saturday Review*, ©1963 by James Baldwin. Copyright renewed. Collected in *The Price of the Ticket*, published by St. Martin's Press. Reprinted by arrangement with the James Baldwin Estate.

Chapter 27: From Giroux, H., "Border Pedagogy in the Age of Postmodernism," in *Journal of Education*, 170, 162–181, copyright © 1988. Reprinted with permission.

Chapter 28: From Nieto, Sonia, *Language, Culture, and Teaching*, copyright © 2002. Reprinted by permission of Lawrence Erlbaum Associates, Inc.

Chapter 29: From Rosenthal, R. and Jacobson, L., *Pygmalion in the Classroom*. Copyright © 1968. Reprinted by permission of Ardent Media.

Chapter 30: From Anyon, J., "Social Class and the Hidden Curriculum of Work," in *Rereading America: Cultural Contexts for Critical Thinking and Writing*, edited by Gary Colombo, et al. St. Martin's, 1992, 521–540. Reprinted with permission.

Chapter 31: From hooks, b., *Where We Stand: Class Matters*, copyright © 2000 by Routledge Publishing, Inc. Reproduced with permission of Routledge Publishing, Inc in the format Textbook via Copyright Clearance Center.

Chapter 33: From Bowers, C. A., "How Computers Contribute to the Ecological Crisis," in *CPSR Newsletter, 8*(3), Summer, 1990. Reprinted with permission.

Chapter 34: From Lyotard, Jean-François., *The Postmodern Condition* (1979), Manchester University Press, 1984. Reprinted with permission.

Preface

Educational Thought in Western Culture

This is a critical text reader of modern and postmodern educational thought. It focuses on Western educational writers and thinkers. As with any compilation of this type, it is selective. Within the limits of the space provided, I, as editor, have tried to be as inclusive as possible. In addition to this Preface, an Introduction, and a Prologue, there are seven major themes around which the readings included were selected:

1. The Aims of Education
2. Society and Education
3. Compulsory Schooling, Education, and the Transmission of Culture
4. Sexuality and Education
5. Race, Multiculturalism, and Education
6. Social Class and Education
7. Technology and Education

Each theme includes modern and postmodern works. In addition to an introductory essay that provides an overview of Educational Thought in Western Culture, shorter essays (including critical questions) introduce each thematic section. Brief introductions with selected questions are also provided before each selection.

This work is consciously interdisciplinary. It is not, however, a work in the philosophy of education. Nor was this work compiled and annotated by a philosopher but instead by a social and cultural theorist, originally trained as a historian of education with secondary training in the philosophy of education and ethnography. This can be regarded as a work in intellectual history and the sociology of knowledge, as well as a work of convenience, a reference tool, a portable library—ideally a useful resource for students, teachers, and scholars.

As mentioned earlier, this book is not intended to be a source book in the philosophy of education. I assume that educational thought reflects a larger range of thought than what comes under the definition of "philosophy." Thus, while the work of the great educational philosopher John Dewey is included, so too is the work of the anthropologist and sociologist Jules Henry, the novelist James Baldwin, and the cultural theorist and feminist bell hooks.

Approximately three fourths of the book is devoted to postmodern writers. This is the case not because the work of postmodern theorists is superior or necessarily more lasting than earlier theorists but because their work is of our own era, and in its immediacy, focused on themes that are our own. An editor and commentator in years to come will almost certainly create a new volume that will supersede the selections made here.

There is a huge amount of material that could have been included in this volume. The initial draft from which this work was cut was nearly four times as long. I have selected essays primarily on the basis of their fitting into one of the seven themes for the book. In general, I have followed the rule that any single work should not take up more than approximately ten published pages. This was an arbitrary decision—what seemed to be a reasonable way of getting as much representation of different authors as possible. Some works are excerpted. As often as possible, I have attempted to include complete works rather than selections—in some cases, choosing pieces of lesser importance than some longer works. For example, John Dewey's "My Pedagogic Creed" was chosen over a more extended selection from his masterwork *Democracy and Education.* I do not wish to suggest the superiority of the shorter piece over the longer, only its better fit in a compilation of this sort.

Finally, I wish to emphasize that this book is described as a "critical reader." I have tried to select texts that are important, provocative, and inherently interesting and which will lead the reader to reflect critically on the meaning of education and schooling in American culture. My introductions to the various parts of the book, as well as the individual selections, are intended to help the reader think and reflect on the meaning and significance of this collection of diverse and important authors.

—*Eugene F. Provenzo, Jr.*

Introduction

In Plato's *Apology,* Socrates (469–399 BCE) comments, "The unexamined life is not worth living for a human being."[1] One can make a similar argument for educators: Being involved in the educational process, whether at the elementary, secondary, or university level, requires one to reflect on the meaning of education—that is, teaching, schooling, and learning. Unfortunately, examining one's life and one's purpose as an educator is seen by many as a luxury, worth neither the time nor the effort necessary. Such a point of view, unfortunately, disconnects many educators from a critical understanding of the work that they do, as well as from the insights of those who have come before them. The pages that follow provide a basic foundation for understanding educational thought and for reflecting on the nature and meaning of education in contemporary culture.

In the West, educational thought can be traced back to Antiquity. Mention of the work of teachers and students can be found in most ancient civilizations. At Sumer (modern Iran), approximately 5,000 years ago, for example, there were written cuneiform records of teachers and their work with students.[2] Educational thought, however, truly began to flourish with the Ancient Greeks and Romans. In the case of Ancient Greece, the philosopher Plato, in his discussions of the ideas of Socrates, developed a fully articulated "philosophy of education," one in which learning takes place through the process of a teacher asking students key questions—what has come to be known as the "Socratic Method."

In his dialogue *The Republic,* Plato (427–347 BCE) argued that different students should receive various types of educations based on their individual interests, abilities, and stations in life. His ideal—some would say utopian ideal—was to create an educational program that would produce philosopher kings or guardians who could effectively rule the State.[3]

Plato's student Aristotle (348–322 BCE) felt that education should be controlled by the State and that individuals learned to be morally virtuous through practice. Thus, as Aristotle argued in *The Ethics,* people "become just by performing just acts, temperate by performing temperate ones, brave by performing brave ones."[4] Thus, education was intended to form the child and help him or her become a more virtuous individual through the process of doing the right thing or acting in a moral way. Education, in Aristotle's philosophy, was seen as being valuable in and of itself—in other words, the process of learning was intrinsically valuable—ultimately good for the individual and the society of which he or she was a part.

There is an important tradition of late Ancient and Medieval writers who address educational issues. The Roman writer Quintilian (35–95), for example, in his *Institutio oratoria,* outlined a model for educating an ideal citizen/orator. In doing so, he defines the curriculum of the Trivium and the Quadrivium, which is followed by schools and universities into the beginning of the 20th century.[5] A few centuries later, Saint Augustine (354–430) developed a philosophy of education in which learners must be aroused by the teacher to discover that which they already hold within themselves.[6]

It is not the purpose of this book to focus on the work of Ancient, Medieval, Renaissance, or even early modern writers on education. While the work of figures such as Thomas Aquinas (1225–1274), Desiderius Erasmus (1466–1536), Jean-Jacques Rousseau (1712–1778), and Johann Friedrich Herbart (1776–1841) could be easily included in this book, I focus largely on contemporary writers. In those cases where I have included older sources, it is because I feel that their ideas are still at work in American education. Thus, I have included selections from late eighteenth-century theorists such as Benjamin Rush (1745–1813), Horace Mann (1796–1859), and John Dewey (1859–1952).

As outlined in the Prologue, I believe that American culture, and in turn education, has gone through a startling transformation in recent years, particularly since the early 1980s. Many factors have contributed to this phenomenon. The introduction of new technologies such as cable television, video and CDs, and most important, inexpensive network computing—that is, the Internet and the World Wide Web—have all transformed education. Changes have also taken place elsewhere. The extension of civil rights not only to minorities but also to women has profoundly changed the character of the culture, as have changes in the structure of traditional families and the workforce.

The authors that I have included in this book tend to reflect this postmodern perspective. I value the views of the authors included in this volume because they tend to tell us much that is useful about who and what we are as a culture and society and, more important in the context of the courses this book will be used for, how and why our educational system functions the way it does.

As you begin to read the various selections included in this book, try to maintain a critical perspective. This is something that I feel is increasingly being lost in American education. Why do we teach what we teach? Who is assigned privilege and advantage by the educational system and why? and so on. These are examples of questions that need to be asked. As you will see, each thematic section of this book, in fact, each selection, raises fundamentally important questions. These questions, and your ability to reflect critically on their importance to the educational system and the culture, are at the center of what I am trying to accomplish with this book. The selected readings are important because they expose you to different perspectives, new ideas, and novel ways of viewing education and society. But it is the questions that I have posed for you, and ultimately the new ones that you ask yourself, that are really important.

Ideally, you will use this book not just for background but also as a means of generating classroom discussion. Think long and hard, reflect, and like the child who has the courage to declare that the emperor is not wearing any clothes, do not be afraid to recognize the truth of what you have learned.

Notes

1. Plato. 1977. *Euthyphro, Apology of Socrates, and Crito,* edited with notes by John Burnet, 38A. Oxford: Clarendon Press.
2. Kramer, Samuel Noah. 1989. *History Begins at Sumer: Thirty-nine Firsts in Man's Recorded History.* Philadelphia: University of Pennsylvania Press.
3. See Hamilton, E., and Cairns, H., eds. 1961. *Plato: Collected Dialogues.* Princeton, N.J.: Princeton University Press. For background on Plato's philosophy of education, see Nettleship, R. L. 1935. *The Theory of Education in Plato's Republic.* Oxford: Clarendon Press.
4. Thomson, J. A. K., trans. 1976. *The Ethics of Aristotle,* 91–92 (1103b). London: Penguin Books.
5. Quintilian. c1951. *Institutio oratoria,* with an English summary and concordance by Charles Edgar Little. Nashville, Tenn.: George Peabody College for Teachers.
6. Augustine's *De Magistro* "On the Teacher." See *Augustine and Liberal Education,* edited by Kim Paffenroth and Kevin L. Hughes. 2000. Aldershot, U.K.: Ashgate.

Prologue

Modern and Postmodern Thought

Western thinking has been dominated since the middle of the eighteenth century by a philosophy of modernism. Modernism focuses on the idea of the autonomous individual as the primary source of meaning and truth in contemporary culture. Innovation and progress are valued over dogma and tradition. Scientific ways of testing and knowing the world take precedence over faith and traditional systems of knowledge. Reason dominates.

Some theorists refer to modernism as the *Enlightenment Project.* Its roots lie in the late Renaissance. It saw the rejection of a magical and mystical world. Its place was taken by a world of science, reason, and supposed objectivity. Faith in science and the idea of progress became a dominant theme in Western intellectual thought.

In the field of education, the American philosopher John Dewey (1859–1952) demonstrated his belief in science and the scientific method when he stated, "Ultimately and philosophically, science is the organ of general social progress."[1] It is a scientific model that has dominated educational thought and reform since the beginning of the twentieth century.

Underlying this model has been the belief that the process of teaching could be reduced down to highly controllable methods and techniques. Psychologists interested in the process of learning, such as Edward Thorndike (1874–1949) and B. F. Skinner (1904–1990), believed that learning involved very specific and repeatable operations or procedures and could ultimately be precisely understood through research based on scientific experimentation.

In reality, scientific models of education have proved less productive than had originally been hoped. In general, over the last twenty-five to thirty years, many scholars have become increasingly skeptical about how much science can help us understand education and society in general. Issues may be too complex, and science too limited, to provide answers about how the world actually works. This certainly seems to be the case in terms of education, which is a far "messier" field than the advocates of scientific models of learning seem to have taken into account. Many individuals have abandoned a purely scientific approach and argue instead that we must deal with the realities of a *postmodern* society or culture.

Postmodernism, by definition, challenges modernist and scientific assumptions. Essentially it argues that a new type of culture and society emerged during the decades following World War II. Postmodernism asks if science is necessarily progressive and will improve our lives. It also challenges the objectivity of science.

An example can be seen by looking at research on nuclear science from a postmodern perspective: Is the world better off because of scientific experimentation with the atom? In some regards, yes. No one who has benefited from a medical technology such as radiation treatment for cancer would argue against its benefits. But what about the victims of Hiroshima and Nagasaki? What is their opinion concerning the benefits regarding the use of the atom?

In this context, the educational theorist Henry A. Giroux argues that we have entered a new period of historical time—that is, a postmodern era:

> Postmodernism in the broadest sense refers to an intellectual position, a form of cultural criticism, as well as to an emerging set of social, cultural, and economic conditions that have come to characterize the age of global capitalism and industrialism. In the first instance, postmodernism represents a form of cultural criticism that radically questions the logic of foundations that has become the epistemological cornerstone of modernism. . . . Postmodernism refers to an increasingly radical change in the relations of production, the nature of the nation-state, the development of new technologies that have redefined the fields of telecommunications and information processing, and the forces at work in the growing globalization and interdependence of the economic, political and cultural spheres.[2]

Other theorists use the term *post-fordism* to describe the complex culture and economic system that has been coming into existence in recent years. According to Stuart Hall,

> "Post-Fordism" is a [broad] term suggesting a whole new epoch distinct from the era of mass production. . . . It covers at least some of the following characteristics: a shift to the new information "technologies"; more flexible, decentralized forms of labor process and work organization; decline of the old manufacturing base and the growth of the "sunrise," computer-based industries; the hiving off or contracting out of functions and services; a greater emphasis on choice and product differentiation, on marketing, packaging, and design, on the "targeting" of consumers by lifestyle, taste, and culture rather than by the categories of social class; a decline in the proportion of the skilled, male, manual working class, the rise of the service industry and "white-collar" classes and the "feminization" of the work force; an economy dominated by the multinationals, with their new international division of labor and their greater autonomy from nation-state control; and the "globalization" of the new financial markets, limited by the communications revolution.[3]

The changes that are part of a postmodern or post-fordian culture are profoundly important in terms of the field of education. Think about the changes that have taken place in American culture since the early 1980s—changes that reflect the emergence of a postmodern culture. Think about the proliferation of personal computers, the Internet and World Wide Web, drugs such as crack cocaine (introduced in the mid-1980s), and AIDS (not even identified as a disease until 1981). Think about *perestroika* and the end of the Soviet Empire, or the rise of China as an economic and political force. Think about changes in the economy (women increasingly entering the workforce), changes in family structures (the growth in the divorce rate), 9/11 and the war on terrorism, and other postmodern forces that have shaped American and world culture in recent years. What roles have these issues and events played in the creation of a new world order?

What does it mean for the United States to be the only military superpower in the world? What does it mean when American children spend more time watching television than going to school? What does it mean when the San Diego Padres baseball team sells sushi as a snack at its games (not just hot dogs, peanuts, popcorn, and cracker jacks)? These are indications of the emergence of a new culture and society in America. How do these facts, in turn, shape and influence what it means to be educated and the activities of schools and the teachers who work in them?

The following selections by George Counts and Vaclav Havel address the types of changes that we are talking about that represent postmodern forces at work. The editorial by Counts was written in 1934 at the height of the Great Depression. It is included because it anticipates, to a remarkable degree, changes that would dominate American culture and education by the end of the century. It is also important because it assigns a special role to education in the creation of the new social system.

In the case of Havel's 1995 speech/essay, "The Need for Transcendence in the Postmodern World," we have one of modern Europe's most celebrated intellectuals describing the emergence of a postmodern culture and the need for contemporary men and women to transcend its limitations.

These two pieces are included in this work as a prologue because they set in context where and what our culture is currently about and, ultimately, what it means to teach and learn in a postmodern culture. Closely related is the piece by Jean-François Lyotard (Chapter 34).

As you read these two selections, keep in mind the following questions:

1. How does postmodernism change the experience of teachers working in the schools?
2. How does postmodernism change the experience of learners and the process of learning?

Notes

1. Dewey, John. 1916. *Democracy and Education*, 239. New York: Macmillan.
2. Aronowitz, Stanley, and Giroux, Henry. 1991. *Postmodern Education: Politics, Culture, and Social Criticism*, 62. Minneapolis: University of Minnesota Press.
3. Quoted in Giroux, Henry, and McLaren, Peter, eds. 1994. *Between Borders: Pedagogy and the Politics of Cultural Studies*, 12. New York: Routledge.

1

"Orientation" Editorial for The Social Frontier *(1934)*

In 1934, the educational theorist George S. Counts (1889–1974), together with other faculty from Teachers College, Columbia University, began the journal *The Social Frontier.* The magazine, which was published until 1943, represented the most intellectually vital and revolutionary journal published in the United States dealing with education and society to emerge from the period prior to World War II.

The initial editorial for the magazine, written by Counts, is a remarkably prophetic piece. According to Counts, American and world culture were in a process of profound transformation, moving from an agrarian to a new urban industrial order. Americans had no choice but to be involved in a process of social reconstruction in which "they must choose whether the great tradition of democracy is to pass away with the individualistic economy to which it has been linked historically or is to undergo the transformation necessary for survival in an age of close economic interdependence."

Counts and his editorial board for *The Social Frontier,* which included figures such as John Dewey and William Heard Kilpatrick, saw the schools, and particularly teachers, playing a critical role in the reinvention of American culture—one that was essential at the height of the Great Depression.

For Counts and his collaborators, education was more than what went on in schools: It represented "all of those formative influences and agencies which serve to induct the individual—whether old or young—into the life and culture of the group."

Counts's editorial anticipated, to a remarkable degree, the profound changes that would occur in American education and culture in the decades following World War II. Counts was clearly aware that changes in the American economy, as well as industrial and technological advances, represented the emergence of a set of forces that would profoundly redefine the meaning of democracy. His ideas are particularly interesting in light of the emergence of the postmodern and global culture that is outlined in the essay by Vaclav Havel, included in this section, as well as the selection by Jean-François Lyotard, included in the Technology and Education section at the conclusion of this book.

As you read Counts's editorial, consider the following questions:

1. How do changes in technology potentially affect the democratic process, as well as the work of educators? Reflect on the impact of technologies such as computers—specifically, personal computers and the Internet—and their role in transforming education, knowledge, and the economy.
2. What are some of the potential sources for education in the culture, other than schools, that Counts referred to in his editorial? How are they different today when compared to 30, 50, and 100 years ago?

1

"Orientation" Editorial for The Social Frontier (1934)

George S. Counts

American Society, along with world society, is passing through an age of profound transition. This fact has been proclaimed with ever greater emphasis and frequency by the march of ideas and events since the Civil War and particularly since the opening of the present century. It is proclaimed in the advance of science, technology, and invention, in the growing mastery of natural forces, in the changing forms of economy and government, in the increasing instability of the whole social structure, in the swelling armaments and the intensification of international rivalries, and in the wars, revolutions, and social calamities which seem to have become the order of the day throughout the world. Also it is proclaimed in the obsolescence of inherited conceptions of human relationships, in the decline of faith in traditional moral and religious doctrines, in the popularity of cults of cynicism and disillusionment, and in the appearance of revolutionary political theories, philosophies, and programs.

While the transition presents many facets, in its basic terms in the United States it is a movement from a simple agrarian and trading economy to a highly complex urban and industrial order with agriculture transformed into single-crop specialties. Since the days of Andrew Jackson the nation has evolved out of a loose aggregation of relatively self-contained rural households and neighborhoods into a vast society marked by minute differentiation of structure and function, close integration of parts, and common dependence on a far-flung productive and distributive mechanism whose operation requires an ever increasing measure of cooperation, general planning, and unified direction.

Source: Counts, George S. 1934. "Orientation." *The Social Frontier* 1 (October): 3–4.

In a word, for the American people the age of individualism in economy is closing, and an age of collectivism is opening. Here is the central and dominating reality in the present epoch.

This fact means that the nation has entered a period freighted with unmeasured opportunities and responsibilities—a period when, in the words of Emerson, "the old and the new stand side by side, and admit of being compared; when the energies of all men are searched by fear and by hope; when the historic glories of the old can be compensated by the rich possibilities of the new era." In the years and decades immediately ahead the American people will be called upon to undertake arduous, hazardous, and crucial tasks of social reconstruction: they will be compelled to make some of the grand choices of history, to determine in which direction they are to move, to make decisions which will deeply affect the life of their country for generations and indeed for centuries—decisions concerning the incidence of economic and political power, the distribution of wealth and income, the relations of classes, races, and nationalities, and the ends for which men and women are to live. Moreover, owing to the revolutionary conquest of mechanical energy during the past one hundred years, the American people stand today on the threshold of unprecedented and unimagined potentialities of material and spiritual development. Also they stand in the imminent presence of economic collapse, political reaction, cultural regimentation, and war. They must choose among the diverse roads now opening before them. In particular they must choose whether the great tradition of democracy is to pass away with the individualistic economy to which it has been linked historically or is to undergo the transformation necessary for survival in an age of close economic interdependence.

In the making of these choices, persons and institutions engaged in the performance of educational functions will inevitably play an important role. To the extent that they operate in the real world, they will make their influence felt. Indeed, even if they should pursue a policy of evasion, in actual fact they would be throwing their influence on the side of outmoded anarchy and disorder. Whatever course they pursue, they will either retard or hasten the adjustment to the new realities; they will either make easy or difficult the transfer of the democratic ideal from individual to social foundations. They will be called upon, not only to bring the heritage of knowledge, thought, and attitude abreast of general social advance, but also to make broad choices concerning alliances to be consummated, values to be preserved, interests to be defended, social goals to be striven for.

Already a few voices have been raised within the ranks of educational workers in acceptance of the challenge of social reconstruction. But as yet these voices are too timid to be effective, too tentative to be convincing, and too individual to speak a language of clear-cut purpose. They belong to persons who singly and in isolation have captured this or the other meaning of unfolding events. Before these persons, and perhaps countless others who have thus far remained inarticulate, can hope to become a positive creative force in American society and education, they must come into closer communication, clarify their thought and purposes, draw like-minded individuals into their ranks, and merge isolated and discordant voices into a mighty instrument of group consensus, harmonious expression, and collective action. To contribute to the achievement of this object, [*The Social Frontier*] is being launched.

The journal makes no pretense to absolute objectivity and detachment, knowing such a goal to be impossible of achievement in that realm of practical affairs to which education belongs and in which positive decisions must be made. It represents a point of view, it has a frame of reference, it stands on a particular interpretation of American history. It accepts the analysis of the current epoch presented above and outlined in greater detail in *Conclusions and Recommendations, Report on the Social Studies* of the Commission of the American Historical Association.

The Social Frontier assumes that the age of individualism in economy is closing and that an age marked by close integration of social life and by collective planning and control is opening. For weal or woe it accepts as irrevocable this deliverance of the historical process. It intends to go forward to meet the new age and to proceed as rationally as possible to the realization of all possibilities for the enrichment and refinement of human life. It will nurse no fantasies of returning to the simple household and neighborhood economy of the time of Thomas Jefferson; it will seek no escape from the responsibilities of today, either by longing for a past now gone beyond recovery or by imagining a future bearing the features of Utopia. It proposes to take seriously the affirmation of the Declaration of Independence that "all men are created equal" and are entitled to "life, liberty, and the pursuit of happiness." Also it proposes, in the light of this great humanist principle applied to the collective realities of industrial civilization, to pass every important educational event, institution, theory, and program under critical review. Finally, it will devote its pages positively to the development of the thought of all who are interested in making education discharge its full responsibility in the present age of social transition. Its editorial staff and board of directors hope that it will help fight the great educational battles—practical and theoretical—which are already looming above the horizon. And they trust that it will engage in the battles of the twentieth and not of the eighteenth century.

The Social Frontier acknowledges allegiance to no narrow conception of education. While recognizing the school as society's central educational agency, it refuses to *limit* itself to a consideration of the work of this institution. On the contrary, it includes within its field of interest all of those formative influences and agencies which serve to induct the individual—whether old or young—into the life and culture of the group. It regards education as an aspect of a culture in process of evolution. It therefore has no desire to promote a restricted and technical professionalism. Rather does it address itself to the task of considering the broad role of education in advancing the welfare and interests of the great masses of the people who do the work of society—those who labor on farms and ships and in the mines, shops, and factories of the world.

2

"The Need for Transcendence in the Postmodern World" (1994)

Vaclav Havel (1936–) is a celebrated Czech writer and dramatist, as well as the last President of Czechoslovakia and the first President of the Czech Republic. He delivered this speech in Independence Hall, Philadelphia, on July 4, 1994. In it, Havel argues that we are in a transitional period, one that is seeing the end of an era of modernism and the emergence of something new—postmodernism.

Havel makes clear that what we are going through is not something new but similar to other transitional periods, such as the Hellenistic era in the Ancient Mediterranean world or the Renaissance in Italy. As people experienced in earlier transitional periods, we are experiencing a mixing and blending of cultures, an amalgamation of world cultures, through the process of globalization.

According to Havel, in the new postmodern era, our modern faith in science and its objectivity is being challenged. The world is confusing, chaotic, and disturbing. There are no certainties or absolutes of the type found in more traditional cultures or in our own earlier history. Havel asks us to recognize that we, as living beings, are not just an accidental anomaly but somehow connected to the larger universe. In addition, we are not wholly autonomous beings but connected to the larger living organism that is the Earth (Gaia). For Havel, human beings have a transcendent quality—one that is anchored in our awareness that we are not alone, nor are we totally autonomous as human beings.

Havel's essay raises multiple questions for educators:

1. How does the postmodern experience change the meaning of learning, what needs to be learned, and, in turn, the work of teachers?
2. What should a postmodern curriculum look like? How can it help us achieve a transcendent understanding of the very fragile world in which we live?

2

"The Need for Transcendence in the Postmodern World" (1994)

Vaclav Havel

In this postmodern world, cultural conflicts are becoming more dangerous than at any time in history. A new model of coexistence is needed, based on man's transcending himself.

There are thinkers who claim that, if the modern age began with the discovery of America, it also ended in America. This is said to have occurred in the year 1969, when America sent the first men to the moon. From this historical moment, they say, a new age in the life of humanity can be dated.

I think there are good reasons for suggesting that the modern age has ended. Today, many things indicate that we are going through a transitional period, when it seems that something is on the way out and something else is painfully being born. It is as if something were crumbling, decaying, and exhausting itself, while something else, still indistinct, were arising from the rubble.

Periods of history when values undergo a fundamental shift are certainly not unprecedented. This happened in the Hellenistic period, when from the ruins of the classical world the Middle Ages were gradually born. It happened during the Renaissance, which opened the way to the modern era. The distinguishing features of such transitional periods are a mixing and blending of cultures and a plurality or parallelism of intellectual and spiritual worlds. These are periods when all consistent value systems collapse, when cultures distant in time and space are discovered or rediscovered. They are periods when there is a tendency to quote, to imitate, and to amplify, rather than to state with authority or integrate. New meaning is gradually born from the encounter, or the intersection, of many different elements.

Source: Havel, Vaclav. 1995. "The Need for Transcendence in the Postmodern World." *The Futurist* 29 (July–August): 46–50.

Today, this state of mind or of the human world is called postmodernism. For me, a symbol of that state is a Bedouin mounted on a camel and clad in traditional robes under which he is wearing jeans, with a transistor radio in his hands and an ad for Coca-Cola on the camel's back. I am not ridiculing this, nor am I shedding an intellectual tear over the commercial expansion of the West that destroys alien cultures. I see it rather as a typical expression of this multicultural era, a signal that an amalgamation of cultures is taking place. I see it as proof that something is happening, something is being born, that we are in a phase when one age is succeeding another, when everything is possible. Yes, everything is possible, because our civilization does not have its own unified style, its own spirit, its own aesthetic.

Science and Modern Civilization

This is related to the crisis, or to the transformation, of science as the basis of the modern conception of the world.

The dizzying development of this science, with its unconditional faith in objective reality and its complete dependency on general and rationally knowable laws, led to the birth of modern technological civilization. It is the first civilization in the history of the human race that spans the entire globe and firmly binds together all human societies, submitting them to a common global destiny. It was this science that enabled man, for the first time, to see Earth from space with his own eyes; that is, to see it as another star in the sky.

At the same time, however, the relationship to the world that modern science fostered and shaped now appears to have exhausted its potential. It is increasingly clear that, strangely, the relationship is missing something. It fails to connect with the most intrinsic nature of reality and with natural human experience. It is now more of a source of disintegration and doubt than a source of integration and meaning. It produces what amounts to a state of schizophrenia: Man as an observer is becoming completely alienated from himself as a being.

Classical modern science described only the surface of things, a single dimension of reality. And the more dogmatically science treated it as the only dimension, as the very essence of reality, the more misleading it became. Today, for instance, we may know immeasurably more about the universe than our ancestors did, and yet, it increasingly seems they knew something more essential about it than we do, something that escapes us. The same thing is true of nature and of ourselves. The more thoroughly all our organs and their functions, their internal structure, and the biochemical reactions that take place within them are described, the more we seem to fail to grasp the spirit, purpose, and meaning of the system that they create together and that we experience as our unique "self."

And thus today we find ourselves in a paradoxical situation. We enjoy all the achievements of modern civilization that have made our physical existence on this earth easier in so many important ways. Yet we do not know exactly what to do with ourselves, where to turn. The world of our experiences seems chaotic, disconnected, confusing. There appear to be no integrating forces, no unified meaning, no true inner understanding of phenomena in our experience of the world. Experts can explain anything in the objective world to us, yet we understand our own lives less and less. In short, we live in the postmodern world, where everything is possible and almost nothing is certain.

When Nothing Is Certain

This state of affairs has its social and political consequences. The single planetary civilization to which we all belong confronts us with global challenges. We stand helpless before them because our civilization has essentially globalized only the surface of our lives. But our inner self continues to have a life of its own. And the fewer answers the era of rational knowledge provides to the basic questions of human Being, the more deeply it would seem that people, behind its back as it were, cling to the ancient certainties of their tribe. Because of this, individual cultures, increasingly lumped together by contemporary civilization, are realizing with new urgency their own inner autonomy and the inner differences of others.

Cultural conflicts are increasing and are understandably more dangerous today than at any other time in history. The end of the era of rationalism has been catastrophic: Armed with the same supermodern weapons, often from the same suppliers, and followed by television cameras, the members of various tribal cults are at war with one another. By day, we work with statistics; in the evening, we consult astrologers and frighten ourselves with thrillers about vampires. The abyss between the rational and the spiritual, the external and the internal, the objective and the subjective, the technical and the moral, the universal and the unique, constantly grows deeper.

Politicians are rightly worried by the problem of finding the key to ensure the survival of a civilization that is global and at the same time clearly multicultural. How can generally respected mechanisms of peaceful coexistence be set up, and on what set of principles are they to be established?

These questions have been highlighted with particular urgency by the two most important political events in the second half of the twentieth century: the collapse of colonial hegemony and the fall of communism. The artificial world order of the past decades has collapsed, and a new, more-just order has not yet emerged. The central political task of the final years of this century, then, is the creation of a new model of coexistence among the various cultures, peoples, races, and religious spheres within a single interconnected civilization. This task is all the more urgent because other threats to contemporary humanity brought about by one-dimensional development of civilization are growing more serious all the time.

Many believe this task can be accomplished through technical means. That is, they believe it can be accomplished through the invention of new organizational, political, and diplomatic instruments. Yes, it is clearly necessary to invent organizational structures appropriate to the present multicultural age. But such efforts are doomed to failure if they do not grow out of something deeper, out of generally held values.

This, too, is well known. And in searching for the most natural source for the creation of a new world order, we usually look to an area that is the traditional foundation of modern justice and a great achievement of the modern age: to a set of values that—among other things—were first declared in this building (Independence Hall). I am referring to respect for the unique human being and his or her liberties and inalienable rights and to the principle that all power derives from the people. I am, in short, referring to the fundamental ideas of modern democracy.

What I am about to say may sound provocative, but I feel more and more strongly that even these ideas are not enough, that we must go farther and deeper. The point is that the solution they offer is still, as it were, modern, derived from the climate of the Enlightenment and from a view of man and his relation to the world that has been characteristic of the Euro-American sphere for the last two centuries. Today, however, we are in a different place and facing a different situation, one to which classically modern solutions in themselves do not give a satisfactory response. After all, the very principle of inalienable human rights, conferred on man by the Creator, grew out of the typically modern notion that man—as a being capable of knowing nature and the world—was the pinnacle of creation and lord of the world.

This modern anthropocentrism inevitably meant that He who allegedly endowed man with his inalienable rights began to disappear from the world: He was so far beyond the grasp of modern science that He was gradually pushed into a sphere of privacy of sorts, if not directly into a sphere of private fancy—that is, to a place where public obligations no longer apply. The existence of a higher authority than man himself simply began to get in the way of human aspirations.

Two Transcendent Ideas

The idea of human rights and freedoms must be an integral part of any meaningful world order. Yet, I think it must be anchored in a different place, and in a different way, than has been the case so far. If it is to be more than just a slogan mocked by half the world, it cannot be expressed in the language of a departing era, and it must not be mere froth floating on the subsiding waters of faith in a purely scientific relationship to the world.

Paradoxically, inspiration for the renewal of this lost integrity can once again be found in science, in a science that is new—let us say post-modern—a science producing ideas that in a certain sense allow it to transcend its own limits. I will give two examples:

The first is the Anthropic Cosmological Principle. Its authors and adherents have pointed out that from the countless possible courses of its evolution the universe took the only one that enabled life to emerge. This is not yet proof that the aim of the universe has always been that it should one day see itself through our eyes. But how else can this matter be explained?

I think the Anthropic Cosmological Principle brings us to an idea perhaps as old as humanity itself: that we are not at all just an accidental anomaly, the microscopic caprice of a tiny particle whirling in the endless depths of the universe. Instead, we are mysteriously connected to the entire universe, we are mirrored in it, just as the entire evolution of the universe is mirrored in us.

Until recently, it might have seemed that we were an unhappy bit of mildew on a heavenly body whirling in space among many that have no mildew on them at all. This was something that classical science could explain. Yet, the moment it begins to appear that we are deeply connected to the entire universe, science reaches the outer limits of its powers. Because it is founded on the search for universal laws, it cannot deal with singularity, that is, with uniqueness. The universe is a unique event and a unique story, and so far we are the unique point of that story. But unique events and stories are the domain of poetry, not science. With the formulation of the Anthropic Cosmological Principle, science has found itself on the border between formula and story, between science and myth. In that, however, science has paradoxically returned, in roundabout way, to man, and offers him—in new clothing—his lost integrity. It does so by anchoring him once more in the cosmos.

The second example is the Gaia Hypothesis. This theory brings together proof that the dense network of mutual interactions between the organic and inorganic portions of the earth's surface form a single system, a kind of mega-organism, a living planet—Gaia—named after an ancient goddess who is recognizable as an archetype of the Earth Mother in perhaps all religions. According to the Gaia Hypothesis, we are parts of a greater whole. Our destiny is not dependent merely on what we do for ourselves but also on what we do for Gaia as a whole. If we endanger her, she will dispense with us in the interests of a higher value—that is, life itself.

Toward Self-Transcendence

What makes the Anthropic Principle and the Gaia Hypothesis so inspiring? One simple thing: Both remind us, in modern language, of what we have long suspected, of what we have long projected into our forgotten myths and what perhaps has always lain dormant within us as archetypes. That is, the awareness of our being anchored in the earth and the universe, the awareness that we are not here alone nor for ourselves alone, but that we are an integral part of higher, mysterious entities against whom it is not advisable to blaspheme. This forgotten awareness is encoded in all religions. All cultures anticipate it in various forms. It is one of the things that form the basis of man's understanding of himself, of his place in the world, and ultimately of the world as such.

A modern philosopher once said: "Only a God can save us now."

Yes, the only real hope of people today is probably a renewal of our certainty that we are rooted in the earth and, at the same time, the cosmos. This awareness endows us with the capacity for self-transcendence. Politicians at international forums may reiterate a thousand times that the basis of the new world order must be universal respect for human rights, but it will mean nothing as long as this imperative does not derive from the respect of the miracle of Being, the miracle of the universe, the miracle of nature, the miracle of our own existence. Only someone who submits to the authority of the universal order and of creation, who values the right to be a part of it and a participant in it, can genuinely value himself and his neighbors, and thus honor their rights as well.

It logically follows that, in today's multicultural world, the truly reliable path to coexistence, to peaceful coexistence and creative cooperation, must start from what is at the root of all cultures and what lies infinitely deeper in human hearts and minds than political opinion, convictions, antipathies, or sympathies—it must be rooted in self-transcendence:

- Transcendence as a hand reached out to those close to us, to foreigners, to the human community, to all living creatures, to nature, to the universe.
- Transcendence as a deeply and joyously experienced need to be in harmony even with what we ourselves are not, what we do not understand, what seems distant from us in time and space, but with which we are nevertheless mysteriously linked because, together with us, all this constitutes a single world.
- Transcendence as the only real alternative to extinction.

The Declaration of Independence states that the Creator gave man the right to liberty. It seems man can realize that liberty only if he does not forget the One who endowed him with it.

PART I

The Aims of Education

Part I includes selections from authors who focus on the question, What is the aim or purpose of education? Implicit in many of these discussions are definitions of what education is and what it means to be educated.

In terms of the modern framing of the debate over what we should teach in the schools, perhaps no author is as important as Herbert Spencer (1820–1903). In his 1861 book *Education: Intellectual, Moral and Physical,* Spencer asked the fundamental question underlying not only all curriculum development but also education in general: "What knowledge is of most worth?"

It is this question, What is the aim or purpose of education? and its corollary, What is it that should be taught? that are among the most fundamental of all questions in the field of education.

As you read the following selections related to the aims of education, keep in mind the following questions:

1. In a democracy, who should determine what the aims of the educational system should be?
2. Should the aims or purposes of education be the same for all students, or should they be different for students with different needs?
3. How essential is it to have a personal aim as an educator—what Dewey referred to as a "pedagogic creed"? What might such a creed entail for you?

3

"My Pedagogic Creed" (1897)

John Dewey (1859–1952) is widely considered the premier philosopher of American culture, as well as its most innovative educational thinker. Beginning in the early 1890s, he focused on educational issues as a major aspect of his writing and thought. In 1894, he became a professor at the University of Chicago, where he founded the first laboratory school in the United States. The Laboratory School was particularly important because it provided Dewey a place to test out his educational theories in actual practice. While his first major work on education was *School and Society,* which was published in 1899, it was preceded two years earlier by his piece "My Pedagogic Creed," which outlines his personal educational philosophy and what he believed the aims of education should be.

Dewey's "Pedagogic Creed" is important because it defines his belief that education is not simply a process of transmission or transference but involves the child learning through an active process of participation in society. School, for Dewey, is primarily a social institution.

In reading Dewey's essay, consider the following questions:

1. What is implied by the assumption that learning by the student is ultimately a social act rather than simply a transfer of knowledge? How does this concept shape or influence what schools should be like?
2. What type of curriculum is best suited to learning on the part of the student? How does the curriculum found in most schools today conform to Dewey's ideas?
3. What would Dewey say about standardized testing and the type of curricular reforms that have been enacted in recent years as a result of legislation such as the No Child Left Behind Act?

3

"My Pedagogic Creed" (1897)

John Dewey

ARTICLE I—What Education Is

I believe that all education proceeds by the participation of the individual in the social consciousness of the race. This process begins unconsciously almost at birth, and is continually shaping the individual's powers, saturating his consciousness, forming his habits, training his ideas, and arousing his feelings and emotions. Through this unconscious education the individual gradually comes to share in the intellectual and moral resources which humanity has succeeded in getting together. He becomes an inheritor of the funded capital of civilization. The most formal and technical education in the world cannot safely depart from this general process. It can only organize it or differentiate it in some particular direction.

I believe that the only true education comes through the stimulation of the child's powers by the demands of the social situations in which he finds himself. Through these demands he is stimulated to act as a member of a unity, to emerge from his original narrowness of action and feeling, and to conceive of himself from the standpoint of the welfare of the group to which he belongs. Through the responses which others make to his own activities he comes to know what these mean in social terms. The value which they have is reflected back into them. For instance, through the response which is made to the child's instinctive babblings the child comes to know what those babblings mean; they are transformed into articulate language and thus the child is introduced into the consolidated wealth of ideas and emotions which are now summed up in language.

Source: Dewey, John. 1897. "My Pedagogic Creed." *The School Journal* 54 (January 16): 77–80.

I believe that this educational process has two sides—one psychological and one sociological—and that neither can be subordinated to the other or neglected without evil results following. Of these two sides, the psychological is the basis. The child's own instincts and powers furnish the material and give the starting point for all education. Save as the efforts of the educator connect with some activity which the child is carrying on of his own initiative independent of the educator, education becomes reduced to a pressure from without. It may, indeed, give certain external results, but cannot truly be called educative. Without insight into the psychological structure and activities of the individual, the educative process will, therefore, be haphazard and arbitrary. If it chances to coincide with the child's activity it will get a leverage; if it does not, it will result in friction, or disintegration, or arrest of the child nature.

I believe that knowledge of social conditions, of the present state of civilization, is necessary in order properly to interpret the child's powers. The child has his own instincts and tendencies, but we do not know what these mean until we can translate them into their social equivalents. We must be able to carry them back into a social past and see them as the inheritance of previous race activities. We must also be able to project them into the future to see what their outcome and end will be. In the illustration just used, it is the ability to see in the child's babblings the promise and potency of a future social intercourse and conversation which enables one to deal in the proper way with that instinct.

I believe that the psychological and social sides are organically related and that education cannot be regarded as a compromise between the two, or a superimposition of one upon the other. We are told that the psychological definition of education is barren and formal—that it gives us only the idea of a development of all the mental powers without giving us any idea of the use to which these powers are put. On the other hand, it is urged that the social definition of education, as getting adjusted to civilization, makes of it a forced and external process, and results in subordinating the freedom of the individual to a preconceived social and political status.

I believe that each of these objections is true when urged against one side isolated from the other. In order to know what a power really is we must know what its end, use, or function is; and this we cannot know save as we conceive of the individual as active in social relationships. But, on the other hand, the only possible adjustment which we can give to the child under existing conditions, is that which arises through putting him in complete possession of all his powers. With the advent of democracy and modern industrial conditions, it is impossible to foretell definitely just what civilization will be twenty years from now. Hence it is impossible to prepare the child for any precise set of conditions. To prepare him for the future life means to give him command of himself; it means so to train him that he will have the full and ready use of all his capacities; that his eye and ear and hand may be tools ready to command, that his judgment may be capable of grasping the conditions under which it has to work, and the executive forces be trained to act economically and efficiently. It is impossible to reach this sort of adjustment save as constant regard is had to the individual's own powers, tastes, and interests—say, that is, as education is continually converted into psychological terms.

In sum, I believe that the individual who is to be educated is a social individual and that society is an organic union of individuals. If we eliminate the social factor from the child we are left only with an abstraction; if we eliminate the individual factor from society, we are left only with an inert and lifeless mass. Education, therefore, must begin with a psychological insight into the child's capacities, interests, and habits. It must be controlled at every point by reference to these same considerations. These powers, interests, and habits must be continually interpreted; we must know what they mean. They must be translated into terms of their social equivalents—into terms of what they are capable of in the way of social service.

ARTICLE II—What the School Is

I believe that the school is primarily a social institution. Education being a social process, the school is simply that form of community life in which all those agencies are concentrated that will be most effective in bringing the child to share in the inherited resources of the race, and to use his own powers for social ends.

I believe that education, therefore, is a process of living and not a preparation for future living.

I believe that the school must represent present life—life as real and vital to the child as that which he carries on in the home, in the neighborhood, or on the playground.

I believe that education which does not occur through forms of life, or that are worth living for their own sake, is always a poor substitute for the genuine reality and tends to cramp and to deaden.

I believe that the school, as an institution, should simplify existing social life—should reduce it, as it were, to an embryonic form. Existing life is so complex that the child cannot be brought into contact with it without either confusion or distraction; he is either overwhelmed by the multiplicity of activities which are going on, so that he loses his own power of orderly reaction, or he is so stimulated by these various activities that his powers are prematurely called into play and he becomes either unduly specialized or else disintegrated.

I believe that as such simplified social life, the school life should grow gradually out of the home life, that it should take up and continue the activities with which the child is already familiar in the home.

I believe that it should exhibit these activities to the child and reproduce them in such ways that the child will gradually learn the meaning of them and be capable of playing his own part in relation to them.

I believe that this is a psychological necessity, because it is the only way of securing continuity in the child's growth, the only way of giving a background of past experience to the new ideas given in school.

I believe that it is also a social necessity because the home is the form of social life in which the child has been nurtured and in connection with which he has had his moral training. It is the business of the school to deepen and extend his sense of the values bound up in his home life.

I believe that much of present education fails because it neglects this fundamental principle of the school as a form of community life. It conceives the school as a place where certain information is to be given, where certain lessons are to be learned, or where certain habits are to be formed. The value of these is conceived as lying largely in the remote future; the child must do these things for the sake of something else he is to do; they are mere preparation. As a result they do not become a part of the life experience of the child and so are not truly educative.

I believe that the moral education centers upon this conception of the school as a mode of social life, that the best and deepest moral training is precisely that which one gets through having to enter into proper relations with others in a unity of work and thought. The present educational systems, so far as they destroy or neglect this unity, render it difficult or impossible to get any genuine, regular moral training.

I believe that the child should be stimulated and controlled in his work through the life of the community.

I believe that under existing conditions far too much of the stimulus and control proceeds from the teacher, because of neglect of the idea of the school as a form of social life.

I believe that the teacher's place and work in the school is to be interpreted from this same basis. The teacher is not in the school to impose certain ideas or to form certain habits in the child, but is there as a member of the community to select the influences which shall affect the child and to assist him in properly responding to these influences.

I believe that the discipline of the school should proceed from the life of the school as a whole and not directly from the teacher.

I believe that the teacher's business is simply to determine on the basis of larger experience and riper wisdom, how the discipline of life shall come to the child.

I believe that all questions of the grading of the child and his promotion should be determined by reference to the same standard. Examinations are of use only so far as they test the child's fitness for social life and reveal the place in which he can be of the most service and where he can receive the most help.

ARTICLE III—The Subject-Matter of Education

I believe that the social life of the child is the basis of concentration, or correlation, in all his training or growth. The social life gives the unconscious unity and the background of all his efforts and of all his attainments.

I believe that the subject-matter of the school curriculum should mark a gradual differentiation out of the primitive unconscious unity of social life.

I believe that we violate the child's nature and render difficult the best ethical results, by introducing the child too abruptly to a number of special studies, of reading, writing, geography, etc., out of relation to this social life.

I believe, therefore, that the true center of correlation on the school subjects is not science, nor literature, nor history, nor geography, but the child's own social activities.

I believe that education cannot be unified in the study of science, or so called nature study, because apart from human activity, nature itself is not a unity; nature in itself is a number of diverse objects in space and time, and to attempt to make it the center of work by itself is to introduce a principle of radiation rather than one of concentration.

I believe that literature is the reflex expression and interpretation of social experience, that hence it must follow upon and not precede such experience. It, therefore, cannot be made the basis, although it may be made the summary, of unification.

I believe once more that history is of educative value in so far as it presents phases of social life and growth. It must be controlled by reference to social life. When taken simply as history it is thrown into the distant past and becomes dead and inert. Taken as the record of man's social life and progress it becomes full of meaning. I believe, however, that it cannot be so taken excepting as the child is also introduced directly into social life.

I believe accordingly that the primary basis of education is in the child's powers at work along the same general constructive lines as those which have brought civilization into being.

I believe that the only way to make the child conscious of his social heritage is to enable him to perform those fundamental types of activity which make civilization what it is.

I believe, therefore, in the so-called expressive or constructive activities as the center of correlation.

I believe that this gives the standard for the place of cooking, sewing, manual training, etc., in the school.

I believe that they are not special studies which are to be introduced over and above a lot of others in the way of relaxation or relief, or as additional accomplishments. I believe rather that they represent, as types, fundamental forms of social activity and that it is possible and desirable that the child's introduction into the more formal subjects of the curriculum be through the medium of these activities.

I believe that the study of science is educational in so far as it brings out the materials and processes which make social life what it is.

I believe that one of the greatest difficulties in the present teaching of science is that the material is presented in purely objective form, or is treated as a new peculiar kind of experience which the child can add to that which he has already had. In reality, science is of value because it gives the ability to interpret and control the experience already had. It should be introduced, not as so much new subject-matter, but as showing the factors already involved in previous experience and as furnishing tools by which that experience can be more easily and effectively regulated.

I believe that at present we lose much of the value of literature and language studies because of our elimination of the social element. Language is almost always treated in the books of pedagogy simply as the expression of thought. It is true that language is a logical instrument, but it is fundamentally and primarily a social instrument. Language is the device for communication; it is the tool through which one individual comes to share the ideas and feelings of others. When treated simply as a way of getting individual information, or as a means of showing off what one has learned, it loses its social motive and end.

I believe that there is, therefore, no succession of studies in the ideal school curriculum. If education is life, all life has, from the outset, a scientific aspect, an aspect of art and culture, and an aspect of communication. It cannot, therefore, be true that the proper studies for one grade are mere reading and writing, and that at a later grade, reading, or literature, or science may be introduced. The progress is not in the succession of studies but in the development of new attitudes towards, and new interests in, experience.

I believe finally, that education must be conceived as a continuing reconstruction of experience; that the process and the goal of education are one and the same thing.

I believe that to set up any end outside of education, as furnishing its goal and standard, is to deprive the educational process of much of its meaning and tends to make us rely upon false and external stimuli in dealing with the child.

ARTICLE IV—The Nature of Method

I believe that the question of method is ultimately reducible to the question of the order of development of the child's powers and interests. The law for presenting and treating material is the law implicit within the child's own nature. Because this is so I believe the following statements are of supreme importance as determining the spirit in which education is carried on:

1. I believe that the active side precedes the passive in the development of the child nature; that expression comes before conscious impression; that the muscular development precedes the sensory; that movements come before conscious sensations; I believe that consciousness is essentially motor or impulsive; that conscious states tend to project themselves in action.

I believe that the neglect of this principle is the cause of a large part of the waste of time and strength in school work. The child is thrown into a passive, receptive, or absorbing attitude. The conditions are such that he is not permitted to follow the law of his nature; the result is friction and waste.

I believe that ideas (intellectual and rational processes) also result from action and devolve for the sake of the better control of action. What we term reason is primarily the law of orderly or effective action. To attempt to develop the reasoning powers, the powers of judgment, without reference to the selection and arrangement of means in action, is the fundamental fallacy in our present methods of dealing with this matter. As a result we present the child with arbitrary symbols. Symbols are a necessity in mental development, but they have their place as tools for economizing effort; presented by themselves they are a mass of meaningless and arbitrary ideas imposed from without.

2. I believe that the image is the great instrument of instruction. What a child gets out of any subject presented to him is simply the images which he himself forms with regard to it.

I believe that if nine tenths of the energy at present directed towards making the child learn certain things were spent in seeing to it that the child was forming proper images, the work of instruction would be indefinitely facilitated.

I believe that much of the time and attention now given to the preparation and presentation of lessons might be more wisely and profitably expended in training the child's power of imagery and in seeing to it that he was continually forming definite, vivid, and growing images of the various subjects with which he comes in contact in his experience.

3. I believe that interests are the signs and symptoms of growing power. I believe that they represent dawning capacities. Accordingly the constant and careful observation of interests is of the utmost importance for the educator.

I believe that these interests are to be observed as showing the state of development which the child has reached.

I believe that they prophesy the stage upon which he is about to enter.

I believe that only through the continual and sympathetic observation of childhood's interests can the adult enter into the child's life and see what it is ready for, and upon what material it could work most readily and fruitfully.

I believe that these interests are neither to be humored nor repressed. To repress interest is to substitute the adult for the child, and so to weaken intellectual curiosity and alertness, to suppress initiative, and to deaden interest.

To humor the interests is to substitute the transient for the permanent. The interest is always the sign of some power below; the important thing is to discover this power. To humor the interest is to fail to penetrate below the surface, and its sure result is to substitute caprice and whim for genuine interest.

4. I believe that the emotions are the reflex of actions.

I believe that to endeavor to stimulate or arouse the emotions apart from their corresponding activities, is to introduce an unhealthy and morbid state of mind.

I believe that if we can only secure right habits of action and thought, with reference to the good, the true, and the beautiful, the emotions will for the most part take care of themselves.

I believe that next to deadness and dullness, formalism and routine, our education is threatened with no greater evil than sentimentalism.

I believe that this sentimentalism is the necessary result of the attempt to divorce feeling from action.

ARTICLE V—The School and Social Progress

I believe that education is the fundamental method of social progress and reform.

I believe that all reforms which rest simply upon the enactment of law, or the threatening of certain penalties, or upon changes in mechanical or outward arrangements, are transitory and futile.

I believe that education is a regulation of the process of coming to share in the social consciousness and that the adjustment of individual activity on the basis of this social consciousness is the only sure method of social reconstruction.

I believe that this conception has due regard for both the individualistic and socialistic ideals. It is duly individual because it recognizes the formation of a certain character as the only genuine basis of right living. It is socialistic because it recognizes that this right character is not to be formed by merely individual precept, example, or exhortation, but rather by the influence of a certain form of institutional or community life upon the individual, and that the social organism through the school, as its organ, may determine ethical results.

I believe that in the ideal school we have the reconciliation of the individualistic and the institutional ideals.

I believe that the community's duty to education is, therefore, its paramount moral duty. By law and punishment, by social agitation and discussion, society can regulate and form itself in a more or less haphazard and chance way. But through education society can formulate its own purposes, can organize its own means and resources, and thus shape itself with definiteness and economy in the direction in which it wishes to move.

I believe that when society once recognizes the possibilities in this direction, and the obligations which these possibilities impose, it is impossible to conceive of the resources of time, attention, and money which will be put at the disposal of the educator.

I believe that it is the business of every one interested in education to insist upon the school as the primary and most effective interest of social progress and reform in order that society may be awakened to realize what the school stands for, and aroused to the necessity of endowing the educator with sufficient equipment properly to perform his task.

I believe that education thus conceived marks the most perfect and intimate union of science and art conceivable in human experience.

I believe that the art of thus giving shape to human powers and adapting them to social service is the supreme art, one calling into its service the best of artists; that no insight, sympathy, tact, executive power, is too great for such service.

I believe that with the growth of psychological service, giving added insight into individual structure and laws of growth, and with growth of social science, adding to our knowledge of the right organization of individuals, all scientific resources can be utilized for the purposes of education.

I believe that when science and art thus join hands the most commanding motive for human action will be reached, the most genuine springs of human conduct aroused, and the best service that human nature is capable of guaranteed.

I believe, finally, that the teacher is engaged, not simply in the training of individuals, but in the formation of the proper social life.

I believe that every teacher should realize the dignity of his calling; that he is a social servant set apart for the maintenance of proper social order and the securing of the right social growth.

I believe that in this way the teacher always is the prophet of the true God and the usherer in of the true kingdom of God.

4

Cardinal Principles of Secondary Education *(1918)*

In 1918, the National Education Association issued a report on the reorganization of secondary education in the United States. Popularly known as the *Cardinal Principles of Secondary Education,* it represents one of the most important documents in the history of American education. The *Cardinal Principles* affirmed the practical utility of education. Its seven objectives established the idea of education meeting the social needs of the student and the culture—that is, that education should apply to real life.

Consider the following questions as you read from this selection:

1. Should education be the same for every generation? Are there certain absolutes that all children should learn? What would the authors of the *Cardinal Principles* argue?
2. The authors of the *Cardinal Principles* outline seven principles that should be the foundation of a secondary education. These include "1. Health. 2. Command of fundamental processes. 3. Worthy home-membership. 4. Vocation. 5. Citizenship. 6. Worthy use of leisure. 7. Ethical character." Are there topics that you would add to this list, given that it was conceived nearly one hundred years ago? Which items of the original list do you consider most important? Why?

4

Cardinal Principles of Secondary Education *(1918)*

National Education Association

Secondary education should be determined by the needs of the society to be served, the character of the individuals to be educated, and the knowledge of educational theory and practice available. These factors are by no means static. Society is always in process of development; the character of the secondary-school population undergoes modification; and the sciences on which educational theory and practice depend constantly furnish new information. Secondary education, however, like any other established agency of society, is conservative and tends to resist modification. Failure to make adjustments when the need arises leads to the necessity for extensive reorganization at irregular intervals. The evidence is strong that such a comprehensive reorganization of secondary education is imperative at the present time.

1. *Changes in society.* Within the past few decades changes have taken place in American life profoundly affecting the activities of the individual. As a citizen, he must to a greater extent and in a more direct way cope with problems of community life, State and National Governments, and international relationships. As a worker, he must adjust himself to a more complex economic order. As a relatively independent personality, he has more leisure. The problems arising from these three dominant phases of life are closely interrelated and call for a degree of intelligence and efficiency on the part of every citizen that can not be secured through elementary education alone, or even through secondary education unless the scope of that education is broadened.

Source: National Education Association. 1918. *Report of the Commission on the Reorganization of Secondary Education.* U.S. Bureau of Education Bulletin 35: 7–16. Washington, D.C.: Government Printing Office.

The responsibility of the secondary school is still further increased because many social agencies other than the school afford less stimulus for education than heretofore. In many vocations there have come such significant changes as the substitution of the factory system for the domestic system of industry; the use of machinery in place of manual labor; the high specialization of processes with a corresponding subdivision of labor; and the breakdown of the apprentice system. In connection with home and family life have frequently come lessened responsibility on the part of the children; the withdrawal of the father and sometimes the mother from home occupations to the factory or store; and increased urbanization, resulting in less unified family life. Similarly, many important changes have taken place in community life, in the church, in the State, and in other institutions. These changes in American life call for extensive modifications in secondary education.

2. *Changes in the secondary-school population.* In the past 25 years there have been marked changes in the secondary-school population of the United States. . . . The character of the secondary-school population has been modified by the entrance of large numbers of pupils of widely varying capacities, aptitudes, social heredity, and destinies in life. Further, the broadening of the scope of secondary education has brought to the school many pupils who do not complete the full course but leave at various stages of advancement. The needs of these pupils can not be neglected, nor can we expect in the near future that all pupils will be able to complete the secondary school as full-time students. . . .

3. *Changes in educational theory.* The sciences on which educational theory depends have within recent years made significant contributions. In particular, educational psychology emphasizes the following factors:

(a) Individual differences in capacities and aptitudes among secondary-school pupils. Already recognized to some extent, this factor merits fuller attention.

(b) The reexamination and reinterpretation of subject values and the teaching methods with reference to "general discipline." While the final verdict of modern psychology has not as yet been rendered, it is clear that former conceptions of "general values" must be thoroughly revised.

(c) Importance of applying knowledge. Subject values and teaching methods must be tested in terms of the laws of learning and the application of knowledge to the activities of life, rather than primarily in terms of the demands of any subject as a logically organized science.

(d) Continuity in the development of children. It has long been held that psychological changes at certain stages are so pronounced as to overshadow the continuity of development. On this basis secondary education has been sharply separated from elementary education. Modern psychology, however, goes to show that the development of the individual is in most respects a

> continuous process and that, therefore, any sudden or abrupt break between the elementary and the secondary school or between any two successive stages of education is undesirable.

The foregoing changes in society, in the character of the secondary-school population, and in educational theory, together with many other considerations, call for extensive modifications of secondary education . . .

This commission, therefore, regards the following as the main objectives of education:

1. Health.
2. Command of fundamental processes.
3. Worthy home-membership.
4. Vocation.
5. Citizenship.
6. Worthy use of leisure.
7. Ethical character.

The naming of the above objectives is not intended to imply that the process of education can be divided into separated fields. This cannot be, since the pupil is indivisible. Nor is the analysis all-inclusive. Nevertheless, we believe that distinguishing and naming these objectives will aid in directing efforts; and we hold that they should constitute the principal aims in education. . . .

1. *Health.* Health needs cannot be neglected during the period of secondary education without serious danger to the individual and the race. The secondary school should therefore provide health instruction, inculcate health habits, organize an effective program of physical activities, regard health needs in planning work and play, and cooperate with home and community in safeguarding and promoting health interests. . . .

2. *Command of fundamental processes.* Much of the energy of the elementary school is properly devoted to teaching certain fundamental processes, such as reading, writing, arithmetical computations, and the elements of oral and written expression. The facility that a child of 12 or 14 may acquire in the use of these tools is not sufficient for the needs of modern life. This is particularly true of the mother tongue. . . . Throughout the secondary school, instruction and practice must go hand in hand, but as . . . much theory should be taught at any one time as will show results in practice.

3. *Worthy home-membership.* Worthy home-membership as an objective calls for the development of those qualities that make the individual a worthy

member of a family, both contributing to and deriving benefit from that membership.

This objective applies to both boys and girls. The social studies should deal with the home as a fundamental social institution and clarify its relation to the wider interests outside. Literature should interpret and idealize the human elements that go to make the home. . . . In the education of every high-school girl, the household arts should have a prominent place because of their importance to the girl herself and to others whose welfare will be directly in her keeping. . . .

4. *Vocation.* Vocational education should equip the individual to secure a livelihood for himself and those dependent on him, to serve well through his vocation, to maintain the right relationships toward his fellow workers and society, and, as far as possible, to find in that vocation his own best development.

This ideal demands that the pupil explore his own capacities and aptitudes, and make a survey of the world's work, to the end that he may select his vocation wisely. Hence, an effective program of vocational guidance in the secondary school is essential.

The extent to which the secondary school should offer training for a specific vocation depends upon the vocation, the facilities that the school can acquire, and the opportunity that the pupil may have to obtain such training later. To obtain satisfactory results those proficient in that vocation should be employed as instructors and the actual conditions of the vocation should be utilized either within the high school or in cooperation with the home, farm, shop, or office. Much of the pupil's time will be required to produce such efficiency.

5. *Civic education should develop in the individual those qualities whereby he will act well his part as a member of neighborhood, town or city, State, and Nation, and give him a basis for understanding international problems. . . .*

While all subjects should contribute to good citizenship, the social studies—geography, history, civics, and economics—should have this as their dominant aim. Too frequently, however, does mere information, conventional in value and remote in its bearing, make up the content of the social studies. History should so treat the growth of institutions that their present value may be appreciated. Geography should show the interdependence of men while it shows their common dependence on nature. Civics should concern itself less with constitutional questions and remote governmental functions and should direct attention to social agencies close at hand and to the informal activities of daily life that regard and seek the common good. Such agencies as child-welfare organizations and consumers' leagues afford specific opportunities for the expression of civic qualities by the older pupils. . . .

The comprehension of the ideals of American democracy and loyalty to them should be a prominent aim of civic education. The pupil would feel that he will be responsible, in cooperation with others, for keeping the Nation true to the best inherited conceptions of democracy, and he should also realize that democracy itself is an ideal to be wrought out by his own and succeeding generations. . . .

6. *Worthy use of leisure.* Education should equip the individual to secure from his leisure the re-creation of body, mind, and spirit, and the enrichment and enlargement of his personality.

This objective calls for the ability to utilize the common means of enjoyment, such as music, art, literature, drama, and social intercourse, together with the fostering in each individual of one or more avocational interests.

Heretofore the high school has given little conscious attention to this objective. It has so exclusively sought intellectual discipline that it has seldom treated literature, art, and music so as to evoke the right emotional response and produce positive enjoyment. Its presentation of science should aim, in part, to arouse a genuine appreciation of nature.

The school has failed also to organize and direct the social activities of young people as it should. One of the surest ways in which to prepare pupils worthily to utilize leisure in adult life is by guiding and directing their use of leisure in youth. The school should, therefore, see that adequate recreation is provided both within the school and by other proper agencies in the community. The school, however, has a unique opportunity in this field because it includes in its membership representatives from all classes of society and consequently is able through social relationships to establish bonds of friendship and common understanding that cannot be furnished by other agencies. Moreover, the school can so organize recreational activities that they will contribute simultaneously to other ends of education, as in the case of the school pageant or festival.

7. *Ethical character.* In a democratic society ethical character becomes paramount among objectives of the secondary school. Among the means for developing ethical character may be mentioned the wise selection of content and methods of instruction in all subjects of study, the social contacts of pupils with one another and with their teachers, the opportunities afforded by the organization and administration of the school for the development on the part of pupils of the sense of personal responsibility and initiative, and, above all, the spirit of service and the principles of true democracy which should permeate the entire school—principal, teachers, and pupils.

5

"A Morally Defensible Mission for Schools in the 21st Century" (1997)

Nel Noddings is among the leading figures in the philosophy of education in the United States. An experienced secondary mathematics teacher and teacher educator, she is a professor of philosophy of education at Teachers College, Columbia University and the Lee L. Jacks Professor of Education Emerita at Stanford University.

In the essay "A Morally Defensible Mission for Schools in the 21st Century," Noddings argues that the current aims of our educational system are inadequate to meet the needs of students. Opposing the standards movement, she maintains that the main purpose of our schools should be to "encourage the growth of competent, caring, loving, and lovable people"—what she defines in her earlier work as an "ethics of care."

Noddings argues that we must create learning environments that focus first and foremost on the personal and humane development of students. Academic competition and national standards are a distraction from more important themes of caring and moral action. Essentially, her philosophy of education maintains that children should be educated to become the best people possible—not simply the best test takers.

When reading the following selection, consider these questions:

1. Is it possible to maintain academic standards and have schools be reflective institutions that cultivate the personal development of students?
2. Whom do standards most benefit? Students? The society? Politicians?

3. What should be the aim of education in the United States? Should it be to produce uniform students who can perform at certain specified levels on standardized tests, or should it be to nurture students to be prepared for life?

5

"A Morally Defensible Mission for Schools in the 21st Century" (1997)

Nel Noddings

Social changes in the years since World War II have been enormous. We have seen changes in work patterns, in residential stability, in style of housing, in sexual habits, in dress, in manners, in language, in music, in entertainment, and perhaps most important of all, in family arrangements. Schools have not responded in an effective way to these changes. They have responded, albeit sluggishly, to technological changes with various additions to curriculum and narrowly prescribed methods of instruction, but they have largely ignored massive social change. When response has occurred, it has been piecemeal, designed to address isolated bits of the problem. Thus, recognizing that some children come to school hungry, schools provide meals for poor children. Alarmed by the increase in teenage pregnancies and sexually transmitted diseases, schools provide courses on sex education. Many more examples could be offered, but no one of these, nor any collection of them, adequately meets the educational needs of today's students.

What do we want for our children? What do they need from education, and what does our society need? The popular response today is that students need more academic training, that the country needs more people with greater mathematical and scientific competence, that a more adequate academic preparation will save people from poverty, crime, and other evils of current society. Most of

---

Source: Noddings, Nel. 1997. "A Morally Defensible Mission for Schools in the 21st Century." In *Transforming Public Education: A New Course for America's Future*, edited by Evan Clinchy, 27–37. New York: Teachers College Press.

these claims are either false or, at best, only partly true. For example, we do not need more physicists and mathematicians; many people highly trained in these fields are unable to find work. Further, the vast majority of adults do not use algebra in their work, and forcing all students to study it is a simplistic response to the real issues of equity and mathematical literacy. And, clearly, more education will not save people from poverty unless a sufficient number of unfortunate people either reject that education or are squeezed out of it; that is, unless the society is willing to pay everyone a living wage. Much work that is now low paid but essential to our society will have to be done even if everyone is "well educated," and no person who does honest, useful work—regardless of her educational attainments—should live in poverty. A society that permits this is not an educational failure; it is a moral failure.

Our society does not need to make its children first in the world in mathematics and science. It needs to care for its children—to reduce violence, to respect honest work of every kind, to reward excellence at every level (Gardner, 1961), to ensure a place for every child and emerging adult in the economic and social world, to produce people who can care competently for their own families and contribute effectively to their communities. In direct opposition to the current emphasis on academic standards, a national curriculum, and national testing, I have argued (Noddings, 1992) that our main educational aim should be to encourage the growth of competent, caring, loving, and lovable people. This is a morally defensible aim for education in the 21st century. I have argued (Noddings, 1992) that liberal education (defined as a set of traditional disciplines) is an outmoded and dangerous model of education for today's young. The popular slogan today is, "All children can learn!" The slogan is so generous and optimistic in its tone that one hesitates to attack it, but it really is virtually meaningless without an object for the verb "learn." What can all children learn? Anyone who has taught in the public schools knows that children's talents and interests vary enormously. As a former high school mathematics teacher, I am convinced that many children—even many who try very hard—cannot learn, for example, the intricacies of mathematical proof. Their inability to comprehend sophisticated mathematical material does not in any way reduce their human worth. Must we declare everyone equal in all things in order to cherish each child and nurture his growth? By trying so hard to pretend that all children are equal in all things, we destroy the very possibility of promoting their real, unique talents. John Dewey (1916) remarked on the attitude of the new education toward this tendency:

> The general aim translates into the aim of regard for individual differences among children. Nobody can take the principle of consideration of native powers into account without being struck by the fact that these powers differ in different individuals. The difference applies not merely to their intensity, but even more to their quality and arrangement. As Rousseau said:

> "Each individual is born with a distinctive temperament. . . . We indiscriminately employ children of different bents on the same exercises; their education destroys the special bent and leaves a dull uniformity. Therefore after we have wasted our efforts in stunting the true gifts of nature we see the short-lived and illusory brilliance we have substituted die away, while the natural abilities we have crushed do not revive." (p. 116)

Some colleagues in mathematics education grant part of my argument; they admit that many students do not grasp mathematical proof. But their solution is to reduce or even eliminate proof from the curriculum and to try to devise a curriculum at which all children can succeed. Clearly, this does an injustice to the mathematically talented.

To insist that all children should get the same dose of academic English, social studies, science, and mathematics invites an important question unaddressed by the sloganeers: Why should children learn what we insist they "can" learn? Is this the material people really need in order to live intelligently, morally, and happily? Or are arguments for traditional liberal education badly mistaken? Worse, are they perhaps mere political maneuverings?

In suggesting that advocates of liberal (academic) education for all might be guilty of political maneuvering, I do not mean to create an educational conspiracy theory. On the contrary, I believe that most advocates honestly believe that their recommendations are in the best interests of children. However, I also believe that these recommendations and the elaborate plans laid for carrying them out do indeed act like political maneuvers; they distract us from the fundamental problems we should address. We cannot eliminate poverty by forcing academic requirements on all children. More reasonably, we might argue that eliminating poverty would improve education and reduce the need for coercion. Children whose lives are physically, materially, and emotionally secure are likely to respond with enthusiasm to literature, science, and history taught well in a relevant social context.

Thus, my argument against liberal education is not a complaint against literature, history, physical science, mathematics, or any other subject. It is an argument, first, against an ideology of control that forces all students to study a particular, narrowly prescribed curriculum devoid of content they might really care about. Second, it is an argument in favor of greater respect for a wonderful range of human capacities now largely ignored in schools. Third, it is an argument against the persistent undervaluing of skills, attitudes, and capacities traditionally associated with women. This last is an argument that has been eloquently made by Jane Roland Martin, whose chapter also appears in this volume.

Michael Apple (1993) has also expressed concerns about the movement toward standardization of curriculum. Implementing a system purporting to improve social conditions is worse than doing nothing if it both fails to change those conditions and, in its failed attempts, justifies the status quo. This is what Apple fears—that in the interests of national competitiveness and the privileged classes, children of the poor will be more rigidly ranked and more firmly stuck in their lower places than ever before:

> The "same treatment" by sex, race and ethnicity, or class is not the same at all. A democratic curriculum and pedagogy must begin with a recognition of "the different social positionings and cultural repertoire in the classrooms, and the power relations between them." Thus, if we are concerned with "really equal treatment," as I think we must be, we must base a curriculum on a recognition of those differences that empower and depower our students in identifiable ways. (p. 1)

I would go further and insist that the starting point has to be provision for individual interests as Rousseau and Dewey saw them. Education organized around a reasonable number of broad talents and interests, augmented and filled out by serious inquiry into common human problems, stands the best chance of achieving a meaningful equality. Such education, in which students are active co-creators of curriculum, is a truly liberal education for both personal and public life in a democracy.

Glimpses of an Alternative

What do we want for our children? Most of us hope that our children will find someone to love, find useful work they enjoy or at least do not hate, establish a family, and maintain bonds with friends and relatives. These hopes are part of our interest in shaping an acceptable child (Ruddick, 1980). What kind of mates, parents, friends, and neighbors will our children be? I would hope that all of our children—both girls and boys—would be prepared to do the work of attentive love. This work must be done in every family situation, whether the family is conventionally or unconventionally constituted. Both men and women, if they choose to be parents, should participate in the joys and responsibilities of direct parenting, of acting as psychological parent. Too often, women have complained about bearing this responsibility almost entirely. When men volunteer to help with child care or help with housework, the very language suggests that the tasks are women's responsibilities. Men "help" in tasks they do not perceive as their own. That has to change.

In education today, there is great concern about women's participation in mathematics and science. Some researchers even refer to something called the "problem of women and mathematics." Women's lack of success or participation in fields long dominated by men is seen as a problem to be treated by educational means. But researchers do not seem to see a problem in men's lack of participation in nursing, elementary school teaching, or full-time parenting.

Our society values activities traditionally associated with men above those traditionally associated with women. (For an extended and powerful argument on this problem, see Martin, 1985.)

The new education I envision puts a very high valuation on the traditional occupations of women. Care for children, the aged, and the ill must be shared by all capable adults, not just women, and everyone should understand that these activities bring special rewards as well as burdens. Work with children can be especially rewarding and provides an opportunity to enjoy childhood vicariously. For example, I have often wondered why high school students are not more often invited to revisit the literature of childhood in their high school English classes. A careful study of fairy tales, augmented by essays on their psychology, might be more exciting and more generally useful than, for example, the study of Hamlet. When we consider the natural interest we have in ourselves—past, present, and future—literature that allows us to look both forward and backward is wonderful. Further, there are opportunities for lessons in geography, history, art, and music.

Our children should learn something about life cycles and stages. When I was in high school, my Latin class read Cicero's essay "On Old Age." With all his talk of wisdom, of milk, honey, wine, and cheese, of meditating in the afternoon breeze, I was convinced that old age had its own romance. Looking at the present condition of many elderly, I see more than enough horror to balance whatever romance there may be. But studies of early childhood, adulthood, and old age (with or without Latin) seem central to education for real life. Further, active association with people of all ages should be encouraged. Again, one can see connections with standard subjects—statistical studies in math; the history and sociology of welfare, medical care, and family life; geographical and cultural differences. We see also that the need for such studies is a result of the social changes discussed earlier. Home life does not provide the experience in these areas that it once did, and yet the need is greater than it has ever been.

Relations with intimate others are the beginning and one of the significant ends of moral life. If we regard our relations with intimate others as central in moral life, we must provide all our children with practice in caring. Children can work together formally and informally on a host of school projects and, as they get older, they can help younger children, contribute to the care of building and grounds, and eventually do volunteer work—carefully supervised—in the community. Looking at Howard Gardner's (1983) multiple intelligences, we see that children can contribute useful service in a wide variety of ways; some have artistic talents, some interpersonal gifts, some athletic or kinesthetic abilities, some spiritual gifts. A moral policy, a defensible mission, for education recognizes a multiplicity of human capacities and interests. Instead of preparing everyone for college in the name of democracy and equality, schools should instill in students a respect for all forms of honest work done well

(Gardner, 1961). Preparation for the world of work, parenting, and civic responsibility is essential for all students. All of us must work, but few of us do the sort of work implied by preparation in algebra and geometry. Almost all of us enter into intimate relationships, but schools largely ignore the centrality of such interests in our lives. And although most of us become parents, evidence suggests that we are not very good at parenting, and again the schools largely ignore this huge human task.

When I suggest that a morally defensible mission for education necessarily focuses on matters of human caring, people sometimes agree but fear the loss of an intellectual mission for the schools. There are at least two powerful responses to this fear. First, anyone who supposes that the current drive for uniformity in standards, curriculum, and testing represents an intellectual agenda needs to reflect on the matter. Indeed, many thoughtful educators insist that such moves are truly anti-intellectual, discouraging critical thinking, creativity, and novelty. Further, in their emphasis on equality, they may lead to even grosser levels of mediocrity. Second, and more important from the perspective adopted here, a curriculum centered on themes of care can be as richly intellectual as we and our students want to make it. Those of us advocating genuine reform—better, transformation—will surely be accused of anti-intellectualism, just as John Dewey was in the middle of this century. But the accusation is false, and we should have the courage to face it down.

Let's consider a few possibilities. Themes that are especially important to young people include love and friendship. Both can be studied in intellectual depth, but the crucial emphasis should be on relevance for self-understanding and growth. Friends are especially important to teenagers, and they need guidance in making and maintaining friendships.

Aristotle is one philosopher who wrote eloquently on friendship, and he assessed it as central in moral life. In the Nicomachean Ethics (trans. 1985), Aristotle wrote that the main criterion of friendship is that a friend wishes a friend well for her own sake. When we befriend others, we want good things for them not because those things may enhance our welfare but because they are good for our friends. Aristotle organized friendships into various categories: those motivated by common business or political purposes, those maintained by common recreational interests, and those created by mutual admiration of the other's virtue. The last was, for Aristotle, the highest form of friendship and, of course, the one most likely to endure.

Students need to understand, as Aristotle did, that friendship can be genuine and yet depend on mutual interests that may be transient. Some friendships do not extend beyond football season, army service, or common work in the same company. They may still be characterized by wishing the best for one's friend. The kind of friendship that grows out of mutual admiration and likability is rare and beautiful and brings with it a special moral obligation. Among the good things we want for our friends is moral growth, an increase in virtue. Although Aristotle did not employ the word virtue in our modern sense, it still makes sense to say that we want our friends to grow both in requisite excellences and in virtue construed as moral virtue. This means that true friends will protect each other not only from external evil but also from evil that arises internally. When we care, as we must about a friend, we continually support the quest for a better self.

How do friendships occur? What draws people together? Here students should have opportunities to see how far Aristotle's description will carry them. They should hear about Damon and Pythias, of course. But they should also examine some incongruous friendships: Huckleberry Finn and the slave, Jim; Miss Celie and Shug in Alice Walker's *The Color Purple*; Lenny and George in *Of Mice and Men*; Jane and Maudie in Doris Lessing's *The Diaries of Jane Somers*. What do each of these characters give to the friendship? Can friendship be part of a personal quest for fulfillment? When does a personal objective go too far and negate Aristotle's basic criterion?

Students should be encouraged to examine the concept of loyalty. Is there such a thing as unconditional friendship—staying friends no matter what? One aspect of this question concerns exploitation and requires a careful analysis of equal relations and what makes them equal. We can rarely browbeat others into carrying their share of obligation, and if caring relations are important to us, we can find better approaches. But we need to attend to this set of problems. Young women especially need guidance on how to maintain relationships without contributing to their own exploitation.

Another aspect is perhaps even more troubling for most of us. When should moral principles outweigh the demands of friendship? The question is often cast this way, even though many of us find the wording misleading. What the questioner wants us to consider is whether we should protect friends who have done something morally wrong. A few years ago, there was a terrifying example of this problem in a town close to my own. A teenage boy killed a girl and bragged about it to his friends. His friends, in what they interpreted as an act of loyalty, did not even report the murder.

From the perspective of caring, there is no inherent conflict between moral requirements and friendship, because we have a primary obligation to promote our friends' moral growth. But lots of concrete conflicts can arise when we have to consider exactly what to do. Instead of juggling principles as we might when we say, "Friendship is more important than a little theft" or "Murder is more important than friendship," we begin by asking ourselves whether our friends have committed caring acts. If they have not, something has to be done. In the case of something as horrible as murder, the act must be reported. But true friends would also go beyond initial judgment and action to ask how they can follow through with appropriate help for the murderer. When we adopt caring as an ethical approach, our moral work just begins where other approaches pronounce Q.E.D. Caring requires staying with, or what Ruddick (1980) has called "holding." We do not let our friends fall if we can help it, and if they do, we hold on and pull them back up.

Friendship, as an equal relation, makes demands on both parties. Young people should understand that it is sometimes necessary to break off a relationship in which they are exploited, abused, or pushed to do things they regard as harmful or wrong. Quitting such a relationship is not "breaking a friendship" because, in actuality, there is no friendship without mutual acceptance of the main criterion.

Gender differences in friendship patterns should also be discussed. It may be harder for males to reject relations in which they are pushed to do socially unacceptable acts because those acts are often used as tests of manhood. Females, in contrast, find it more difficult to separate themselves from abusive relations. In both cases, young people have to learn not only to take appropriate responsibility for the moral growth of others but also to insist that others accept responsibility for their own behavior. It is often a fine line, and since there are no formulas to assist us, we remain vulnerable in all our moral relations.

With much more space, we could explore many themes of care for both their relevance to real lives and their intellectual richness. (For some suggestions on how to teach such themes, see Noddings, 1992, 1995.)

Some Recommendations

A transformation of the sort envisioned here requires organizational and structural changes to support those in curriculum and instruction. It requires a move away from the ideology of control, from the mistaken notion that iron-fisted accountability will ensure the products we set out as desirable. It just won't happen. We should have learned by now that both children and adults can accomplish wonderful things in an atmosphere of love and trust and that they will (if they are healthy) resist—sometimes to their own detriment—in environments of coercion.

The traditional organization of schooling is intellectually and morally inadequate for contemporary society. We live in an age troubled by social problems that force us to reconsider what we do in schools. So many of us think that we can improve education merely by designing a better curriculum, finding and implementing a better form of instruction, or instituting a better form of classroom management. These things won't work.

We need to give up the notion of an ideal of the educated person and replace it with a multiplicity of models designed to accommodate the multiple capacities and interests of students. We need to recognize multiple identities.

For example, an eleventh grader may be a Black, a woman, a teenager, a Smith, an American, a New Yorker, a Methodist, a person who loves math, and so on. As she exercises these identities, she may use different languages, adopt different postures, and relate differently to those around her. But whoever she is at a given moment, whatever she is engaged in, she needs—as we all do—to be cared for. Her need for care may require formal respect, informal interaction, expert advice, just a flicker of recognition, or sustained affection. To give the care she needs requires a set of capacities in each of us to which schools give too little attention.

I have argued that education should be organized around themes of care rather than the traditional disciplines. All students should be engaged in a general education that guides them in caring for self, intimate others, global others, plants, animals and the environment, objects and instruments, and ideas. Moral life so defined should be frankly embraced as the main goal of education. Such an aim does not work against intellectual development or academic achievement. On the contrary, it supplies a firm foundation for both.

How can we begin? Here is what I think we must do:

First, be clear and unapologetic about our goal. The main aim of education should be to produce competent, caring, loving, and lovable people. Stating such an aim does not standardize either the curriculum or a mode of pedagogy. It opens the way to continuous dialogue and debate: What do we mean by competence? What does it mean to care? What can we (as parents and teachers) do to develop children who are loving and lovable?

Second, take care of affiliative needs. There are many things we can do with little cost to meet these needs. We can keep teachers and students together (by mutual consent) for several years instead of the traditional (and arbitrary) one year. We can keep students together and in one building for considerable periods of time—long enough for them to think of the physical place as their own. Administrators and policymakers can support teachers in their efforts to care and legitimize time spent on building relations of care and trust.

Third, relax the impulse to control. This is a hard recommendation to make and an even harder one to follow in an era reeking of distrust and filled with demands for accountability. But, surely, if we value a truly democratic way of life, we must give teachers, students, and parents greater opportunities to participate and exercise judgment. We need responsible experimentation, not a petrification of current mediocrity. Indeed, it is odd that, in a liberal democracy that prides itself on independence and resistance to governmental interference, so many well-meaning people should be pressing for more and tighter control of what goes on in schools. We should take the time to know what is actually going on in our schools, but we need not (and should not, I would say) prescribe beforehand everything that they must do. Study and appraise their outcomes both critically and appreciatively, but do not prescribe outcomes! We can learn from responsible experimentation.

Fourth, get rid of program hierarchies. This will take time, but we must begin now to provide excellent programs for all our children. Programs for the non-college-bound should be just as rich, desirable, and rigorous as those for the college-bound. What a student wants to do or to study should guide what is required by way of preparation. Here we should not worry greatly about students "changing their minds." Right now we are so afraid that if students prepare for something particular, they may change their minds and all that preparation will be wasted. Therefore, we busily prepare them uniformly for nothing. We forget that when people have a goal in mind, they learn well, and that even if they change their minds, they may well have acquired the skills and habits of mind they will need for further learning. In addition to preparation for work or future study, we must also give all students what all students need—genuine opportunities to explore the questions central to human life.

Fifth, give at least part of every day to themes of care. If we want to decrease violence and increase responsibility, we simply must spend time in dialogue with our children about the full range of existential questions, including both moral and spiritual matters. In all classes, opportunities can be found to discuss common human predicaments, outstanding acts of compassion, examples of towering genius, and the great joys potential in everyday life. We can give students practice in caring and time to reflect on and discuss their efforts. To nurture caring in our children, we have to show, first, that we care for them. This means listening as well as talking, following their legitimate interests as well as guiding them away from dangerous and undesirable interests.

Finally, we must teach them, and show by our example, that caring in every domain implies competence. When we care, we accept the responsibility to work continuously on our competence so that the recipient of our care—person, animal, object, or idea—is enhanced. There is nothing mushy about caring. It is the strong, resilient backbone of human life.

References

Apple, M. (1993). The politics of official knowledge: Does a national curriculum make sense? *Discourse*, 14(1), 1–16.

Aristotle. (1985). *Nicomachean ethics* (Terence Irwin, Trans.). Indianapolis: Hackett.

Dewey, J. (1916). *Democracy and education.* New York: Macmillan.

Gardner, H. (1983). *Frames of mind.* New York: Basic Books.

Gardner, J. (1961). *Excellence: Can we be equal and excellent too?* New York: Harper.

Martin, J. R. (1985). *Reclaiming a conversation: The ideal of the educated woman.* New Haven: Yale University Press.

Noddings, N. (1992). *The challenge to care in the schools.* New York: Teachers College Press.

Noddings, N. (1995). Teaching themes of care. *Phi Delta Kappan*, 76(3), 675–679.

Ruddick, S. (1980). Maternal thinking. *Feminist Studies*, 6(2), 342–367.

PART II

Society and Education

Part II focuses on the relationship between society and education. Included in this section are several selections from sources such as Thomas Jefferson, Benjamin Rush, and Horace Mann. I include these materials because they address the role education played in the formation of American culture. They also challenge our tendency to assume that institutions such as schools have always been the way they are today instead of conscious creations at specific moments in historical time.

In this context, the first selection, from Thomas Jefferson's 1781 *Notes on the State of Virginia,* asserts that the schools will play a very specific role in the new nation. Similarly, Benjamin Rush's essay, written a few years later, addresses the same issue, in his case, the belief that the schools and the education of children should largely serve the needs of the state.

The selections from Horace Mann's 1848 report of the Massachusetts school board describe his view of the common or public schools literally as an engine of civilization—conserving and maintaining the culture. His ideas contrast markedly with those of George S. Counts, nearly a century later, who called for the schools to provide the means of creating a new social order.

As you read the following selections related to the aims of education, keep in mind the following questions:

1. In a democracy, who should determine what the aims of the educational system should be?
2. Should the aims or purposes of education be the same for all students or different for students with different needs?

6

Selection From Notes on the State of Virginia *(1781)*

Of all of the political leaders to emerge from the American Revolution, perhaps none was more interested in educational issues than Thomas Jefferson (1743–1826). While Jefferson devoted no single work to his ideas on education, he explored the subject throughout his life. His single greatest accomplishment in the area was his role in establishing the University of Virginia.

Jefferson believed that education was essential to American society. In his General Education Bills of 1779 and 1817, he argued that an elementary education should be provided by the state to all of its citizens. Such an education would include a basic background in reading, history, geography, arithmetic, and grammar.

Secondary education would be provided to those who could purchase it as a luxury or to the most gifted students (rich or poor), who would be awarded scholarships. Twenty secondary schools would be located throughout the state, making them easily accessible to the entire population. These schools would teach English grammar, classical languages, modern languages such as French, and a range of scientific subjects.

At the college or university level, Jefferson called for a reorganization of the curriculum at William and Mary in Williamsburg, Virginia; the establishment of a state university, what became the University of Virginia; as well as the establishment of a national university. With regard to a national university, Jefferson's proposals were never realized.

Jefferson's *Notes on the State of Virginia* was written in 1781. In the following selection, he outlines the basic organization of his three-tiered system of education.

As you read this selection, think about the following questions:

1. What role does education play in the lives of the citizens in Jefferson's democracy?
2. To what extent do Jefferson's ideas anticipate the establishment of universal public education at the elementary level (common schools) by the mid-nineteenth century?

6

Selection From Notes on the State of Virginia *(1781)*

Thomas Jefferson

Another object of the revisal is to diffuse knowledge more generally through the mass of the people. This bill proposes to lay off every county into small districts of five or six miles square, called hundreds, and in each of them to establish a school for teaching reading, writing, and arithmetic. The tutor to be supported by the hundred, and every person in it entitled to send their children three years gratis, and as much longer as they please, paying for it. These schools to be under a visitor, who is annually to chuse the boy of best genius in the school, of those whose parents are too poor to give them further education, and to send him forward to one of the grammar schools, of which twenty are proposed to be erected in different parts of the country, for teaching Greek, Latin, geography, and the higher branches of numerical arithmetic. Of the boys thus sent in any one year, trial is to be made at the grammar schools one or two years, and the best genius of the whole selected, and continued six years, and the residue dismissed. By this means twenty of the best geniuses will be raked from the rubbish annually, and be instructed, at the public expence, so far as the grammar schools go. At the end of six years instruction, one half are to be discontinued (from among whom the grammar schools will probably be supplied with future masters); and the other half, who are to be chosen for the superiority of their parts and disposition, are to be sent and continued three years in the study of such sciences as they shall chuse, at William and Mary college, the plan of which is proposed to be enlarged, as will be hereafter explained, and extended to all the useful sciences. The ultimate

Source: Jefferson, Thomas. 1781. *Notes on the State of Virginia.* Brooklyn, N. Y.: Historical Printing Club, 1894.

result of the whole scheme of education would be the teaching all the children of the state reading, writing, and common arithmetic; turning out ten annually of superior genius, well taught in Greek, Latin, geography, and the higher branches of arithmetic; turning out ten others annually, of still superior parts, who, to those branches of learning, shall have added such of the sciences as their genius shall have led them to; the furnishing to the wealthier part of the people convenient schools, at which their children may be educated, at their own expence.

The general objects of this law are to provide an education adapted to the years, to the capacity, and the condition of every one, and directed to their freedom and happiness. Specific details were not proper for the law. These must be the business of the visitors entrusted with its execution. The first stage of this education being the schools of the hundreds, wherein the great mass of the people will receive their instruction, the principal foundations of future order will be laid here. Instead therefore of putting the Bible and Testament into the hands of the children, at an age when their judgments are not sufficiently matured for religious enquiries, their memories may here be stored with the most useful facts from Grecian, Roman, European and American history. The first elements of morality too may be instilled into their minds; such as, when further developed as their judgments advance in strength, may teach them how to work out their own greatest happiness, by shewing them that it does not depend on the condition of life in which chance has placed them, but is always the result of a good conscience, good health, occupation, and freedom in all just pursuits.

Those whom either the wealth of their parents or the adoption of the state shall destine to higher degrees of learning, will go on to the grammar schools, which constitute the next stage, there to be instructed in the languages. The learning Greek and Latin, I am told, is going into disuse in Europe. I know not what their manners and occupations may call for, but it would be very ill-judged in us to follow their example in this instance. There is a certain period of life, say from eight to fifteen or sixteen years of age, when the mind, like the body, is not yet firm enough for laborious and close operations. If applied to such, it falls an early victim to premature exertion, exhibiting indeed at first, in these young and tender subjects, the flattering appearance of their being men while they are yet children, but ending in reducing them to be children when they should be men. The memory is then most susceptible and tenacious of impressions, and the learning of languages being chiefly a work of memory, it seems precisely fitted to the powers of this period, which is long enough too for acquiring the most useful languages ancient and modern. I do not pretend that language is science. It is only an instrument for the attainment of science. But that time is not lost which is employed in providing tools for future operation; more especially as in this case the books put into the hands of the youth for this purpose may be such as will at the same time impress their minds with useful facts and good principles. If this period be suffered to pass in idleness, the mind becomes lethargic and impotent, as would the body it inhabits if unexercised during the same time. The sympathy between body and mind during their rise, progress, and decline is too strict and obvious to endanger our being misled while we reason from the one to the other.

As soon as they are of sufficient age, it is supposed they will be sent on from the grammar schools to the university, which constitutes our third and last stage, there to study those sciences which may be adapted to their views. By that part of our plan which prescribes the selection of the youths of genius from among the classes of the poor, we hope to avail the state of those talents which nature has sown as liberally among the poor as the rich, but which perish without use, if not sought for and cultivated.

But of all the views of this law none is more important, none more legitimate, than that of rendering the people safe, as they are the ultimate guardians of their own liberty. For this purpose the reading in the first stage, where *they* will receive their whole education, is proposed, as has been said, to be chiefly historical. History by apprising them of the past will enable them to judge of the future; it will avail them of the experience of other times and other nations; it will qualify them as judges of the actions and designs of men; it will enable them to know ambition under every disguise it may assume; and knowing it, to defeat its views. In every government on earth is some trace of human weakness, some germ of corruption and degeneracy, which cunning will discover, and wickedness insensibly open, cultivate, and improve. Every government degenerates when trusted to the rulers of the people alone. The people themselves therefore are its only safe depositories. And to render even them safe their minds must be improved to a certain degree. This indeed is not all that is necessary, though it be essentially necessary. An amendment of our constitution must here come in aid of the public education. The influence over government must be shared among all the people. If every individual which composes their mass participates of the ultimate authority, the government will be safe because the corrupting the whole mass will exceed any private resources of wealth; and public ones cannot be provided but by levies on the people. In this case every man would have to pay his own price. The government of Great-Britain has been corrupted, because but one man in ten has a right to vote for members of parliament. The sellers of the government therefore get nine-tenths of their price clear. It has been thought that corruption is restrained by confining the right of suffrage to a few of the wealthier of the people, but it would be more effectually restrained by an extension of that right to such numbers as would bid defiance to the means of corruption.

Lastly, it is proposed, by a bill in this revisal, to begin a public library and gallery, by laying out a certain sum annually in books, paintings, and statues.

7

"Thoughts Upon the Mode of Education Proper in a Republic" (1786)

Benjamin Rush (1745–1813) was a signer of the *Declaration of Independence* and one of the leading public figures of the early republic. A doctor by profession, he wrote extensively on issues of public concern, including education. In his 1786 essay, Rush argued that the citizens of a nation need to be politically and socially shaped early in their lives. The purpose of schools was to create a unified or homogenous set of values with common goals and purposes. Rush considered the needs of the individual to be subordinate to those of the state. He believed that "it is possible to convert men into republican machines. This must be done, if we expect them to perform their parts properly, in the great machine of the government of the state." For Rush, the individual and the state "must be fitted to each other by means of education before they can be made to produce regularity and unison in government."

Consider the following questions as you read Rush's "Thoughts":

1. What role should the state have in the education of its children?
2. Whose interests are to be served first in the education of the American people: those of the state or those of the individual?

7

"Thoughts Upon the Mode of Education Proper in a Republic" (1786)

Benjamin Rush

The business of education has acquired a new complexion by the independence of our country. The form of government we have assumed has created a new class of duties to every American. It becomes us, therefore, to examine our former habits upon this subject, and, in laying the foundations for nurseries of wise and good men, to adapt our modes of teaching to the peculiar form of our government.

The first remark that I shall make upon this subject is that an education in our own is to be preferred to an education in a foreign country. The principle of patriotism stands in need of the reinforcement of prejudice. And it is well known that our strongest prejudices in favour of our country are formed in the first one and twenty years of our lives. The policy of the Lacedemonians is well worthy of our imitation. When Antipater demanded fifty of their children as hostages for the fulfillment of a distant engagement, those wise republicans refused to comply with his demand, but readily offered him double the number of their adult citizens, whose habits and prejudices could not be shaken by residing in a foreign country. Passing by, in this place, the advantages to the community from the early attachment of youth to the laws and constitution of their country, I shall only remark that young men who have trodden the paths of science together, or have joined in the same

---

Source: Rush, Benjamin. 1806. *Essays, Literary, Moral, and Philosophical,* 2d ed., 8–13. Philadelphia: Thomas and William Bradford.

sports, whether of swimming, skating, fishing, or hunting, generally feel, thro' life, such ties to each other, as add greatly to the obligations of mutual benevolence. . . .

While we inculcate these republican duties upon our pupil, we must not neglect, at the same time, to inspire him with republican principles. He must be taught that there can be no durable liberty but in a republic, and that government, like all other sciences, is of a progressive nature. The chains which have bound this science in Europe are happily unloosed in America. Here it is open to investigation and improvement. While philosophy has protected us by its discoveries from a thousand natural evils, government has unhappily followed with an unequal pace. It would be to dishonour human genius, only to name the many defects which still exist in the best systems of legislation. We daily see matter of a perishable nature rendered durable by certain chemical operations. In like manner, I conceive that it is possible to combine power in such a way as not only to increase the happiness, but to promote the duration of republican forms of government far beyond the terms limited for them by history, or the common opinions of mankind.

To assist in rendering religious, moral, and political instructions more effectual upon the minds of our youth, it will be necessary to subject their bodies to physical discipline. To obviate the inconveniences of their studious and sedentary mode of life, they should live upon a temperate diet, consisting chiefly of broths, milk, and vegetables. The black broth of Sparta and the barley broth of Scotland have been alike celebrated for their beneficial effects upon the minds of young people. They should avoid tasting Spirituous liquors. They should also be accustomed occasionally to work with their hands, in the intervals of Study, and in the busy seasons of the year in the country. Moderate sleep, silence, occasional solitude, and cleanliness should be inculcated upon them, and the utmost advantage should be taken of a proper direction of those great principles in human conduct—sensibility, habit, imitations, and association.

The influence of these physical causes will be powerful upon the intellects, as well as upon the principles and morals of young people.

To those who have studied human nature, it will not appear paradoxical to recommend, in this essay, a particular attention to vocal music. Its mechanical effects in civilizing the mind, and thereby preparing it for the influence of religion and government, have been so often felt and recorded, that it will be unnecessary to mention facts in favour of its usefulness, in order to excite a proper attention to it.

I cannot help bearing a testimony, in this place, against the custom, which prevails in some parts of America, (but which is daily falling into disuse in Europe) of crowding boys together under one roof for the purpose of education. The practice is the gloomy remains of monkish ignorance and is as unfavorable to the improvements of the mind in useful learning as monasteries are to the spirit of religion. I grant this mode of secluding boys from the intercourse of private families has a tendency to make them scholars, but our business is to make them men, citizens, and Christians. The vices of young people are generally learned from each other. The vices of adults seldom infect them. By separating them from each other, therefore, in their hours of relaxation from study, we secure their morals from a principal source of corruption, while we improve their manners, by subjecting them to those restraints which the difference of age and sex naturally produce in private families.

From the observations that have been made it is plain that I consider it is possible to convert men into republican machines. This must be done if we expect them to perform their parts properly in the great machine of the government of the state. That republic is sophisticated with monarchy or aristocracy that does not revolve upon the wills of the people, and these must be fitted to each other by means of education before they can be made to produce regularity and unison in government.

8

Selections From Report No. 12 of the Massachusetts School Board *(1848)*

Horace Mann (1796–1859) has often been called the "schoolmaster of the republic." A lawyer by training, he became the first Secretary of Education for the state of Massachusetts, a position he served in from 1837 to 1848. Like Thomas Jefferson, he believed that public education should be provided by the state for all of its children. More than any single figure, Mann is responsible for the establishment of common schools (free public schools common to all children) in the United States.

Mann's ideas are most clearly outlined in his Twelve Annual Reports as Massachusetts's Secretary of Education. Selections from the last report, which was published in 1848, follow this introduction.

As you read these selections, consider the following questions:

1. What role should the state play in the education of its children?
2. How important is universal education as a means of socializing Americans and training them to be good citizens?

8

Selections From Report No. 12 of the Massachusetts School Board *(1848)*

Horace Mann

Under the Providence of God, our means of education are the grand machinery by which the "raw material" of human nature can be worked up into inventors and discoverers, into skilled artisans and scientific farmers, into scholars and jurists, into the founders of benevolent institutions, and the great expounders of ethical and theological science. By means of early education, these embryos of talent may be quickened, which will solve the difficult problems of political and economical law; and by them, too, the genius may be kindled which will blaze forth in the Poets of Humanity. Our schools, far more than they have done, may supply the Presidents and Professors of Colleges, and Superintendents of Public Instruction, all over the land; and send, not only into our sister states, but across the Atlantic, the men of practical science, to superintend the construction of the great works of art. Here, too, may those judicial powers be developed and invigorated, which will make legal principles so clear and convincing as to prevent appeals to force; and, should the clouds of war ever lower over our country, some hero may be found—the nursling of our schools, and ready to become the leader of our armies—that best of all heroes, who will secure the glories of a peace, unstained by the magnificent murders of the battle-field. . . .

Without undervaluing any other human agency, it may be safely affirmed that the Common School, improved and energized as it can easily be, may

Source: Massachusetts Board of Education. 1848. *Twelfth Annual Report of the Board of Education*, 37–38, 42, 53, 55, 57–60, 76–80, 84–90. Boston: Dutton and Wentworth State Printers.

become the most effective and benignant of all the forces of civilization. Two reasons sustain this position. In the first place, there is a universality in its operation, which can be affirmed of no other institution whatever. If administered in the spirit of justice and conciliation, all the rising generation may be brought within the circle of its reformatory and elevating influences. And, in the second place, the materials upon which it operates are so pliant and ductile as to be susceptible of assuming a greater variety of forms than any other earthly work of the Creator. The inflexibility and ruggedness of the oak, when compared with the lithe sapling or the tender germ, are but feeble emblems to typify the docility of childhood, when contrasted with the obduracy and intractableness of man. It is these inherent advantages of the Common School, which, in our own State, have produced results so striking, from a system so imperfect, and an administration so feeble. In teaching the blind, and the deaf and dumb, in kindling the latent spark of intelligence that lurks in an idiot's mind, and in the more holy work of reforming abandoned and outcast children, education has proved what it can do, by glorious experiments. These wonders, it has done in its infancy, and with the lights of a limited experience; but, when its faculties shall be fully developed, when it shall be trained to wield its mighty energies for the protection of society against the giant vices which now invade and torment it—against intemperance, avarice, war, slavery, bigotry, the woes of want and the wickedness of waste—then, there will not be a height to which these enemies of the race can escape, which it will not scale, nor a Titan among them all, whom it will not slay.

I proceed, then, in endeavoring to show how the true business of the schoolroom connects itself, and becomes identical, with the great interests of society. The former is the infant, immature state of those interests; the latter, their developed, adult state. As "the child is father to the man," so may the training of the schoolroom expand into the institutions and fortunes of the State. . . .

Intellectual Education, as a Means of Removing Poverty, and Securing Abundance

Another cardinal object which the government of Massachusetts, and all the influential men in the State should propose to themselves, is the physical well-being of all the people—the sufficiency, comfort, competence of every individual, in regard to food, raiment, and shelter. And these necessaries and conveniences of life should be obtained by each individual for himself, or by each family for themselves, rather than accepted from the hand of charity, or extorted by poor-laws. It is not averred that this most desirable result can, in all instances, be obtained; but it is, nevertheless, the end to be aimed at. True statesmanship and true political economy, not less than true philanthropy, present this perfect theory as the goal, to be more and more closely approximated by our imperfect practice. The desire to achieve such a result cannot be regarded as an unreasonable ambition; for, though all mankind were well-fed, well-clothed, and well-housed, they might still be but half-civilized. . . .

According to the European theory, men are divided into classes—some to toil and earn, others to seize and enjoy. According to the Massachusetts theory, all are to have an equal chance for earning, and equal security in the enjoyment of what they earn. The latter tends to equality of condition; the former to the grossest inequalities. Tried by any Christian standard of morals, or even by any of the better sort of heathen standards, can any one hesitate, for a moment, in declaring which of the two will produce the greater amount of human welfare; and which, therefore, is the more conformable to the Divine will? The European theory is blind to what constitutes the highest glory, as well as the highest duty, of a State. . . .

I suppose it to be the universal sentiment of all those who mingle any ingredient of benevolence with their notions on Political Economy, that vast and overshadowing private fortunes are among the greatest dangers to which the happiness of the people in a republic can be subjected. Such fortunes would create a feudalism of a new kind, but one more oppressive and unrelenting than that of the Middle Ages. The feudal lords in England, and on the continent, never held their retainers in a more abject condition of servitude than the great majority of foreign manufacturers and capitalists hold their operatives and laborers at the present day. The means employed are different, but the similarity in results is striking. What force did then, money does now. The villein of the Middle Ages had no spot of earth on which he could live, unless one were granted to him by his lord. The operative or laborer of the present day has no employment, and therefore no bread, unless the capitalist will accept his services. The vassal had no shelter but such as his master provided for him. Not one in five thousand of English operatives, or farm laborers, is able to build or own even a hovel; and therefore they must accept such shelter as Capital offers them. The baron prescribed his own terms to his retainers; those terms were peremptory, and the serf must submit or perish. The British manufacturer or farmer prescribes the rate of wages he will give to his work-people; he reduces these wages under whatever pretext he pleases, and they too have no alternative but submission or starvation. In some respects, indeed, the condition of the modern dependant is more forlorn than that of the corresponding serf class in former times. Some attributes of the patriarchal relation did spring up between the lord and his lieges, to soften the harsh relations subsisting between them. Hence came some oversight of the condition of children, some relief in sickness, some protection and support in the decrepitude of age. But only in instances comparatively few have kindly offices smoothed the rugged relation between British Capital and British Labor. The children of the work-people are abandoned to their fate; and, notwithstanding the privations they suffer, and the dangers they threaten, no power in the realm has yet been able to secure them an education; and when the adult laborer is prostrated by sickness, or eventually worn out by toil and age, the poor-house, which has all along been his destination, becomes his destiny.

Now two or three things will doubtless be admitted to be true, beyond all controversy, in regard to Massachusetts. By its industrial condition, and its business operations, it is exposed, far beyond any other state in the Union, to the fatal extremes of overgrown wealth and desperate poverty. Its population is more dense than that of any other state. It is four or five times more dense than the average of all the other states, taken together; and density of population has always been one of the proximate causes of social inequality. According to population and territorial extent, there is far more capital in Massachusetts—capital which is movable, and instantaneously available—than in any other state in the Union; and probably both these qualifications respecting population and territory could be omitted without endangering the truth of the assertion. It has been recently stated, in a very respectable public journal, on the authority of a writer conversant with the subject, that, from the last of June, 1846, to the 1st of August, 1848, the amount of money invested, by the citizens of Massachusetts, "in manufacturing cities, railroads, and other improvements," is "fifty-seven millions of dollars, of which more than fifty has been paid in and expended." The dividends to be received by the citizens of Massachusetts from June, 1848, to April, 1849, are estimated, by the same writer, at ten millions, and the annual increase of capital at "little short of twenty-two millions." If this be so, are we not in danger of naturalizing and domesticating among ourselves those hideous evils which are always engendered between Capital and Labor, when all the capital is in the hands of one class, and all the labor is thrown upon another?

Now, surely, nothing but Universal Education can counter-work this tendency to the domination of capital and the servility of labor. If one class possesses all the wealth and the education, while the residue of society is ignorant and poor, it matters not by what name the relation between them may be called; the latter, in fact and in truth, will be the servile dependents and subjects of the former. But if education be equably diffused, it will draw property after it, by the strongest of all attractions; for such a thing never did happen, and never can happen, as that an intelligent and practical body of men should be permanently poor. Property and labor, in different classes, are essentially antagonistic; but property and labor, in the same class, are essentially fraternal. The people of Massachusetts have, in some degree, appreciated the truth, that the unexampled prosperity of the State—its comfort, its competence, its general intelligence and virtue—is attributable to the education, more or less perfect, which all its people have received; but are they sensible of a fact equally important?—namely, that it is to this same education that two thirds of the people are indebted for not being, to-day, the vassals of as severe a tyranny, in the form of capital, as the lower classes of Europe are bound to in the form of brute force.

Education, then, beyond all other devices of human origin, is the great equalizer of the conditions of men—the balance-wheel of the social machinery. I do not here mean that it so elevates the moral nature as to make men disdain and abhor the oppression of their fellow men. This idea pertains to another of its attributes. But I mean that it gives each man the independence and the means by which he can resist the selfishness of other men. It does better than to disarm the poor of their hostility towards the rich; it prevents being poor. Agrarianism is the revenge of poverty against wealth. The wanton destruction of the property of others—the burning of hay-ricks and corn-ricks, the demolition of machinery, because it supersedes hand-labor, the sprinkling of vitriol on rich dresses—is only agrarianism run mad. Education prevents both the revenge and the madness. On the other hand, a fellow feeling for one's class or caste is the common instinct of hearts not wholly sunk in selfish regards for person, or for family. The spread of education, by enlarging the cultivated class or caste, will open a wider area over which the social feelings will expand; and, if this education should be universal and complete, it would do more than all things else to obliterate factitious distinctions in society.

The main idea set forth in the creeds of some political reformers, or revolutionizers, is that some people are poor because others are rich. This idea supposes a fixed amount of property in the community, which, by fraud or force, or arbitrary law, is unequally divided among men; and the problem presented for solution is how to transfer a portion of this property from those who are supposed to have too much to those who feel and know that they have too little. At this point, both their theory and their expectation of reform stop. But the beneficent power of education would not be exhausted, even though it should peaceably abolish all the miseries that spring from the coexistence, side by side, of enormous wealth and squalid want. It has a higher function. Beyond the power of diffusing old wealth, it has the prerogative of creating new. It is a thousand times more lucrative than fraud, and adds a thousandfold more to a nation's resources than the most successful conquests. Knaves and robbers can obtain only what was before possessed by others. But education creates or develops new treasures—treasures not before possessed or dreamed of by any one. . . .

If a savage will learn how to swim, he can fasten a dozen pounds' weight to his back, and transport it across a narrow river, or other body of water of moderate width. If he will invent an axe, or other instrument, by which to cut down a tree, he can use the tree for a float, and one of its limbs for a paddle, and can thus transport many times the former weight, many times the former distance. Hollowing out his log, he will increase, what may be called, its tonnage—or, rather, its poundage—and, by sharpening its ends, it will cleave the water both more easily and more swiftly. Fastening several trees together, he makes a raft, and thus increases the buoyant power of his embryo water-craft. Turning up the ends of small poles, or using knees of timber instead of straight pieces, and grooving them together, or filling up the interstices between them, in some other way, so as to make them water-tight, he brings his rude raft literally into ship-shape. Improving upon hull below and rigging above, he makes a proud merchantman, to be wafted by the winds from continent to continent. But, even this does not content the adventurous naval architect. He frames iron arms for his ship; and, for oars, affixes iron wheels, capable of swift revolution, and stronger than the strong sea. Into iron-walled cavities in her bosom, he puts iron organs of massive structure and strength, and of cohesion insoluble by fire. Within these, he kindles a small volcano; and then, like a sentient and rational existence, this wonderful creation of his hands cleaves oceans, breasts tides, defies tempests, and bears its living and jubilant freight around the globe. Now, take away intelligence from the ship-builder, and the steamship—that miracle of human art—falls back into a floating log; the log itself is lost; and the savage swimmer, bearing his dozen pounds on his back, alone remains.

And so it is, not in one department only, but in the whole circle of human labors. The annihilation of the sun would no more certainly be followed by darkness, than the extinction of human intelligence would plunge the race at once into the weakness and helplessness of barbarism. To have created such beings as we are, and to have placed them in this world, without the light of the sun, would be no more cruel than for a government to suffer its laboring classes to grow up without knowledge. . . .

For the creation of wealth, then—for the existence of a wealthy people and a wealthy nation—intelligence is the grand condition. The number of improvers will increase, as the intellectual constituency, if I may so call it, increases. In former times, and in most parts of the world even at the present day, not one man in a million has ever had such a development of mind, as made it possible for him to become a contributor to art or science. Let this development precede, and contributions, numberless, and of inestimable value, will be sure to follow. That Political Economy, therefore, which busies itself about capital and labor, supply and demand, interest and rents, favorable and unfavorable balances of trade, but leaves out of account the element of a wide-spread mental development, is nought but stupendous folly. The greatest of all the arts in political economy is to change a consumer into a producer; and the next greatest is to increase the producer's producing power—an end to be directly attained, by increasing his intelligence. . . .

Political Education

The necessity of general intelligence—that is, of education, (for I use the terms as substantially synonymous; because general intelligence can never exist without general education, and general education will be sure to produce general intelligence)—the necessity of general intelligence, under a republican form of government, like most other very important truths, has become a very trite one. It is so trite, indeed, as to have lost much of its force by its familiarity. Almost all the champions of education seize upon this argument, first of all, because it is so simple as to be understood by the ignorant, and so strong as to convince the skeptical. Nothing would be easier than to follow in the train of so many writers, and to demonstrate, by logic, by history, and by the nature of the case, that a republican form of government, without intelligence in the people, must be, on a vast scale, what a mad-house, without superintendent or keepers, would be, on a small one—the despotism of a few succeeded by universal anarchy, and anarchy by despotism, with no change but from bad to worse. Want of space and time alike forbid me to attempt any full development of the merits of this theme; but yet, in the closing one of a series of reports, partaking somewhat of the nature of a summary of former arguments, an omission of this topic would suggest to the comprehensive mind the idea of incompleteness.

That the affairs of a great nation or state are exceedingly complicated and momentous, no one will dispute. Nor will it be questioned that the degree of intelligence that superintends, should be proportioned to the magnitude of the interests superintended. He who scoops out a wooden dish needs less skill than the maker of a steam-engine or a telescope. The dealer in small wares requires less knowledge than the merchant who exports and imports to and from all quarters of the globe. An ambassador cannot execute his functions with the stock of attainments or of talents sufficient for a parish clerk. Indeed, it is clear, that the want of adequate intelligence—of intelligence commensurate with the nature of the duties to be performed—will bring ruin or disaster upon any department. A merchant loses his intelligence, and he becomes a bankrupt. A lawyer loses his intelligence, and he forfeits all the interests of his clients. Intelligence abandons a physician, and his patients die, with more than the pains of natural dissolution. Should judges upon the bench be bereft of this guide, what havoc would be made of the property and the innocence of men! Let this counsellor be taken from executive officers, and the penalties due to the wicked would be visited upon the righteous, while the rewards and immunities of the righteous would be bestowed upon the guilty. And so, should intelligence desert the halls of legislation, weakness, rashness, contradiction, and error would glare out from every page of the statute book. Now, as a republican government represents almost all interests, whether social, civil or military, the necessity of a degree of intelligence adequate to the due administration of them all is so self-evident that a bare statement is the best argument.

But in the possession of this attribute of intelligence, elective legislators will never far surpass their electors. By a natural law, like that which regulates the equilibrium of fluids, elector and elected, appointer and appointee, tend to the same level. It is not more certain that a wise and enlightened constituency will refuse to invest a reckless and profligate man with office, or discard him if accidentally chosen, than it is that a foolish or immoral constituency will discard or eject a wise man. This law of assimilation, between the choosers and the chosen, results, not only from the fact that the voter originally selects his representative according to the affinities of good or of ill, of wisdom or of folly, which exist between them; but if the legislator enacts or favors a law which is too wise for the constituent to understand, or too just for him to approve, the next election will set him aside as certainly as if he had made open merchandise of the dearest interests of the people, by perjury and for a bribe. And if the infinitely Just and Good, in giving laws to the Jews, recognized the "hardness of their hearts," how much more will an earthly ruler recognize the baseness or wickedness of the people, when his heart is as hard as theirs! In a republican government, legislators are a mirror reflecting the moral countenance of their constituents. And hence it is, that the establishment of a republican government, without well-appointed and efficient means for the universal education of the people, is the most rash and fool-hardy experiment ever tried by man. Its fatal results may not be immediately developed—they may not follow as the thunder follows the lightning—for time is an element in maturing them, and the calamity is too great to be prepared in a day; but, like the slow-accumulating avalanche, they will grow more terrific by delay, and, at length, though it may be at a late hour, will overwhelm with ruin whatever lies athwart their path. It may be an easy thing to make a Republic; but it is a very laborious thing to make Republicans; and woe to the republic that rests upon no better foundations than ignorance, selfishness, and passion. Such a Republic may grow in numbers and in wealth. As an avaricious man adds acres to his lands, so its rapacious government may increase its own darkness by annexing provinces and states to its ignorant domain. Its armies may be invincible, and its fleets may strike terror into nations on the opposite sides of the globe, at the same hour. Vast in its extent, and enriched with all the prodigality of nature, it may possess every capacity and opportunity of being great, and of doing good. But if such a Republic be devoid of intelligence, it will only the more closely resemble an obscene giant who has waxed strong in his youth, and grown wanton in his strength; whose brain has been developed only in the region of the appetites and passions, and not in the organs of reason and conscience; and who, therefore, is boastful of his bulk alone, and glories in the weight of his heel and in the destruction of his arm. Such a Republic, with all its noble capacities for beneficence, will rush with the speed of a whirlwind to an ignominious end; and all good men of after-times would be fain to weep over its downfall, did not their scorn and contempt at its folly and its wickedness repress all sorrow for its fate. . . .

However elevated the moral character of a constituency may be, however well informed in matters of general science or history, yet they must, if citizens of a Republic, understand something of the true nature and functions of the government under which they live. That any one who is to participate in the government of a country, when he becomes a man, should receive no instruction respecting the nature and functions of the government he is afterwards to administer is a political solecism. In all nations, hardly excepting the most rude and barbarous, the future sovereign receives some training which is supposed to fit him for the exercise of the powers and duties of his anticipated station. Where, by force of law, the government devolves upon the heir, while yet in a state of legal infancy, some regency, or other substitute, is appointed, to act in his stead, until his arrival at mature age; and, in the meantime, he is subjected to such a course of study and discipline, as will tend to prepare him, according to the political theory of the time and the place, to assume the reins of authority at the appointed age. If, in England, or in the most enlightened European monarchies, it would be a proof of restored barbarism to permit the future sovereign to grow up without any knowledge of his duties—and who can doubt that it would be such a proof—then, surely, it would be not less a proof of restored, or of never-removed barbarism, amongst us, to empower any individual to use the elective franchise, without preparing him for so momentous a trust. Hence, the constitution of the United States, and of our own State, should be made a study in our Public Schools. The partition of the powers of government into the three co-ordinate branches—legislative, judicial, and executive—with the duties appropriately devolving upon each; the mode of electing or of appointing all officers, with the reason on which it was founded; and, especially, the duty of every citizen, in a government of laws, to appeal to the courts for redress, in all cases of alleged wrong, instead of undertaking to vindicate his own rights by his own arm; and, in a government where the people are the acknowledged sources of power, the duty of changing laws and rulers by an appeal to the ballot, and not by rebellion, should be taught to all the children until they are fully understood.

Had the obligations of the future citizen been sedulously inculcated upon all the children of this Republic, would the patriot have had to mourn over so many instances, where the voter, not being able to accomplish his purpose by voting, has proceeded to accomplish it by violence; where, agreeing with his fellow citizens, to use the machinery of the ballot, he makes a tacit reservation, that, if that machinery does not move according to his pleasure, he will wrest or break it? If the responsibleness and value of the elective franchise were duly appreciated, the day of our State and National elections would be among the most solemn and religious days in the calendar. Men would approach them, not only with preparation and solicitude, but with the sobriety and solemnity, with which discreet and religious-minded men meet the great crises of life. No man would throw away his vote, through caprice or wantonness, any more than he would throw away his estate, or sell his family into bondage. No man would cast his vote through malice or revenge, any more than a good surgeon would amputate a limb, or a good navigator sail through perilous straits, under the same criminal passions.

But, perhaps, it will be objected, that the constitution is subject to different readings, or that the policy of different administrations has become the subject of party strife; and, therefore, if any thing of constitutional or political law is introduced into our schools, there is danger that teachers will be chosen on account of their affinities to this or that political party; or that teachers will feign affinities which they do not feel, in order that they may be chosen; and so each schoolroom will at length become a miniature political club-room, exploding with political resolves, or flaming out with political addresses, prepared, by beardless boys, in scarcely legible hand-writing, and in worse grammar.

With the most limited exercise of discretion, all apprehensions of this kind are wholly groundless. There are different readings of the constitution, it is true; and there are partisan topics which agitate the country from side to side; but the controverted points, compared with those about which there is no dispute, do not bear the proportion of one to a hundred. And what is more, no man is qualified, or can be qualified, to discuss the disputable questions, unless previously and thoroughly versed in those questions, about which there is no dispute. In the terms and principles common to all, and recognized by all, is to be found the only common medium of language and of idea, by which the parties can become intelligible to each other; and there, too, is the only common ground, whence the arguments of the disputants can be drawn.

It is obvious, on the other hand, that if the tempest of political strife were to be let loose upon our Common Schools, they would be overwhelmed with sudden ruin. Let it be once understood, that the schoolroom is a legitimate theatre for party politics, and with what violence will hostile partisans struggle to gain possession of the stage, and to play their parts upon it! Nor will the stage be the only scene of gladiatorial contests. These will rage in all the avenues that lead to it. A preliminary advantage, indispensable to ultimate success, will be the appointment of a teacher of the true faith. As the great majority of the schools in the State are now organized, this can be done only by electing a prudential committee, who will make what he calls political soundness paramount to all other considerations of fitness. Thus, after petty skirmishings among neighbors, the fierce encounter will begin in the district's primary assembly—in the schoolroom itself. This contest being over, the election of the superintending, or town's committee, must be determined in the same way, and this will bring together the combustibles of each district, to burn with an intenser and a more devouring flame, in the town meeting. It is very possible, nay, not at all improbable, that the town may be of one political complexion, while a majority of the districts are of the opposite. Who shall moderate the fury of these conflicting elements when they rage against each other, and who shall save the dearest interests of the children from being consumed in the fierce combustion? If parents find that their children are indoctrinated into what they call political heresies, will they not withdraw them from the school; and, if they withdraw them from the school, will they not resist all appropriations to support a school from which they derive no benefit?

But, could the schools, themselves, survive these dangers for a single year, it would be only to encounter others still more perilous. Why should not the same infection that poisons all the relations of the schoolroom, spread itself abroad, and mingle with all questions of external organization and arrangement? Why should not political hostility cause the dismemberment of districts, already too small; or, what would work equal injury, prevent the union of districts, whose power of usefulness would be doubled by a combination of their resources? What better could be expected, than that one set of school books should be expelled, and another introduced, as they might be supposed, however remotely, to favor one party or the other; or, as the authors of the books might belong to one party or the other? And who could rely upon the reports, or even the statistics of a committee, chosen by partisan votes, goaded on by partisan impulses, and responsible to partisan domination; and this, too, without any opportunity of control or check from the minority? Nay, if the schools could survive long enough to meet the crisis, why should not any and every measure be taken, either to maintain an existing political ascendancy, or to recover a lost one, in a school district, or in a town, which has even been taken by unscrupulous politicians, to maintain or to recover an ascendancy at the polls? Into a district, or into a town, voters may be introduced from abroad, to turn the scale. An employer may dismiss the employed, for their refusal to submit to his dictation; or make the bread that is given to the poor man's children, perform the double office of payment for labor to be performed, and of a bribe for principle to be surrendered. And, beyond all this, if the imagination can conceive any thing more deplorable than this, what kind of political doctrines would be administered to the children, amid the vicissitudes of party domination—their alternations of triumph and defeat? This year, under the ascendancy of one side, the constitution declares one thing: and commentaries, glosses, and the authority of distinguished names, all ratify and confirm its decisions. But victory is a fickle goddess. Next year, the vanquished triumph; and constitution, gloss, and authority, make that sound doctrine, which was pestilent error before, and that false, which was true. Right and wrong have changed sides. The children must now join in chorus to denounce what they had been taught to reverence before, and to reverence what they had been taught to denounce. In the mean time, those great principles, which, according to Cicero, are the same at Rome and at Athens, the same now and forever—and which, according to Hooker, have their seat in the bosom of God, become the fittest emblems of chance and change.

Long, however, before this series of calamities would exhaust itself upon our schools, these schools themselves would cease to be. The plough-share would have turned up their foundations. Their history would have been brought to a close—a glorious and ascending history, until struck down by the hand of political parricide; then, suddenly falling with a double ruin—with death, and with ignominy. But to avoid such a catastrophe, shall all teaching, relative to the nature of our government, be banished from our schools; and shall our children be permitted to grow up in entire ignorance of the political history of their country? In the schools of a republic, shall the children be left without any distinct knowledge of the nature of a republican government; or only with such knowledge as they may pick up from angry political discussions, or from party newspapers; from caucus speeches, or Fourth of July orations—the Apocrypha of Apocrypha?

Surely, between these extremes, there must be a medium not difficult to be found. And is not this the middle course, which all sensible and judicious men, all patriots, and all genuine republicans, must approve?—namely, that those articles in the creed of republicanism, which are accepted by all, believed in by all, and which form the common basis of our political faith, shall be taught to all. But when the teacher, in the course of his lessons or lectures on the fundamental law, arrives at a controverted text, he is either to read it without comment or remark; or, at most, he is only to say that the passage is the subject of disputation, and that the schoolroom is neither the tribunal to adjudicate, nor the forum to discuss it.

Such being the rule established by common consent, and such the practice, observed with fidelity under it, it will come to be universally understood, that political proselytism is no function of the school; but that all indoctrination into matters of controversy between hostile political parties is to be elsewhere sought for, and elsewhere imparted. Thus, may all the children of the Commonwealth receive instruction in the great essentials of political knowledge—in those elementary ideas without which they will never be able to investigate more recondite and debatable questions—thus, will the only practicable method be adopted for discovering new truths, and for discarding—instead of perpetuating—old errors; and thus, too, will that pernicious race of intolerant zealots, whose whole faith may be summed up in two articles—that they, themselves, are always infallibly right, and that all dissenters are certainly wrong—be extinguished—extinguished, not by violence, nor by proscription, but by the more copious inflowing of the light of truth.

9

Selection From Dare the Schools Build a New Social Order? *(1932)*

In 1932, George S. Counts wrote a brief book titled *Dare the Schools Build a New Social Order?* The book was written at the height of the Great Depression. It called for schools and teachers to take on an active role in reconstructing the society.

Counts argues that schools reflect the culture of which they are a part and that they are "driven by the very forces that are transforming the rest of the social order."

Counts believes that the schools in the United States are essentially conservative. Even progressive education, which he believed philosophically had the potential to transform traditional learning, was largely under the control and influence of an elite business class. Lacking a clearly articulated set of social objectives, Counts saw the movement as incomplete.

Although Counts recognizes that any education, to a certain degree, involves the imposition of values on the child, he also sees it as a means by which to critically understand and challenge the world. It is in this context—that is, having the child learn through the curriculum of the schools to be a critical and reflective thinker and, in turn, a member of the democracy—that Counts sets himself apart from many earlier thinkers in the field.

As you read this selection, consider the following questions:

1. Is it possible that progressive education was a good idea that, for various social and political reasons, was imperfectly implemented in American education?
2. What are the implications for the curriculum of having students learn to become critical and engaged thinkers? What are the implications for teaching?

9

Selection From Dare the Schools Build a New Social Order? *(1932)*

George S. Counts

Like all simple and unsophisticated peoples we Americans have a sublime faith in education. Faced with any difficult problem of life we set our minds at rest sooner or later by the appeal to the school. We are convinced that education is the one unfailing remedy for every ill to which man is subject, whether it be vice, crime, war, poverty, riches, injustice, racketeering, political corruption, race hatred, class conflict, or just plain original sin. We even speak glibly and often about the general reconstruction of society through the school. We cling to this faith in spite of the fact that the very period in which our troubles have multiplied so rapidly has witnessed an unprecedented expansion of organized education. This would seem to suggest that our schools, instead of directing the course of change, are themselves driven by the very forces that are transforming the rest of the social order.

The bare fact, however, that simple and unsophisticated peoples have unbounded faith in education does not mean that the faith is untenable. History shows that the intuitions of such folk may be nearer the truth than the weighty and carefully reasoned judgments of the learned and the wise. Under certain conditions education may be as beneficent and as powerful as we are wont to think. But if it is to be so, teachers must abandon much of their easy optimism, subject the concept of education to the most rigorous scrutiny, and be prepared to deal much more fundamentally, realistically, and positively with the American social situation than has been their habit in the past. Any

Source: Counts, George S. 1932. *Dare the Schools Build a New Social Order?* 3–12. New York: John Day.

individual or group that would aspire to lead society must be ready to pay the costs of leadership: to accept responsibility, to suffer calumny, to surrender security, to risk both reputation and fortune. If this price, or some important part of it, is not being paid, then the chances are that the claim to leadership is fraudulent. Society is never redeemed without effort, struggle, and sacrifice. Authentic leaders are never found breathing that rarefied atmosphere lying above the dust and smoke of battle. With regard to the past we always recognize the truth of this principle, but when we think of our own times we profess the belief that the ancient roles have been reversed and that now prophets of a new age receive their rewards among the living.

That the existing school is leading the way to a better social order is a thesis which few informed persons would care to defend. Except as it is forced to figh[illegible] for its own life during times of depression, its course is too serene and [illegible]bled. Only in the rarest of instances does it wage war on behalf of [illegible]deal. Almost everywhere it is in the grip of conservative forces [illegible] cause of perpetuating ideas and institutions suited to an age [illegible]re is one movement above the educational horizon which [illegible]omise of genuine and creative leadership. I refer to the [illegible]ovement. Surely in this union of two of the great [illegible]people, the faith in progress and the faith in education, [illegible]hope for light and guidance. Here is a movement which [illegible]be completely devoted to the promotion of social welfare [illegible]ation.

[illegible] a casual examination of the program and philosophy of the Progressive schools, however, raises many doubts in the mind. To be sure, these schools have a number of large achievements to their credit. They have focused attention squarely upon the child; they have recognized the fundamental importance of the interest of the learner; they have defended the thesis that activity lies at the root of all true education; they have conceived learning in terms of life situations and growth of character; they have championed the rights of the child as a free personality. Most of this is excellent, but in my judgment it is not enough. It constitutes too narrow a conception of the meaning of education; it brings into the picture but one-half of the landscape.

If an educational movement, or any other movement, calls itself progressive, it must have orientation; it must possess direction. The word itself implies moving forward, and moving forward can have little meaning in the absence of clearly defined purposes. We cannot, like Stephen Leacock's horseman, dash off in all directions at once. Nor should we, like our presidential candidates, evade every disturbing issue and be all things to all men. Also we must beware lest we become so devoted to motion that we neglect the question of direction and be entirely satisfied with movement in circles. Here, I think, we find the fundamental weakness, not only of Progressive Education, but also of American education generally. Like a baby shaking a rattle, we seem to be utterly content with action, provided it is sufficiently vigorous and noisy. In the last analysis a very large part of American educational thought, inquiry, and experimentation is much ado about nothing. And, if we are permitted to push the analogy of the rattle a bit further, our consecration to motion is encouraged and supported in order to keep us out of mischief. At least we know that so long as we thus busy ourselves we shall not incur the serious displeasure of our social elders.

The weakness of Progressive Education thus lies in the fact that it has elaborated no theory of social welfare, unless it be that of anarchy or extreme individualism. In this, of course, it is but reflecting the viewpoint of the members of the liberal-minded upper middle class who send their children to the Progressive schools—persons who are fairly well-off, who have abandoned the faiths of their fathers, who assume an agnostic attitude towards all important questions, who pride themselves on their open-mindedness and tolerance, who favor in a mild sort of way fairly liberal programs of social reconstruction, who are full of good will and humane sentiment, who have vague aspirations for world peace and human brotherhood, who can be counted upon to respond moderately to any appeal made in the name of charity, who are genuinely distressed at the sight of *unwonted* forms of cruelty, misery, and suffering, and who perhaps serve to soften somewhat the bitter clashes of those real forces that govern the world; but who, in spite of all their good qualities, have no deep and abiding loyalties, possess no convictions for which they would sacrifice overmuch, would find it hard to live without their customary material comforts, are rather insensitive to the accepted forms of social injustice, are content to play the role of interested spectator in the drama of human history, refuse to see reality in its harsher and more disagreeable forms, rarely move outside the pleasant circles of the class to which they belong, and in the day of severe trial will follow the lead of the most powerful and respectable forces in society and at the same time find good reasons for so doing. These people have shown themselves entirely incapable of dealing with any of the great crises of our time—war, prosperity, or depression. At bottom they are romantic sentimentalists, but with a sharp eye on the main chance. That they can be trusted to write our educational theories and shape our educational programs is highly improbable.

Among the members of this class the number of children is small, the income relatively high, and the economic functions of the home greatly reduced. For these reasons an inordinate emphasis on the child and child interests is entirely welcome to them. They wish to guard their offspring from too strenuous endeavor and from coming into too intimate contact with the grimmer aspects of industrial society. They wish their sons and daughters to succeed according to the standards of their class and to be a credit to their parents. At heart feeling themselves members of a superior human strain, they do not want their children to mix too freely with the children of the poor or of the less fortunate races. Nor do they want them to accept radical social doctrines, espouse unpopular causes, or lose themselves in quest of any Holy Grail. According to their views education should deal with life, but with life at a distance or in a highly diluted form. They would generally maintain that life should be kept at arm's length, if it should not be handled with a poker.

If Progressive Education is to be genuinely progressive, it must emancipate itself from the influence of this class, face squarely and courageously every social issue, come to grips with life in all of its stark reality, establish an organic relation with the community, develop a realistic and comprehensive theory of welfare, fashion a compelling and challenging vision of human destiny, and become less frightened than it is today at the bogies of *imposition* and *indoctrination.* In a word, Progressive Education cannot place its trust in a child centered school.

This brings us to the most crucial issue in education—the question of the nature and extent of the influence which the school should exercise over the development of the child. The advocates of extreme freedom have been so successful in championing what they call the rights of the child that even the most skillful practitioners of the art of converting others to their opinions disclaim all intention of molding the learner. And when the word indoctrination is coupled with education there is scarcely one among us possessing the hardihood to refuse to be horrified. This feeling is so widespread that even Mr. Lunacharsky, Commissar of Education in the Russian Republic until 1929, assured me on one occasion that the Soviet educational leaders do not believe in the indoctrination of children in the ideas and principles of communism. When I asked him whether their children become good communists while attending the schools, he replied that the great majority do. On seeking from him an explanation of this remarkable phenomenon he said that Soviet teachers merely tell their children the truth about human history. As a consequence, so he asserted, practically all of the more intelligent boys and girls adopt the philosophy of communism. I recall also that the Methodist sect in which I was reared always confined its teachings to the truth!

The issue is no doubt badly confused by historical causes. The champions of freedom are obviously the product of an age that has broken very fundamentally with the past and is equally uncertain about the future. In many cases they feel themselves victims of narrow orthodoxies which were imposed upon them during childhood and which have severely cramped their lives. At any suggestion that the child should be influenced by his elders they therefore envisage the establishment of a state church, the formulation of a body of sacred doctrine, and the teaching of this doctrine as fixed and final. If we are forced to choose between such an unenlightened form of pedagogical influence and a condition of complete freedom for the child, most of us would in all probability choose the latter as the lesser of two evils. But this is to create a wholly artificial situation: the choice should not be limited to these two extremes. Indeed today neither extreme is possible. I believe firmly that a critical factor must play an important role in any adequate educational program, at least in any such program fashioned for the modern world. An education that does not strive to promote the fullest and most thorough understanding of the world is not worthy of the name. Also there must be no deliberate distortion or suppression of facts to support any theory or point of view. On the other hand, I am prepared to defend the thesis that all education contains a large element of imposition, that in the very nature of the case this is inevitable, that the existence and evolution of society depend upon it, that it is consequently eminently desirable, and that the frank acceptance of this fact by the educator is a major professional obligation. I even contend that failure to do this involves the clothing of one's own deepest prejudices in the garb of universal truth and the introduction into the theory and practice of education of an element of obscurantism. . . .

PART III

Compulsory Schooling, Education, and the Transmission of Culture

Who should control the education of children, and whether or not people should be compelled to go to school and learn certain specific things, represents one of the classic debates of educational policy and practice. In a democracy, does the state have the right and obligation to make sure that children learn certain things (reading, writing, numeracy, civics)? Should parents have the right to proscribe and define what their children learn? What happens when the desires and needs of the state are in conflict with those of the family? Whose point of view should predominate?

Issues such as those outlined in the previous paragraph have made their way as high as the Supreme Court. In *Pierce v. the Society of Sisters* (1925) and *Wisconsin v. Yoder* (1972), parents challenged, on the basis of their religious beliefs, whether or not their children could be compelled to attend state schools. In the case of *Pierce,* a 1922 Oregon compulsory education law requiring parents, or guardians, to send their children to public schools rather than private Catholic schools was overturned. In *Wisconsin v. Yoder,* three Amish families in Wisconsin objected to the requirement that their children attend school until the age of sixteen. Attendance at school beyond the level of learning to read the Bible was seen by these families as a distraction from the traditions of their community and their religious beliefs. The Supreme Court ruled that compulsory education laws violated the right of the Amish families to freely exercise their religious beliefs.

As seen in the readings included in this section of the book, some critics maintain that the state and the educational system have a vested interest in the education of children. The state of Massachusetts in 1852, and eventually the rest of the states in the Union, reinforced its right through the passage of compulsory education laws.

Critics of compulsory education challenge what values and beliefs are transmitted to children by means of compulsory education. Educational critics such as Paul Goodman, Paulo Freire, and Ivan Illich see compulsory education as often mis-serving the needs of minority groups or the oppressed, while serving the purposes of those in power.

As you read the selections in this section of the book, keep in mind the following questions:

1. If education is inherently valuable and worthwhile for individuals, why should they be compelled to attend school?
2. What are the rights of the individual, and what are the rights of the state when it comes to education?
3. Does the state have its own primary interest at work in the education of children, or does it have the interests of the child first and foremost?
4. How is a nation shaped into a coherent political and economic system? Is education a critical part of this process?
5. Does compulsory education have different implications for different students based on race or socioeconomic background?
6. To what extent are teachers agents of the state in the enforcement of compulsory education?

10

Massachusetts Compulsory School Law (1852)

In 1852, Massachusetts passed the first statewide law in the United States requiring children between the ages of eight and fourteen to attend school for twelve weeks a year. Parents or guardians who did not send their children to be educated would be fined.

As you read the following selection, consider these questions:

1. What are the reasons that the state would want to educate students to a certain level?
2. Why might some parents not want to see their children educated by the state?
3. If there is a conflict between the state and parents over the education of a child, who should prevail?

10

Massachusetts Compulsory School Law (1852)

General Court of Massachusetts

An Act Concerning the Attendance of Children at School

BE IT ENACTED BY THE SENATE AND HOUSE OF REPRESENTATIVES IN GENERAL COURT ASSEMBLED, AND BY THE AUTHORITY OF THE SAME, AS FOLLOWS:

Sect. 1. Every person who shall have any child under his control, between the ages of eight and fourteen years, shall send such child to some public school within the town or city in which he resides, during at least twelve weeks, if the public schools within such town or city shall be so long kept, in each and every year during which such child shall be under his control, six weeks of which shall be consecutive.

Sect. 2. Every person who shall violate the provisions of the first section of this act shall forfeit, to the use of such town or city, a sum not exceeding twenty dollars, to be recovered by complaint or indictment.

Sect. 3. It shall be the duty of the school committee in the several towns or cities to inquire into all cases of violation of the first section of this act, and to ascertain of the persons violating the same, the reasons, if any, for such violation, and they shall report such cases, together with such reasons, if any, to the town

Source: From *Acts and Resolves Passed by the General Court of Massachusetts in the Year 1852,* 170–171. Boston: White and Potter.

or city in their annual report; but they shall not report any cases such as are provided for by the fourth section of this act.

Sect. 4. If, upon inquiry by the school committee, it shall appear, or if upon the trial of any complaint or indictment under this act it shall appear, that such child has attended some school, not in the town or city in which he resides, for the time required by this act, or has been otherwise furnished with the means of education for a like period of time, or has already acquired those branches of learning which are taught in common schools, or if it shall appear that his bodily or mental condition has been such as to prevent his attendance at school, or his acquisition of learning for such a period of time, or that the person having the control of such child, is not able, by reason of poverty, to send such child to school, or to furnish him with the means of education, then such person shall be held not to have violated the provisions of this act.

Sect. 5. It shall be the duty of the treasurer of the town or city to prosecute all violations of this act. (*Approved by the Governor, May 18, 1852.*)

11

Selection From Compulsory Mis-Education *(1964)*

By the early 1960s, radical educators began to question the value of compulsory education. Among the most prominent was Paul Goodman (1911–1972), whose *Compulsory Mis-Education* was published in 1964. *Compulsory Mis-Education* proposed a number of alternatives to compulsory schooling, including alternative programs and nontraditional teachers. Ideas such as these were developed in even more detail by theorists such as Ivan Illich.

As you read the selection, consider the following questions:

1. Do all children necessarily learn in the same way? Is a traditional school setting necessarily good for many students?
2. Are traditional teachers the only people who should educate children, or are there members of the community who can work with them equally well?
3. What is defined as necessary knowledge that should be taught, and why?

11

Selection From Compulsory Mis-Education *(1964)*

Paul Goodman

The compulsory system has become a universal trap, and it is no good. Very many of the youth, both poor and middle class, might be better off if the system simply did not exist, even if they then had no formal schooling at all. (I am extremely curious for a philosophic study of Prince Edward County in Virginia, where for some years schooling did not exist for Negro children.)

But what would become of these children? For very many, both poor and middle class, their homes are worse than the schools, and the city streets are worse in another way. Our urban and suburban environments are precisely not cities or communities where adults naturally attend to the young and educate to a viable life. Also, perhaps especially in the case of the overt drop-outs, the state of their body and soul is such that we must give them refuge and remedy, whether it be called school, settlement house, youth worker, or work camp.

There are thinkable alternatives. Throughout this little book, as occasion arises, I shall offer alternative proposals that I as a single individual have heard of or thought up. Here are half a dozen directly relevant to the subject we have been discussing, the system as compulsory trap. In principle, when a law begins to do more harm than good, the best policy is to alleviate it or try doing without it.

1. Have "no school at all" for a few classes. These children should be selected from tolerable, though not necessarily cultured, homes. They should be neighbors and numerous enough to be a society for one another and so that

---

Source: Goodman, Paul. 1964. *Compulsory Mis-Education and the Community of Scholars*, 31–34. New York: Vintage Books.

they do not feel merely "different." Will they learn the rudiments anyway? This experiment cannot do the children any academic harm, since there is good evidence that normal children will make up the first seven years school-work with four to seven months of good teaching.

2. Dispense with the school building for a few classes; provide teachers and use the city itself as the school—its streets, cafeterias, stores, movies, museums, parks, and factories. Where feasible, it certainly makes more sense to teach using the real subject-matter than to bring an abstraction of the subject-matter into the school building as "curriculum." Such a class should probably not exceed 10 children for one pedagogue. The idea—it is the model of Athenian education—is not dissimilar to Youth gang work, but not applied to delinquents and not playing to the gang ideology.

3. Along the same lines, but both outside and inside the school building, use appropriate *unlicensed* adults of the community—the druggist, the storekeeper, the mechanic—as the proper educators of the young into the grown-up world. By this means we can try to overcome the separation of the young from the grown-up world so characteristic in modern urban life, and to diminish the omnivorous authority of the professional school-people. Certainly it would be a useful and animating experience for the adults. (There is the beginning of such a volunteer program in the New York and some other systems.)

4. Make class attendance not compulsory, in the manner of A. S. Neill's Summerhill. If the teachers are good, absence would tend to be eliminated; if they are bad, let them know it. The compulsory law is useful to get the children away from the parents, but it must not result in trapping the children. A fine modification of this suggestion is the rule used by Frank Brown in Florida; he permits the children to be absent for a week or a month to engage in any worthwhile enterprise or visit any new environment.

5. Decentralize an urban school (or do not build a new big building) into small units, 20 to 50, in available store-fronts or clubhouses. These tiny schools, equipped with record-player and pin-ball machine, could combine play, socializing, discussion, and formal teaching. For special events, the small units can be brought together into a common auditorium or gymnasium, so as to give the sense of the greater community. Correspondingly, I think it would be worthwhile to give the Little Red Schoolhouse a spin under modern urban conditions, and see how it works out—that is, to combine all the ages in a little room for 25 to 30, rather than to grade by age.

6. Use a pro rata part of the school money to send children to economically marginal farms for a couple of months of the year, perhaps 6 children from mixed backgrounds to a farmer. The only requirement is that the farmer feed them and not beat them; best, of course, if they take part in the farm-work. This

will give the farmer cash, as part of the generally desirable program to redress the urban-rural ratio to something nearer to 70% to 30%. (At present, less than 8% of families are rural.) Conceivably, some of the urban children will take to the other way of life, and we might generate a new kind of rural culture.

I frequently suggest these and similar proposals at teachers colleges, and I am looked at with an eerie look—do I really mean to diminish the state-aid grant for each student-day? But mostly the objection is that such proposals entail intolerable administrative difficulties.

Above all, we must apply these or any other proposals to particular individuals and small groups, without the obligation of uniformity. There is a case for uniform standards of achievement, lodged in the Regents, but they cannot be reached by uniform techniques. The claim that standardization of procedure is more efficient, less costly, or alone administratively practical, is often false. Particular inventiveness requires thought, but thought does not cost money.

12

"Vulnerability and Education" (1966)

In his essay "Vulnerability and Education," the anthropologist and sociologist Jules Henry (1904–1969) makes clear that one of the primary purposes that schools have is making students vulnerable. In doing so, schools are provided a means by which to control and shape people in order to maintain the social system. Henry maintains that people are not entirely powerless but that they can resist the control that is imposed over them.

In reading the following essay, consider these questions:

1. Is making people vulnerable a necessary and useful thing? If so, is school an appropriate place to do so?
2. Should socializing children to fear and feel vulnerable be part of learning?
3. Is teaching children to resist being vulnerable an appropriate activity for schools, or for parents? Does teaching children to resist contradict the function of schools in some way?
4. Is it important for teachers to be made aware of the fact that they are not only the transmitters of cultural values to children but also one of the means by which society makes children vulnerable?

12

"Vulnerability and Education" (1966)

Jules Henry

This paper would never have been written were it not for Raymond Callahan's distinguished book *Education and the Cult of Efficiency*, in which he discusses the extreme vulnerability of school administrators.* He argues that, up to the second decade of this century, they were vulnerable largely because of the power exercised over education by business. Reading the book, I said to myself: 'All are vulnerable. Mankind is a vulnerable animal and suffers from feelings of vulnerability day in, day out, awake and in his dreams.'

As a college teacher, I am aware of the excruciating vulnerability of students; and my own sensation of vulnerability as a student will never leave me. I am remotely like the old professor in the movie *Wild Strawberries* who, at the peak of his fame, when he was about to receive the highest scholastic honour in the country and a salute of cannons, had a dream the night before of failing an examination. It is not very long since I ceased to have such dreams; they are the primeval dreams of confronting life's test and failing.

Social scientists consider protection a requisite for society, but it is also essential that society make men vulnerable. If a man is invulnerable society cannot reach him, and if society produces men who cannot be reached, it cannot endure. Thus society will protect us only if we consent to being relatively defenseless. To the end that man can be injured and thus brought to heel, an array of frightful devices has been created so that men will be meek and mild, even to being meek and mild in order to be violent and terrible, like the soldier who obeys orders to kill. From all this it follows that in order for society to survive it must create a vulnerable character structure in its members. The combination of factors that make us thus vulnerable I call the *vulnerability system*.

Source: Henry, Jules. 1966. "Vulnerability and Education." *Teachers College Record* 68 (2): 135–145.

* Raymond Callahan, *Education and the Cult of Efficiency*, University of Chicago Press, 1964.

Bringing Men to Heel

Where is man vulnerable and how is his vulnerability accomplished? To begin with we must have a clear idea of the areas of existence in which man is exposed to injury. First there is his reputation—his good name. Since a person protects it by learning the norms of his social class and never deviating, reputation depends on careful study of norms and obedience to them, however one may despise them. Of course it is always better if one believes in them, and this is the effortless way of maintaining a good reputation, of being socially invulnerable. But maintaining a good reputation must involve also a certain amount of concealment—of hiding one's deviations. Since deviation can be in thought as well as in action, invulnerability of reputation involves learning how to conceal deviant thoughts. Hence the person with an invulnerable reputation knows how to conceal his socially unacceptable thoughts—if he ever has any. Of course, the best way to handle deviant thoughts is NOT to have any. This requires either looking away quickly from the socially unpleasant; or better still, never looking at anything closely.

How does society make people excruciatingly sensitive to the possibilities of and dangers in losing reputation, and how does society make one sensitive to one's vulnerability? It is done through placing reputation—the social person—in the centre of consideration and making reputation destiny; by degrading the inner self to second, third, or merely adventitious place, and making the social facade supreme, so that at every step the self will be sacrificed to the facade.

How is this manoeuvre accomplished? Surely it can be accomplished best through acquiescence and through disregarding and even punishing the emerging self. It is not so much, however, that the child is punished for asserting his selfhood, but that the thrusting upward of the self is not even seen; what is seen by the parent is largely what is relevant to social requirements; what contributes to a good name; what makes one socially invulnerable. In this way the spirit is pruned, largely insensibly, of everything that is not socially acceptable and self becomes identical with reputation. This need not be so, for it is possible for a person to lose his good name and yet accomplish good things in the name of his self. Great reformers and creators have often done this.

Dependence and Inflated Images

An important function of the feeling of vulnerability is to make us dependent. As small children we are overwhelmed by our vulnerability and so lean on parents, who have in this way become exalted in our eyes. Thus another function of vulnerability is to enlarge the image of those who could harm us and those who protect us. Society is built on a foundation of inflated images derived from vulnerability and upheld by the feeling that what is important are the norms and not ourselves.

While in our culture dependence on parents is necessary and very real in childhood, the function of the inflated parental image is to project the child's feeling of vulnerability far beyond the boundaries of realism—in order that society itself may be protected. Thus behind every inflated authority image lies society's fear that it is vulnerable. Behind every inflated image lies society's determination to cancel independence. The child's vulnerability is sustained and intensified by the elementary school, where he is at the teacher's mercy. The teacher, clearly through no fault of her own, is the agent of vulnerability, and she transmits the sense of vulnerability to the child through two weapons thrust into her hands, sometimes against her will—discipline and the power to fail the child. Before these absolute weapons the child is even more vulnerable than with his parents; for with his parents the agony of vulnerability is allayed in part by love, and he can, within limits, fight back. In school, however, this usually is not the case; for in the first place, in the contemporary overcrowded class room, fighting back is a negation of necessary order and routine, and fear of failure is the pulse of school life. Remove the fear of failure and education in America would stop as if its heart had been cut out. Yet we cannot blame the feeling of vulnerability on fear of failure, for after all, without fear of failure nobody would try for success, and without striving for success there could be no contemporary culture. Thus another characteristic of vulnerability—its roots in the idea of success.

The Lifetime Fears

Fear of failure does not begin in school, for in our culture even the basic biological functions of early childhood are amalgamated with the ideas of success and failure. Moving one's bowels at the right time and in the right place is a great success for a baby; while losing control and doing it on the living-room rug is a failure, a source of shame and disgrace for many children. Even taking the right amount of milk from the bottle, and eating all one's spinach before getting dessert are successes, while leaving food on one's plate, or eating sloppily so that milk dribbles on one's shirt may be considered failures. Thus a baby is already psychologically vulnerable at the mouth and bowel, and thus in our culture fear of failure is built right into the biological functions. In this way the soul is prepared for the intensified fear of failure instilled all through school, including college and graduate school.

Related to such fears is the college student's query of 'Will I make it?,' and for many college is a four-year opium sleep in which the answer to the question is postponed, while the student commits himself to the pleasures of a coeducational school as a courting pavilion, while at the same time trying to make himself invulnerable to the dangers of the socio-economic system. And, this is the paradox—that even as the undergraduate is presumably arming, he gives himself up to pleasure in order to forget the enemy.

Thus fear of failure is the dark aspect of the hope and striving for success. For most of us, our abilities, our good looks and our social techniques, our pleasant, public relations 'hellos,' our ability to laugh at anybody's jokes, our capacity to hold conventional opinions and never to value or fight for any position in an argument too much never seem quite adequate to ward off all the chances of failure. If a young person is successful in competition for one grade, one scholarship, one boy or girl, or one position today, can he be sure of being successful next time? In our culture a person's armour of personal capabilities is never predictably adequate, so that like the stock market and the gross national product, one can never be sure that if his capabilities are high today they will not crash tomorrow.

From this long training in feeling vulnerable the graduate student enters the academic world with a greater concern with reputation than with self and an overpowering fear of failure. Under these conditions he is bound to be a failure to his self and at this point the coup de grace is often administered to it.

Vulnerability in the Schools

In the world outside the university many institutions ensure that the sense of vulnerability will never be lost. Every teacher in a public school system, for example, knows that if he asserts hisself the probabilities of getting a raise or even keeping his job are reduced. But behind the principal who makes this clear to him is a superintendent who can punish the principal; and behind the superintendent is a board of education, while behind them is a state department of education ready to punish them all. Behind the state department are the people. Now the circle is complete, for the people, after all, are interested largely in preserving their good names. Since so many among them have given up self-striving, why should they allow it to anybody else? Furthermore they are frightened about what might happen to their non-conforming children.

It is now time to ask: 'How shall a person who wishes to assert himself in the school system become invulnerable or at least reduce his vulnerability?' By self-assertion I do not necessarily mean yelling at the principal, although it is rarely that assertion of one's self does not entail standing up to a superior.

By assertion of the self, I mean doing and saying what is in harmony with a self that is striving for something significant, for something which would be a step in the direction of self-realization—in the direction of something that would enable one to say to one's self, 'I have made myself more significant in my own eyes.' It is this 'ownmost self,' as Martin Heidegger has called it, that studies and evaluates remorselessly, that I am talking about.

For a teacher, assertion of the self would involve saying what he thinks most enlightening to the students; refusing to use stupid books, or reinterpreting them to make sense; deviating from the embalmed curriculum, and so on. Alone, he obviously can do this only within limits—although, when we come to think of it, the country is so starved for teachers now that after a squabble a teacher can often go around the corner to the next school district and get another job; while principals who once never thought twice before letting a teacher go, now think a hundred times.

On the other hand, going it alone is foolish, not so much because of the teacher's vulnerability but because, if his ideas are good, other teachers should share and express them; and if the majority of teachers in the same school do, it is difficult to withstand them. If a teacher acts alone and is forced to lie down or quit, the sense of vulnerability is intensified throughout the school system. The sense of vulnerability functions in a school system to frighten the teachers into becoming stupid; and since when they become stupid, so do the pupils, we end up with the understanding that vulnerability in the teacher helps educate children to stupidity. In this way society gets what it wants.

The Example of Paradise

The functioning of the vulnerability system is illustrated by the case of Virginia Franklin, a high-school teacher in Paradise, California, as reported in *Life, 26 April 1963.*

I quote from the article:

> The rage in Paradise centres on a high-school teacher named Virginia Franklin. She believes America is served best by training children to make up their own minds. Her social-studies classes, filled with debate, are encouraged to read material of widely divergent points of view, from the liberal to the extremes of the right wing.
>
> Although Mrs. Franklin earned an award from the Freedoms Foundation, she gained the enmity of the local American Legion post and others, including the John Birch Society. She was, of course, accused of being a communist, and one of her students was discovered spying on her in class by means of a tape recorder hidden in a hole carved in a text book. Fortunately Mrs. Franklin is such a good teacher that she had the support of her principal, her superintendent and a small majority of the people who voted in the election for a new member of the school board. Mrs. Franklin's supporter won.

This case has many features of the vulnerability system as it operates in our country. It is seen to have its roots in irrational fear and hate, and it takes possession of a revered symbol, in this case love of country. But it appropriates the fear symbol also which, in this case, is communism, for the extreme right considers itself the sole defender of the country. Mrs. Franklin would have been vulnerable had she stood alone; but what is most striking is that, although the principal, the superintendent and the school board supported her during the outbreak of lunacy, the other teachers did not come forward.

The comment of Dr. George Baron of the Institute of Education of the University of London is vital in connection with the case. Writing in the *Teachers College Record* (May 1964), he says:

> The Hell in Paradise case . . . gives to an English reader at first the impression of a closed, insular little society in which all is distrust and suspicion. . . .
>
> There was, it would seem, no structure of accepted authority and custom to which the participants could appeal, no firmly held views on what was the nature of the trust that parent, teacher and pupil must have in each other and in each other's roles, in the school situation. Moreover . . . neither teacher nor principal was effectively supported by any professional associations; *no university appears to have lent its weight to the cause of the teacher's freedom, and no figures of significance in the intellectual and political life of the nation seized on the incident as one to be lifted out of its purely parochial context.* It was left then, for the . . . small community of Paradise to decide unaided issues that have occupied men for centuries.

Thus Dr. Baron sees to the core: the distrust and suspicion which spread like cancer; the readiness of hate and fear-motivated organizations to usurp power where no clear authority exists; and the oceanic lack of involvement of the American people in their own vulnerable predicament. This is brought out by Dr. Baron's remarks that no professional association, no university—especially professors of education—came forward to be heard on the matter. Like the New Yorkers who watched from behind their blinds while a woman was stabbed to death, they remained uninvolved. As long as Americans are uninvolved in one another, each stands alone in his vulnerability. We conclude from this that a consequence of extreme vulnerability, wherein all men stand alone, is to make all men vulnerable; to bring all men to heel. Commenting further Dr. Baron says:

> This is markedly different from the situation in England—or, indeed, in Europe generally—where the universities, the schools, and the professions together have a coherence that protects them and individual teachers and practitioners from local and other external pressures.

In conclusion he says:

> Given the place accorded to the local community in school affairs [in the United States], the isolation of the teacher, the seriousness of the heed paid to the views of

> children and adolescents, the political function ascribed to the school [as a controller of political ideas], and the fear of uncontrolled unusual ideas, other Paradises are inevitable. Teachers and parents who support mildly controversial ideas, even though they are commonplace throughout the western world, must then live with the fear of being denounced and persecuted.

It is now necessary to ask the question, 'Where were the professors of education?' As a matter of fact, where are professors altogether in the social studies issue? We can examine some of the factors that might prevent them from taking strong positions on sharpening the social studies. In the first place the professors of education in those institutions which are in the most strategic position to make their opinions felt, are subject to the same pressures toward ineffectualness as Mrs. Franklin. Their situation is aggravated, however, by the fact that although their universities may be tolerant, the state departments, fearful of their own position, cannot afford to liberalize the social studies, and therefore the professors cannot afford to be different.

The Roots of Incompetence

Since a consequence of vulnerability is to prevent social change, and since in our culture there is always a strong push for enlightened social change, we conclude that usually the function of the vulnerability system is to prevent enlightenment and the consequent change. Put another way, the function of the vulnerability system is often to guarantee darkness and incompetence. As a matter of fact, the people who are in the positions most strategic for social change are usually the most vulnerable. In government an outstanding example of this is the United States Department of Labour, which, although originally established to look after the interests of labour, was quickly deprived of power because of the danger of too great closeness of labour and government. Shorn of real power, the Department of Labor became a frozen bureaucracy dedicated largely to collecting statistics and keeping out of trouble with Congress, the Department of State and organized labour itself, who came to look upon the Department as largely a do-nothing outfit, uninterested in labour's welfare and under the thumb of Congress and business.

In education the group most strategic for social change is the teachers, and we know that the teachers are a vulnerable group. . . . Fifty years ago labour was in a similar position, and it is only through organizing that it lost its vulnerability. As soon as this happened, however, labour lost interest in social change also. This suggests that although a vulnerable group cannot institute social change, once it has become invulnerable it may lose its interest in social change.

As a group becomes invulnerable, either through organization or through freezing in self-protective attitudes, it also becomes incompetent, because within the cake of protection that freezes around it there are frozen also the skills the group is seeking to protect. Hence teachers don't change, superintendents don't change, and workers do not take the trouble to educate themselves beyond the skills guaranteed to them by their organization. Over the years invulnerability through hiding has become the very factor that has now made educators increasingly vulnerable to the criticism of incompetence.

Scapegoats and Children

In all of this those who suffer most are children, for the defensiveness of everybody—the socially patterned exposure and vulnerability of everybody in the educational system—produces classrooms where off-beat questions are rarely asked. If they arise, they are ignored by the teacher; the readers, written largely by females who make a business of writing mindless stories, confront no issue but the apathy of the children; and, for generations, little changes but the faces.

Attacks on teachers nowadays therefore have some of the spuriousness of attacks on Jews, for whenever a society is under stress the most vulnerable group becomes the scapegoat. Anti-educationalism is a refined form of scapegoating. In the present crisis in education, we see that what really binds the system is the hysterical and stingy public, committed to the high-rising living standard and frightened out of its wits by fear of communism. Meanwhile, in the drive to improve the teaching of science and mathematics we observe a present paradox, for while fear impels us to revolutionize science teaching the danger arises—as witness Mrs. Franklin—that we go backwards in other areas. Even the fear of communism, however, is not the force behind the effort to improve the teaching of science and mathematics. Basically the force is all of business—textiles, oil, supermarkets, rockets and so on, who need the scientist and the mathematician to automate, to analyze, to invent and to compute along with the computers; for business is so vulnerable to competition, to obsolescence, to the stock market, to imports, to a labour movement and to depression that it needs our children's brains as protection. We must not, however, let everything else in our schools remain dead and embalmed while science and mathematics spring to a new and ambiguous life.

The Case of Rene Descartes

Most of us have learned in introductory courses in philosophy that Descartes was so afraid of the church that he had to prove many times that God exists, that he withdrew several of his works on hearing of the condemnation of Galileo, and that he insisted on anonymity. It has not been pointed out that Descartes seems to have avoided discovering calculus because he was afraid that analysis of infinity would be considered blasphemy. Anyone who knows Descartes's capacities, that he started western philosophy on new pathways, that he is a fundamental source of modern phenomenology, and that he invented analytical geometry, could not doubt, after reading his Principles, that he could have discovered calculus had he not been afraid of inquiring into the nature of infinity. Consider the following from Principles XXVI and XXVII:

> That we must not try to dispute about the infinite, but just consider that all that in which we find no limits is indefinite, such as the extension of the world, the divisibility of its parts, the number of the stars, etc.
>
> We will thus never hamper ourselves with disputes about the infinite, since it would be absurd that we who are finite should undertake to decide anything regarding it. . . . That is why we do not care to reply to those who demand whether the half of an infinite line is infinite, and whether an infinite number is even or odd and so on. . . . And for our part, while we regard things in which, in a certain sense, we observe no limits, we shall not for all that state that they are infinite, but merely hold them to be indefinite. Thus because we cannot imagine an extension so great that we cannot at the same time conceive that there may be one yet greater, we shall say that 'the' magnitude of possible things is indefinite.

Now come the lines that make clear that the calculus was definitely within Descartes's reach:

> And because we cannot divide a body into parts which are so small that each part cannot be divided into others yet smaller, we shall consider that the quantity may be divided into parts whose number is indefinite.

Since infinity and the infinitesimal are at the core of the calculus and since Descartes discovered analytical geometry, necessary preliminary to calculus, it is highly probable he would have discovered calculus too if he had not been afraid. Principle XXVII makes the issue even clearer.

> And we shall name these things indefinite rather than infinite in order to reserve to God alone the name of infinite, first of all because in Him alone we observe no limitation whatever, and because we are quite certain that He can have none. [I change now to the French translation, because the issues are clearer there.]* As regards other things we know that they are not thus absolutely perfect because although we observe in them certain properties which appear to have no limit, we yet know that this proceeds from our lack of understanding and not from their natures.

So, he says, man must leave the infinite and the infinitesimal unplumbed because they belong to God and are beyond understanding—even though

---

*See *Philosophical Works of Descartes*, translated into English by Elizabeth S. Haldane and G. R. T. Ross, Cambridge University Press, 1931. The translators indicate that Descartes was enthusiastic about the French translation (from Latin) and that he wrote the Preface.

it was perfectly clear that Descartes understood them. Thus the sensation of vulnerability prevented Descartes from making a great discovery, and from this we conclude that behind many intellectual failures lies a failure of nerve.

Knowledge Bureaucratized

A bureaucracy is a hierarchically organized institution whose purpose is to carry on certain limited functions. Thus a school system, the army, a university, the government are all bureaucracies. It is common knowledge, however, that bureaucracies have three functions, rather than one. Although the first is ostensibly to carry out the tasks for which they are established, the definition of roles and the routinization of procedures in bureaucracies brings it about that an important function of the organization becomes that of preventing anything within it from changing. Even small change might make it necessary for the entire organization to change because each part is so interlocked with every other, that to alter any procedure in a bureaucracy without changing the rest is often like trying to increase the height of one wall of a house without modifying its entire configuration. A third function of a bureaucracy is to perpetuate itself, to prevent itself from disappearing. Given the functions of preventing internal change and struggling to survive, bureaucracies tend to devote much of their time to activities that will prevent change. Under these conditions it is difficult to introduce new knowledge into the system. Often only a general convulsion in the total society can compel a bureaucracy to change; and then it will do so only just enough to avoid going out of business. Obviously these are the conditions for incompetence; bureaucracies create the conditions for their own incompetence and hence for their own destruction. World convulsions have caused radical changes in the administration of the executive in our own government; the changes in the Department of Defense have been a response to world crisis; and the entrenched military brass have almost been swept away because they would not change. And so it goes. The feeling of vulnerability always creates efforts at defense but these very efforts only increase vulnerability over the long run because they cause incompetence. The feeling of vulnerability, efforts at defense by freezing the system, increased vulnerability and ultimate destruction if there is no change—this is the universal law of western civilization.

Competence for What and Whom?

Anybody in our culture who suggested that we did not love our children would be hated; and in harmony with our love of children we want them to have the best education available. Of course, it has to be the best education available for the money we are willing to spend, and we all know that in calculating the amount of money we are able—or rather, are willing—to spend on education, the family standard of living comes first. That is to say, after we have calculated expenditures for food, drink, entertainment, the kind of clothes that will present us and our children to the world in conformity with our class position, expenditures for fishing tackle, guns, high-fi sets, radios (several in one house), TV (two or three in one house), outboard motor boats, two cars, $30 to $40 dresses for the kid's graduation prom, two or more bathing suits for everybody, a summer vacation, a barbecue pit, a nice house with suitable mortgage and upkeep, hairdos, mouthwashes, cosmetics, cigarettes, bowling, movies and repairs on the car; I say, after we have calculated all these expenses—not to mention taxes to state and federal governments—we are willing to give our children the best education to be bought with the money that's left over. Obviously not much is, and the continued defeat of one school bond issue after the other is witness to the contradiction between educational goals and the living standard. Thus education, the very phenomenon that made a rising living standard possible, is being undermined by it.

Another factor contributing heavily to incompetence in education is the war, for since taxes to support it draw heavily on all of us, we are unwilling to be taxed for other things; that is to say, we are unwilling to pay higher education taxes in the interests of our children. When we add the expenditures for the spendthrift commitment to a good time and a rising standard of living, our children get the dirty end of the stick. Let us put it even more clearly: as far as education is concerned, war, a good time and the living standard eat up so much that, in their education, the kids get the crumbs that fall from the table. Educational crumbs can only be educational incompetence. On the other hand in a deeper sense, our children get the best education compatible with a society that requires a high level of stupidity in order to exist as it is. A moment's reflection will convince anyone that this is true. For example, if television had a truly well-educated audience and the newspapers and magazines well-educated readers, the economy would collapse because, since nobody would then be impressed by the advertising, they would not buy. Adults who had been trained by clear-headed, sharp-brained teachers would be imbued with such clarity of vision that they would not put up with many federal and local policies and they certainly would stop smoking. They might even begin to question the need for a standard of living that has spread wall-to-wall carpeting from here to California and given millions more space and more mobility than they can intelligently use. In the light of these terrifying possibilities the thought of an education in depth and sharpness for everybody can only make a thoughtful person anxious, because an education for stupidity is the only one we can afford right now.

I hope it is understood that no criticism is intended of socially necessary education for stupidity. Having been an educator much of my life,

I understand that every civilization needs to introduce a reasonable amount of respectable intellectual sabotage into its educational system lest the young get out of hand and challenge or scorn tradition and accepted canons of truth. Too much striving by intellectual Samsons will only bring the temple down; it surely can do no lasting harm to cut their hair a wee bit. It looks better too: a crowd of crew-cuts or flat-tops looks so much neater than a mob of long-hairs. For a college teacher there is a certain comfort and tranquility in dealing with students who have been trained in elementary and secondary school not to embarrass him by asking impertinent questions; and scarcely a day must pass when he does not give thanks to a system that has provided him with meek students who permit him to grow old without too much intellectual stir—without him feel vulnerable.

Education and War

If we look at education and war from the standpoint of vulnerability, we see that in many ways education in this country today is hostage to our fear of communism; and revision in the courses in maths and science are not going to help the child much, they are just going to make him better for the war machine and for the changing character of American industry which each day becomes more and more dependent on the sciences. Revision of the teaching of sciences and maths will not help the child much because we are not improving his skills in maths and sciences in the interest of his inner self but in the interest of war and business. Furthermore the overwhelming majority of girls will have no use for it, and college students seem to show a declining interest in the sciences. The history of American education in the last hundred years, as set forth cogently by my colleague, Professor Callahan, shows that education has not considered the child's interest but that of industry; and I am not yet convinced that what is good for General Motors is good for our children. Even less am I convinced that what is good for Missile Dynamics is good for our children, or what is good for the Pentagon is good for them. Meanwhile the educational system, pressed by one world movement or local interest after the other, successively breeds one form of incompetence after the other. Each world hysteria generates a powerful group that sees itself as prophet of the system and the system yields to it. It is yield or die, because for the moment they hold overwhelming power.

It thus becomes clear that love of our children is, at best, qualified by our love of fun and the high-rising living standard, and that the Joneses, the McMullins, and the Schwarzes throughout the country do not love their children so much that they are willing to lower their living standard and give up some fun in the interest of raising the level of education to what is more in conformity with the possibilities of the richest and one of the most democratic countries in the world. It is also clear that, although we love our children, it is not so clear that others—like business or the Pentagon—love them in the same way and for the same reasons.

Knowing Our Strength

I have spoken of the vulnerability—the susceptibility to destruction and defeat—of man in our culture. I pointed out that in order for society to continue it has to make us vulnerable—it has to create in us a vulnerable character structure, for did we not feel vulnerable society would have no way of making us toe the mark. I discussed Descartes because I wanted to show how what attacks all of us in the scholarly world—fear of punishment for making the very discoveries which are the goal and glory of our calling—prevented Descartes from discovering the calculus. Anyone who reads history and the social sciences critically learns that behind many intellectual failures is indeed a failure of nerve. The books we are compelled to give our students—largely because there are no better ones—are often boring and irritating, not because their authors lack brains but because they lack courage.

Thus it turns out that incompetence in education is in large part a consequence of fear—fear of one another and fear of communism—and the case of Mrs. Franklin is merely an extreme and overt expression of the widespread but covert process of sabotage that plagues the educational system and helps to make our children stupid. But the incompetence of the educational system is merely one form of bureaucratic incompetence, and all bureaucracies become incompetent because of fear.

The moral of all this is that we must know our strength. Nobody is invulnerable, but nobody is as weak as he thinks he is either. Let everyone, instead of saying to himself, 'I am afraid,' say instead, 'I may be stronger than I think.'

13

"The Banking Model of Education" (1970)

Paulo Freire (1921–1997) was among the most important educational thinkers of the twentieth century. He is best known for his book *Pedagogy of the Oppressed,* in which he argues that much of formal education is based on a banking model in which knowledge is deposited in the mind of the learner in much the same way that money is deposited in a bank. Like John Dewey, he called for an active model in which the individual is engaged in the process of what he or she is learning.

As you read the following selection, keep these questions in mind:

1. What is the role of the teacher when a banking model is at work in education?
2. Who does a banking model of teaching benefit most?
3. How does a banking model compare with an active model of learning?

13

"The Banking Model of Education" (1970)

Paulo Freire

A careful analysis of the teacher-student relationship at any level inside or outside the school reveals its fundamentally *narrative* character. This relationship involves a narrating Subject (the teacher) and patient, listening objects (the students). The contents, whether values or empirical dimensions of reality, tend in the process of being narrated to become lifeless and petrified. Education is suffering from narration sickness.

The teacher talks about reality as if it were motionless, static, compartmentalized, and predictable. Or else he expounds on a topic completely alien to the existential experience of the students. His task is to "fill" the students with the contents of his narration—contents which are detached from reality, disconnected from the totality that engendered them and could give them significance. Words are emptied of their concreteness and become a hollow, alienated, and alienating verbosity.

The outstanding characteristic of this narrative education, then, is the sonority of words, not their transforming power. "Four times four is sixteen; the capital of Para is Belem." The student records, memorizes, and repeats these phrases without perceiving what four times four really means, or realizing the true significance of "capital" in the affirmation "the capital of Para is Belem," that is, what Belem means for Para and what Para means for Brazil.

Narration (with the teacher as narrator) leads the students to memorize mechanically the narrated content. Worse yet, it turns them into "containers," into "receptacles" to be "filled" by the teacher. The more completely she fills the

---

Source: Freire, Paulo. 1970. "The Banking Model of Education." *Pedagogy of the Oppressed,* Chap. 2. New York: Continuum.

receptacles, the better a teacher she is. The more meekly the receptacles permit themselves to be filled, the better students they are.

Education thus becomes an act of depositing, in which the students are the depositories and the teacher is the depositor. Instead of communicating, the teacher issues communiques and makes deposits which the students patiently receive, memorize, and repeat. This is the "banking" concept of education, in which the scope of action allowed to the students extends only as far as receiving, filing, and storing the deposits. They do, it is true, have the opportunity to become collectors or cataloguers of the things they store. But in the last analysis, it is the people themselves who are filed away through the lack of creativity, transformation, and knowledge in this (at best) misguided system. For apart from inquiry, apart from the praxis, individuals cannot be truly human. Knowledge emerges only through invention and re-invention, through the restless, impatient, continuing, hopeful inquiry human beings pursue in the world, with the world, and with each other.

In the banking concept of education, knowledge is a gift bestowed by those who consider themselves knowledgeable upon those whom they consider to know nothing. Projecting an absolute ignorance onto others, a characteristic of the ideology of oppression, negates education and knowledge as processes of inquiry. The teacher presents himself to his students as their necessary opposite; by considering their ignorance absolute, he justifies his own existence. The students, alienated like the slave in the Hegelian dialectic, accept their ignorance as justifying the teacher's existence—but, unlike the slave, they never discover that they educate the teacher.

The *raison d'etre* of libertarian education, on the other hand, lies in its drive towards reconciliation. Education must begin with the solution of the teacher-student contradiction, by reconciling the poles of the contradiction so that both are simultaneously teachers *and* students.

This solution is not (nor can it be) found in the banking concept. On the contrary, banking education maintains and even stimulates the contradiction through the following attitudes and practices, which mirror oppressive society as a whole:

(a) the teacher teaches and the students are taught;

(b) the teacher knows everything and the students know nothing;

(c) the teacher thinks and the students are thought about;

(d) the teacher talks and the students listen—meekly;

(e) the teacher disciplines and the students are disciplined;

(f) the teacher chooses and enforces his choice, and the students comply;

(g) the teacher acts and the students have the illusion of acting through the action of the teacher;

(h) the teacher chooses the program content, and the students (who were not consulted) adapt to it;

(i) the teacher confuses the authority of knowledge with his or her own professional authority, which she or he sets in opposition to the freedom of the students;

(j) the teacher is the Subject of the learning process, while the pupils are mere objects.

It is not surprising that the banking concept of education regards men as adaptable, manageable beings. The more students work at storing the deposits entrusted to them, the less they develop the critical consciousness which would result from their intervention in the world as transformers of that world. The more completely they accept the passive role imposed on them, the more they tend simply to adapt to the world as it is and to the fragmented view of reality deposited in them.

The capability of banking education to minimize or annul the students' creative power and to stimulate their credulity serves the interests of the oppressors, who care neither to have the world revealed nor to see it transformed. The oppressors use their "humanitarianism" to preserve a profitable situation. Thus they react almost instinctively against any experiment in education which stimulates the critical faculties and is not content with a partial view of reality but always seeks out the ties which link one point to another and one problem to another.

Indeed, the interests of the oppressors lie in "changing the consciousness of the oppressed, not the situation which oppresses them";[1] for the more the oppressed can be led to adapt to that situation, the more easily they can be dominated. To achieve this end, the oppressors use the banking concept of education in conjunction with a paternalistic social action apparatus, within which the oppressed receive the euphemistic title of "welfare recipients." They are treated as individual cases, as marginal persons who deviate from the general configuration of a "good, organized, and just" society. The oppressed are regarded as the pathology of the healthy society, which must therefore adjust these "incompetent and lazy" folk to its own patterns by changing their mentality. These marginals need to be "integrated," "incorporated" into the healthy society that they have "forsaken."

The truth is, however, that the oppressed are not "marginals," are not people living "outside" society. They have always been "inside"—inside the structure which made them "beings for others." The solution is not to "integrate" them into the structure of oppression, but to transform that structure so that they can become "beings for themselves." Such transformation, of course, would undermine the oppressors' purposes; hence their utilization of the banking concept of education to avoid the threat of student *conscientizacao.*

The banking approach to adult education, for example, will never propose to students that they critically consider reality. It will deal instead with such vital questions as whether Roger gave green grass to the goat, and insist upon the importance of learning that on the contrary, Roger gave green grass to the rabbit. The "humanism" of the banking approach masks the effort to turn women and men into automatons—the very negation of their ontological vocation to be more fully human.

Those who use the banking approach, knowingly or unknowingly (for there are innumerable well-intentioned bank-clerk teachers who do not realize that they are serving only to dehumanize), fail to perceive that the deposits themselves contain contradictions about reality. But, sooner or later, these contradictions may lead formerly passive students to turn against their domestication and the attempt to domesticate reality. They may discover through existential experience that their present way of life is irreconcilable with their vocation to become fully human. They may perceive through their relations with reality that reality is really a *process,* undergoing constant transformation. If men and women are searchers and their ontological vocation is humanization, sooner or later they may perceive the contradiction in which banking education seeks to maintain them, and then engage themselves in the struggle for their liberation.

But the humanist, revolutionary educator cannot wait for this possibility to materialize. From the outset, her efforts must coincide with those of the students to engage in critical thinking and the quest for mutual humanization. His efforts must be imbued with a profound trust in people and their creative power. To achieve this, they must be partners of the students in their relations with them.

The banking concept does not admit to such partnership—and necessarily so. To resolve the teacher-student contradiction, to exchange the role of depositor, prescriber, domesticator, for the role of student among students would be to undermine the power of oppression and serve the cause of liberation.

Implicit in the banking concept is the assumption of a dichotomy between human beings and the world: a person is merely *in* the world, not *with* the world or with others; the individual is spectator, not re-creator. In this view, the person is not a conscious being (*corpo consciente*); he or she is rather the possessor of a consciousness: an empty "mind" passively open to the reception of deposits of reality from the world outside. For example, my desk, my books, my coffee cup, all the objects before me—as bits of the world which surround me—would be "inside" me, exactly as I am inside my study right now. This view makes no distinction between being accessible to consciousness and entering consciousness. The distinction, however, is essential: the objects which surround me are simply accessible to my consciousness, not located within it. I am aware of them, but they are not inside me.

It follows logically from the banking notion of consciousness that the educator's role is to regulate the way the world "enters into" the students. The teacher's task is to organize a process which already occurs spontaneously to "fill" the students by making deposits of information which he or she considers to constitute true knowledge.[2] And since people "receive" the world as passive entities, education should make them more passive still, and adapt them to the world. The educated individual is the adapted person, because she or he is a better "fit" for the world. Translated into practice, this concept is well suited to the purposes of the oppressors, whose tranquility rests on how well people fit the world the oppressors have created, and how little they question it.

The more completely the majority adapt to the purposes which the dominant minority prescribe for them (thereby depriving them of the right to their own purposes), the more easily the minority can continue to prescribe. The theory and practice of banking education serve this end quite efficiently. Verbalistic lessons, reading requirements,[3] the methods for evaluating knowledge, the distance between the teacher and the taught, the criteria for promotion: Everything in this ready-to-wear approach serves to obviate thinking.

The bank-clerk educator does not realize that there is no true security in his hypertrophied role, that one must seek to live *with* others in solidarity. One cannot impose oneself, nor even merely co-exist with one's students. Solidarity requires true communication, and the concept by which such an educator is guided fears and proscribes communication.

Yet only through communication can human life hold meaning. The teacher's thinking is authenticated only by the authenticity of the students' thinking. The teacher cannot think for her students, nor can she impose her thought on them. Authentic thinking, thinking that is concerned about *reality*, does not take place in ivory tower isolation, but only in communication. If it is true that thought has meaning only when generated by action upon the world, the subordination of students to teachers becomes impossible.

Because banking education begins with a false understanding of men and women as objects, it cannot promote the development of what Fromm calls "biophily," but instead produces its opposite: "necrophily."

While life is characterized by growth in a structured, functional manner, the necrophilous person loves all that does not grow, all that is mechanical. The necrophilous person is driven by the desire to transform the organic into the inorganic, to approach life mechanically, as if all living persons were things. . . . Memory, rather than experience; having, rather than being, is what counts. The necrophilous person can relate to an object—a flower or a person—only if he possesses it; hence a threat to his possession is a threat to himself; if he loses possession he loses contact with the world. . . . He loves control, and in the act of controlling he kills life.[4]

Oppression—overwhelming control—is necrophilic; it is nourished by love of death, not life. The banking concept of education, which serves the interests of oppression, is also necrophilic. Based on a mechanistic, static, naturalistic, spatialized view of consciousness, it transforms students into receiving objects. It attempts to control thinking and action, leads women and men to adjust to the world, and inhibits their creative power.

When their efforts to act responsibly are frustrated, when they find themselves unable to use their faculties, people suffer. "This suffering due to impotence is rooted in the very fact that the human equilibrium has been disturbed."[5] But the inability to act which causes people's anguish also causes them to reject their impotence, by attempting

> . . . to restore [their] capacity to act. But can [they], and how? One way is to submit to and identify with a person or group having power. By this symbolic participation in another person's life, [men have] the illusion of acting, when in reality [they] only submit to and become a part of those who act.[6]

Populist manifestations perhaps best exemplify this type of behavior by the oppressed, who, by identifying with charismatic leaders, come to feel that they themselves are active and effective. The rebellion they express as they emerge in the historical process is motivated by that desire to act effectively. The dominant elites consider the remedy to be more domination and repression, carried out in the name of freedom, order, and social peace (that is, the peace of the elites). Thus they can condemn—logically from their point of view—"the violence of a strike by workers and [can] call upon the state in the same breath to use violence in putting down the strike."[7]

Education as the exercise of domination stimulates the credulity of students, with the ideological intent (often not perceived by educators) of indoctrinating them to adapt to the world of oppression. This accusation is not made in the naive hope that the dominant elites will thereby simply abandon the practice. Its objective is to call the attention of true humanists to the fact that they cannot use banking educational methods in the pursuit of liberation, for they would only negate that very pursuit. Nor may a revolutionary society inherit these methods from an oppressor society. The revolutionary society which practices banking education is either misguided or mistrusting of people. In either event it is threatened by the specter of reaction.

Unfortunately, those who espouse the cause of liberation are themselves surrounded and influenced by the climate which generates the banking concept, and often do not perceive its true significance or its dehumanizing power. Paradoxically, then, they utilize this same instrument of alienation in what they consider an effort to liberate. Indeed, some "revolutionaries" brand as "innocents," "dreamers," or even "reactionaries" those who would challenge this educational practice. But one does not liberate people by alienating them.

Authentic liberation—the process of humanization—is not another deposit to be made in men. Liberation is a praxis: the action and reflection of men and women upon their world in order to transform it. Those truly committed to the cause of liberation can accept neither the mechanistic concept of consciousness as an empty vessel to be filled, nor the use of banking methods of domination (propaganda, slogans—deposits) in the name of liberation.

Those truly committed to liberation must reject the banking concept in its entirety, adopting instead a concept of women and men as conscious beings, and consciousness as consciousness intent upon the world. They must abandon the educational goal of deposit-making and replace it with the posing of the problems of human beings in their relations with the world. "Problem-posing" education, responding to the essence of consciousness—intentionality—rejects communiques and embodies communication. It epitomizes the special characteristic of consciousness: being *conscious of* not only as intent on objects but as turned in upon itself in a Jasperian "split"—consciousness as consciousness *of* consciousness.

Liberating education consists in acts of cognition, not transferrals of information. It is a learning situation in which the cognizable object (far from being the end of the cognitive act) intermediates the cognitive actors—teacher on the one hand and students on the other. Accordingly the practice of problem-posing education entails at the outset that the teacher-student contradiction be resolved. Dialogical relations—indispensable to the capacity of cognitive actors to cooperate in perceiving the same cognizable object—are otherwise impossible.

Indeed, problem-posing education, which breaks with the vertical patterns characteristic of banking education, can fulfil its function as the practice of freedom only if it can overcome the above contradiction. Through dialogue, the teacher-of-the-students and the students-of-the-teacher cease to exist and a new term emerges: teacher-student with students-teachers. The teacher is no longer merely the-one-who-teaches, but one who is himself taught in dialogue with the students, who in turn while being taught also teach. They become jointly responsible for a process in which all grow. In this process, arguments based on "authority" are no longer valid; in order to function, authority must be *on the side of* freedom, not against it. Here, no one teaches another, nor is anyone self-taught. People teach each other, mediated by the world, by the cognizable objects which in banking education are "owned" by the teacher.

The banking concept (with its tendency to dichotomize everything) distinguishes two stages in the action of the educator. During the first he cognizes a cognizable object while he prepares his lessons in his study or his laboratory; during the second, he expounds to his students about that object. The students are not called upon to know, but to memorize the contents narrated by the teacher. Nor do the students practice any act of cognition, since the object towards which that act should be directed is the property of the teacher rather than a medium evoking the critical reflection of both teacher and students. Hence in the name of the "preservation of culture and knowledge" we have a system which achieves neither true knowledge nor true culture.

The problem-posing method does not dichotomize the activity of the teacher-student: she is not "cognitive" at one point and "narrative" at another. She is always "cognitive," whether preparing a project or engaging in dialogue with the students. He does not regard cognizable objects as his private property but as the object of reflection by himself and the students. In this way the problem-posing educator constantly re-forms his reflections in the reflection of the students. The students—no longer docile listeners—are now critical co-investigators in dialogue with the teacher. The teacher presents the material to the students for their consideration, and re-considers her earlier considerations as the students express their own. The role of the problem-posing educator is to create, together with the students, the conditions under which knowledge at the level of the *doxa* is superseded by true knowledge, at the level of the *logos.*

Whereas banking education anesthetizes and inhibits creative power, problem-posing education involves a constant unveiling of reality. The former attempts to maintain the *submersion* of consciousness; the latter strives for the *emergence* of consciousness and *critical intervention* in reality.

Students, as they are increasingly posed with problems relating to themselves in the world and with the world, will feel increasingly challenged and obliged to respond to that challenge. Because they apprehend the challenge as interrelated to other problems within a total context, not as a theoretical question, the resulting comprehension tends to be increasingly critical and thus constantly less alienated. Their response to the challenge evokes new challenges, followed by new understandings; and gradually the students come to regard themselves as committed.

Education as the practice of freedom—as opposed to education as the practice of domination—denies that man is abstract, isolated, independent, and unattached to the world; it also denies that the world exists as a reality apart from people. Authentic reflection considers neither abstract man nor the world without people, but pea-pie in their relations with the world. In these relations consciousness and world are simultaneous: consciousness neither precedes the world nor follows it.

La conscience et le monde sont dormes d'un meme coup: exterieur par essence a la conscience, le monde est, par essence relatif a elle.[8]

In one of our culture circles in Chile, the group was discussing (based on a codification[9]) the anthropological concept of culture. In the midst of the discussion, a peasant who by banking standards was completely ignorant said: "Now I see that without man there is no world." When the educator responded: "Let's say, for the sake of argument, that all the men on earth were to die, but that the earth itself remained, together with trees, birds, animals, rivers, seas, the stars. . . . wouldn't all this be a world?" "Oh no," the peasant replied emphatically, "There would be no one to say: 'This is a world.'"

The peasant wished to express the idea that there would be lacking the consciousness of the world which necessarily implies the world of consciousness. *I* cannot exist without a *not-I.* In turn, the *not-I* depends on that existence. The world which brings consciousness into existence becomes the world *of* that consciousness. Hence, the previously cited affirmation of Sartre: "*La conscience et le mond sont dormes d'un meme coup.*"

As women and men, simultaneously reflecting on themselves and on the world, increase the scope of their perception, they begin to direct their observations towards previously inconspicuous phenomena:

> In perception properly so-called, as an explicit awareness [*Gewahren*], I am turned towards the object, to the paper, for instance. I apprehend it as being this here and now. The apprehension is a singling out, every object having a background in experience. Around and about the paper lie books, pencils, ink-well, and so forth, and these in a certain sense are also "perceived," perceptually there, in the "field of intuition"; but whilst I was turned towards the paper there was no turning in their direction, nor any apprehending of them, not even in a secondary sense. They appeared and yet were not singled out, were not posited on their own account. Every perception of a thing has such a zone of background intuitions or background awareness, if "intuiting" already includes the state of being turned towards, and this also is a "conscious experience," or more briefly a "consciousness of" all indeed that in point of fact lies in the co-perceived objective background.[10]

That which had existed objectively but had not been perceived in its deeper implications (if indeed it was perceived at all) begins to "stand out," assuming the character of a problem and therefore of challenge. Thus, men and women begin to single out elements from their "background awareness" and to reflect upon them. These elements are now objects of their consideration, and, as such, objects of their action and cognition.

In problem-posing education, people develop their power to perceive critically *the way they exist* in the world *with which* and *in which* they find themselves; they come to see the world not as a static reality but as a reality in process, in transformation. Although the dialectical relations of women and men with the world exist independently of how these relations are perceived (or whether or not they are perceived at all), it is also true that the form of action they adopt is to a large extent a function of how they perceive themselves in the world. Hence, the teacher-student and the students-teachers reflect simultaneously on themselves and the world without dichotomizing this reflection from action, and thus establish an authentic form of thought and action.

Once again, the two educational concepts and practices under analysis come into conflict. Banking education (for obvious reasons) attempts, by mythicizing reality, to conceal certain facts which explain the way human beings exist in the world; problem-posing education sets itself the task of demythologizing. Banking education resists dialogue; problem-posing education regards dialogue as indispensable to the act of cognition which unveils reality. Banking education treats students as objects of assistance; problem-posing education makes them critical thinkers. Banking education inhibits creativity and domesticates (although it cannot completely destroy) the *intentionality* of consciousness by isolating consciousness from the world, thereby denying people their ontological and historical vocation of becoming more fully human. Problem-posing education bases itself on creativity and stimulates true reflection and action upon reality, thereby responding to the vocation of persons as beings who are authentic only when engaged in inquiry and creative transformation. In sum: banking theory and practice, as immobilizing and fixating forces, fail to acknowledge men and women as historical beings; problem-posing theory and practice take the people's historicity as their starting point.

Problem-posing education affirms men and women as beings in the process of *becoming*—as unfinished, uncompleted beings in and with a likewise unfinished reality. Indeed, in contrast to other animals who are unfinished, but not historical, people know themselves to be unfinished; they are aware of their incompletion. In this incompletion and this awareness lie the very roots of education as an exclusively human manifestation. The unfinished character of human beings and the transformational character of reality necessitate that education be an ongoing activity.

Education is thus constantly remade in the praxis. In order to *be,* it must *become.* Its "duration" (in the Bergsonian meaning of the word) is found in the interplay of the opposites *permanence* and *change.* The banking method emphasizes permanence and becomes reactionary; problem-posing education—which accepts neither a "well-behaved" present nor a predetermined fixture—roots itself in the dynamic present and becomes revolutionary.

Problem-posing education is revolutionary futurity. Hence it is prophetic (and, as such, hopeful). Hence, it corresponds to the historical nature of humankind. Hence, it affirms women and men as beings who transcend themselves, who move forward and look ahead, for whom immobility represents a fatal threat, for whom looking at the past must only be a means of understanding more clearly what and who they are so that they can more wisely build the fixture. Hence, it identifies with the movement which engages people as beings aware of their incompletion—an historical movement which has its point of departure, its Subjects and its objective.

The point of departure of the movement lies in the people themselves. But since people do not exist apart from the world, apart from reality the movement must begin with the human-world relationship. Accordingly, the point of departure must always be with men and women in the "here and now," which constitutes the situation within which they are submerged, from which they emerge, and in which they intervene. Only by starting from this situation—which determines their perception of it—can they begin to move. To do this authentically they must perceive their state not as fated and unalterable, but merely as limiting—and therefore challenging.

Whereas the banking method directly or indirectly reinforces men's fatalistic perception of their situation, the problem-posing method presents this very situation to them as a problem. As the situation becomes the object of their cognition, the naive or magical perception which produced their fatalism gives way to perception which is able to perceive itself even as it perceives reality, and can thus be critically objective about that reality.

A deepened consciousness of their situation leads people to apprehend that situation as an historical reality susceptible of transformation. Resignation gives way to the drive for transformation and inquiry, over which men feel themselves to be in control, if people, as historical beings necessarily engaged with other people in a movement of inquiry, did not control that movement, it would be (and is) a violation of their humanity. Any situation in which some individuals prevent others from engaging in the process of inquiry is one of violence. The means used are not important; to alienate human beings from their own decision-making is to change them into objects.

This movement of inquiry must be directed towards humanization—the people's historical vocation. The pursuit of full humanity however, cannot be carried out in isolation or individualism, but only in fellowship and solidarity; therefore it cannot unfold in the antagonistic relations between oppressors and oppressed. No one can be authentically human while he prevents others from being so. Attempting *to be more* human, individualistically, leads to *having more,* egotistically a form of dehumanization. Not that it is not fundamental *to have* in order *to be* human. Precisely because it *is* necessary, some men's *having* must not be allowed to constitute an obstacle to others *having,* must not consolidate the power of the former to crush the latter.

Problem-posing education, as a humanist and liberating praxis, posits as fundamental that the people subjected to domination must fight for their emancipation. To that end, it enables teachers and students to become Subjects of the educational process by overcoming authoritarianism and an alienating intellectualism; it also enables people to overcome their false perception of reality. The world—no longer something to be described with deceptive words—becomes the object of that transforming action by men and women which results in their humanization.

Problem-posing education does not and cannot serve the interests of the oppressor. No oppressive order could permit the oppressed to begin to question: Why? While only a revolutionary society can carry out this education in systematic terms, the revolutionary leaders need not take full power before they can employ the method. In the revolutionary process, the leaders cannot utilize the banking method as an interim measure, justified on grounds of expediency with the intention of *later* behaving in a genuinely revolutionary fashion. They must be revolutionary—that is to say dialogical—from the outset.

Notes

1. Simone de Beauvoir; La Pensee de Droite, Aujord'hui (Paris); ST, El Pensamiento politico de la Derecha (Buenos Aires, 1963), p. 34.
2. This concept corresponds to what Sartre calls the "digestive" or "nutritive" concept of education, in which knowledge is "fed" by the teacher to the students to "fill them out." See Jean-Paul Sartre, "Une idee fundamentale de la phenomenologie de Husserl: L'intentionalite," Situations 1 (Paris, 1947).
3. For example, some professors specify in their reading lists that a book should be read from pages 10 to 15—and do this to "help" their students!
4. Fromm, op. cit., p. 41.
5. ibid., p. 31.
6. ibid.
7. Reinhold Niebuhr, *Moral Man and Immoral Society* (New York, 1960), p. 130.
8. Sartre, op. cit., p. 32.
9. See chapter 3.—Translator's note.
10. Edmund Husserl, *Ideas: General Introduction to Pure Phenomenology* (London, 1969), pp. 105–106.

14

"Why We Must Disestablish School" (1970)

Ivan Illich (1926–2002) was a Catholic priest and social activist who is best known for his 1970 book *Deschooling Society*. In *Deschooling Society*, Illich argued that traditional institutionalized schools do not meet the needs of poor children. He called for the establishment of alternative models of schooling to take the place of more traditional models.

The following selection includes most of the first chapter of Illich's work. In it, he outlined alternatives to traditional schooling, and he identified how real learning takes place for most people—that is, outside of traditional school settings.

As you read this selection, consider the following questions:

1. If, as Illich maintains, the most important learning takes place outside of formal schooling, what is it that is learned in schools?
2. How does learning function in more traditional societies? What is considered important to learn? Why?
3. What constitutes an educated person?

14

"Why We Must Disestablish School" (1970)

Ivan Illich

Many students, especially those who are poor, intuitively know what the schools do for them. They school them to confuse process and substance. Once these become blurred, a new logic is assumed: the more treatment there is, the better are the results; or, escalation leads to success. The pupil is thereby "schooled" to confuse teaching with learning, grade advancement with education, a diploma with competence, and fluency with the ability to say something new. His imagination is "schooled" to accept service in place of value. Medical treatment is mistaken for health care, social work for the improvement of community life, police protection for safety, military poise for national security, the rat race for productive work. Health, learning, dignity, independence, and creative endeavor are defined as little more than the performance of the institutions which claim to serve these ends, and their improvement is made to depend on allocating more resources to the management of hospitals, schools, and other agencies in question. In these essays, I will show that the institutionalization of values leads inevitably to physical pollution, social polarization, and psychological impotence: three dimensions in a process of global degradation and modernized misery. I will explain how this process of degradation is accelerated when nonmaterial needs are transformed into demands for commodities; when health, education, personal mobility, welfare, or psychological healing are defined as the result of services or "treatments." I do this because I believe that most of the research now going on

Source: Illich, Ivan. 1970. "Why We Must Disestablish School." *Deschooling Society*, Chap. 1. New York: Harper and Row.

about the future tends to advocate further increases in the institutionalization of values and that we must define conditions which would permit precisely the contrary to happen. We need research on the possible use of technology to create institutions which serve personal, creative, and autonomous interaction and the emergence of values which cannot be substantially controlled by technocrats. We need counterfoil research to current futurology.

I want to raise the general question of the mutual definition of man's nature and the nature of modern institutions which characterizes our world view and language. To do so, I have chosen the school as my paradigm, and I therefore deal only indirectly with other bureaucratic agencies of the corporate state: the consumer-family, the party, the army, the church, the media. My analysis of the hidden curriculum of school should make it evident that public education would profit from the deschooling of society, just as family life, politics, security, faith, and communication would profit from an analogous process.

I begin my analysis, in this first essay, by trying to convey what the deschooling of a schooled society might mean. In this context, it should be easier to understand my choice of the five specific aspects relevant to this process with which I deal in the subsequent chapters.

Not only education but social reality itself has become schooled. It costs roughly the same to school both rich and poor in the same dependency. The yearly expenditure per pupil in the slums and in the rich suburbs of any one of twenty U.S. cities lies in the same range—and sometimes is favorable to the poor. Rich and poor alike depend on schools and hospitals which guide their lives, form their world view, and define for them what is legitimate and what is not. Both view doctoring oneself as irresponsible, learning on one's own as unreliable, and community organization, when not paid for by those in authority, as a form of aggression or subversion. For both groups the reliance on institutional treatment renders independent accomplishment suspect. The progressive underdevelopment of self- and community-reliance is even more typical in Westchester than it is in the northeast of Brazil. Everywhere not only education but society as a whole needs "deschooling."

Welfare bureaucracies claim a professional, political, and financial monopoly over the social imagination, setting standards of what is valuable and what is feasible. This monopoly is at the root of the modernization of poverty. Every simple need to which an institutional answer is found permits the invention of a new class of poor and a new definition of poverty. Ten years ago in Mexico it was the normal thing to be born and to die in one's own home and to be buried by one's friends. Only the soul's needs were taken care of by the institutional church. Now to begin and end life at home become signs either of poverty or of special privilege. Dying and death have come under the institutional management of doctors and undertakers.

Once basic needs have been translated by a society into demands for scientifically produced commodities, poverty is defined by standards which the technocrats can change at will. Poverty then refers to those who have fallen behind an advertised ideal of consumption in some important respect. In Mexico the poor are those who lack three years of schooling, and in New York they are those who lack twelve.

The poor have always been socially powerless. The increasing reliance on institutional care adds a new dimension to their helplessness: psychological impotence, the inability to fend for themselves. Peasants on the high plateau of the Andes are exploited by the landlord and the merchant; once they settle in Lima they are, in addition, dependent on political bosses, and disabled by their lack of schooling. Modernized poverty combines the lack of power over circumstances with a loss of personal potency. This modernization of poverty is a world-wide phenomenon, and lies at the root of contemporary underdevelopment. Of course it appears under different guises in rich and in poor countries.

It is probably most intensely felt in U.S. cities. Nowhere else is poverty treated at greater cost. Nowhere else does the treatment of poverty produce so much dependence, anger, frustration, and further demands. And nowhere else should it be so evident that poverty—once it has become modernized—has become resistant to treatment with dollars alone and requires an institutional revolution.

Today in the United States the black and even the migrant can aspire to a level of professional treatment which would have been unthinkable two generations ago, and which seems grotesque to most people in the Third World. For instance, the U.S. poor can count on a truant officer to return their children to school until they reach seventeen, or on a doctor to assign them to a hospital bed which costs sixty dollars per day—the equivalent of three months' income for a majority of the people in the world. But such care only makes them dependent on more treatment, and renders them increasingly incapable of organizing their own lives around their own experiences and resources within their own communities.

The poor in the United States are in a unique position to speak about the predicament which threatens all the poor in a modernizing world. They are making the discovery that no amount of dollars can remove the inherent destructiveness of welfare institutions, once the professional hierarchies of these institutions have convinced society that their ministrations are morally necessary. The poor in the U.S. inner city can demonstrate from their own experience the fallacy on which social legislation in a "schooled" society is built.

Supreme Court Justice William O. Douglas observed that "the only way to establish an institution is to finance it." The corollary is also true. Only by channeling dollars away from the institutions which now treat health, education, and welfare can the further impoverishment resulting from their disabling side effects be stopped. . . .

Obligatory schooling inevitably polarizes a society; it also grades the nations of the world according to an international caste system. Countries are rated like castes whose educational dignity is determined by the average years of schooling of its citizens, a rating which is closely related to per capita gross national product, and much more painful.

The paradox of the schools is evident: increased expenditure escalates their destructiveness at home and abroad. This paradox must be made a public issue. It is now generally accepted that the physical environment will soon be destroyed by biochemical pollution unless we reverse current trends in the production of physical goods. It should also be recognized that social and personal life is threatened equally by HEW pollution, the inevitable by-product of obligatory and competitive consumption of welfare.

The escalation of the schools is as destructive as the escalation of weapons but less visibly so. Everywhere in the world school costs have risen faster than enrollments and faster than the GNP; everywhere expenditures on school fall even further behind the expectations of parents, teachers, and pupils. Everywhere this situation discourages both the motivation and the financing for large-scale planning for nonschooled learning. The United States is proving to the world that no country can be rich enough to afford a school system that meets the demands this same system creates simply by existing, because a successful school system schools parents and pupils to the supreme value of a larger school system, the cost of which increases disproportionately as higher grades are in demand and become scarce.

Rather than calling equal schooling temporarily unfeasible, we must recognize that it is, in principle, economically absurd, and that to attempt it is intellectually emasculating, socially polarizing, and destructive of the credibility of the political system which promotes it. The ideology of obligatory schooling admits of no logical limits. The White House recently provided a good example. Dr. Hutschnecker, the "psychiatrist" who treated Mr. Nixon before he was qualified as a candidate, recommended to the President that all children between six and eight be professionally examined to ferret out those who have destructive tendencies, and that obligatory treatment be provided for them. If necessary, their re-education in special institutions should be required. This memorandum from his doctor the President sent for evaluation to HEW. Indeed, preventive concentration camps for predelinquents would be a logical improvement over the school system.

Equal educational opportunity is, indeed, both a desirable and a feasible goal, but to equate this with obligatory schooling is to confuse salvation with the Church. School has become the world religion of a modernized proletariat, and makes futile promises of salvation to the poor of the technological age. The nation-state has adopted it, drafting all citizens into a graded curriculum leading to sequential diplomas not unlike the initiation rituals and hieratic promotions of former times. The modern state has assumed the duty of enforcing the judgment of its educators through well-meant truant officers and job requirements, much as did the Spanish kings who enforced the judgments of their theologians through the conquistadors and the Inquisition.

Two centuries ago the United States led the world in a movement to disestablish the monopoly of a single church. Now we need the constitutional disestablishment of the monopoly of the school, and thereby of a system which legally combines prejudice with discrimination. The first article of a bill of rights for a modern, humanist society would correspond to the First Amendment to the U.S. Constitution: "The State shall make no law with respect to the establishment of education." There shall be no ritual obligatory for all.

To make this disestablishment effective, we need a law forbidding discrimination in hiring, voting, or admission to centers of learning based on previous attendance at some curriculum. This guarantee would not exclude performance tests of competence for a function or role, but would remove the present absurd discrimination in favor of the person who learns a given skill with the largest expenditure of public funds or what is equally likely has been able to obtain a diploma which has no relation to any useful skill or job. Only by protecting the citizen from being disqualified by anything in his career in school can a constitutional disestablishment of school become psychologically effective.

Neither learning nor justice is promoted by schooling because educators insist on packaging instruction with certification. Learning and the assignment of social roles are melted into schooling. Yet to learn means to acquire a new skill or insight, while promotion depends on an opinion which others have formed. Learning frequently is the result of instruction, but selection for a role or category in the job market increasingly depends on mere length of attendance.

Instruction is the choice of circumstances which facilitate learning. Roles are assigned by setting a curriculum of conditions which the candidate must meet if he is to make the grade. School links instruction but not learning to these roles. This is neither reasonable nor liberating. It is not reasonable because it does not link relevant qualities or competences to roles, but rather the process by which such qualities are supposed to be acquired. It is not liberating or educational because school reserves instruction to those whose every step in learning fits previously approved measures of social control.

Curriculum has always been used to assign social rank. At times it could be prenatal: karma ascribes you to a caste and lineage to the aristocracy. Curriculum could take the form of a ritual, of sequential sacred ordinations, or it could consist of a succession of feats in war or hunting, or further advancement could be made to depend on a series of previous princely favors. Universal schooling was meant to detach role assignment from personal life history: it was meant to give everybody an equal chance to any office. Even now many people wrongly believe that school ensures the dependence of public trust on relevant learning achievements. However, instead of equalizing chances, the school system has monopolized their distribution.

To detach competence from curriculum, inquiries into a man's learning history must be made taboo, like inquiries into his political affiliation, church attendance, lineage, sex habits, or racial background. Laws forbidding discrimination on the basis of prior schooling must be enacted. Laws, of course, cannot stop prejudice against the unschooled—nor are they meant to force anyone to intermarry with an autodidact but they can discourage unjustified discrimination.

A second major illusion on which the school system rests is that most learning is the result of teaching. Teaching, it is true, may contribute to certain kinds of learning under certain circumstances. But most people acquire most of their knowledge outside school, and in school only insofar as school, in a few rich countries, has become their place of confinement during an increasing part of their lives.

Most learning happens casually, and even most intentional learning is not the result of programmed instruction. Normal children learn their first language casually, although faster if their parents pay attention to them. Most people who learn a second language well do so as a result of odd circumstances and not of sequential teaching. They go to live with their grandparents, they travel, or they fall in love with a foreigner. Fluency in reading is also more often than not a result of such extracurricular activities. Most people who read widely, and with pleasure, merely believe that they learned to do so in school; when challenged, they easily discard this illusion.

But the fact that a great deal of learning even now seems to happen casually and as a by-product of some other activity defined as work or leisure does not mean that planned learning does not benefit from planned instruction and that both do not stand in need of improvement. The strongly motivated student who is faced with the task of acquiring a new and complex skill may benefit greatly from the discipline now associated with the old-fashioned schoolmaster who taught reading, Hebrew, catechism, or multiplication by rote. School has now made this kind of drill teaching rare and disreputable, yet there are many skills which a motivated student with normal aptitude can master in a matter of a few months if taught in this traditional way. This is as true of codes as of their encipherment; of second and third languages as of reading and writing; and equally of special languages such as algebra, computer programming, chemical analysis, or of manual skills like typing, watchmaking, plumbing, wiring, TV repair; or for that matter dancing, driving, and diving.

In certain cases acceptance into a learning program aimed at a specific skill might presuppose competence in some other skill, but it should certainly not be made to depend upon the process by which such prerequisite skills were acquired. TV repair presupposes literacy and some math; diving, good swimming; and driving, very little of either.

Progress in learning skills is measurable. The optimum resources in time and materials needed by an average motivated adult can be easily estimated. The cost of teaching a second Western European language to a high level of fluency ranges between four and six hundred dollars in the United States, and for an Oriental tongue the time needed for instruction might be doubled. This would still be very little compared with the cost of twelve years of schooling in New York City (a condition for acceptance of a worker into the Sanitation Department) almost fifteen thousand dollars. No doubt not only the teacher but also the printer and the pharmacist protect their trades through the public illusion that training for them is very expensive.

At present schools pre-empt most educational funds. Drill instruction which costs less than comparable schooling is now a privilege of those rich enough to bypass the schools, and those whom either the army or big business sends through in-service training. In a program of progressive deschooling of U.S. education, at first the resources available for drill training would be limited. But ultimately there should be no obstacle for anyone at any time of his life to be able to choose instruction among hundreds of definable skills at public expense.

Right now educational credit good at any skill center could be provided in limited amounts for people of all ages, and not just to the poor. I envisage such credit in the form of an educational passport or an "edu-credit card" provided to each citizen at birth. In order to favor the poor, who probably would not use their yearly grants early in life, a provision could be made that interest accrued to later users of cumulated "entitlements." Such credits would permit most people to acquire the skills most in demand, at their convenience, better, faster, cheaper, and with fewer undesirable side effects than in school.

Potential skill teachers are never scarce for long because, on the one hand, demand for a skill grows only with its performance within a community and, on the other, a man exercising a skill could also teach it. But, at present, those using skills which are in demand and do require a human teacher are discouraged from sharing these skills with others. This is done either by teachers who monopolize the licenses or by unions which protect their trade interests. Skill centers which would be judged by customers on their results, and not on the personnel they employ or the process they use, would open unsuspected working opportunities, frequently even for those who are now considered unemployable. Indeed, there is no reason why such skill centers should not be at the work place itself, with the employer and his work force supplying instruction as well as jobs to those who choose to use their educational credits in this way.

In 1956 there arose a need to teach Spanish quickly to several hundred teachers, social workers, and ministers from the New York Archdiocese so that they could communicate with Puerto Ricans. My friend Gerry Morris announced over a Spanish radio station that he needed native speakers from Harlem. Next day some two hundred teen-agers lined up in front of his office, and he selected four dozen of them—many of them school dropouts. He trained them in the use of the U.S. Foreign Service Institute (FSI) Spanish manual, designed for use by linguists with graduate training, and within a week his teachers were on their own—each in charge of four New Yorkers who wanted to speak the language. Within six months the mission was accomplished. Cardinal Spellman could claim that he had 127 parishes in which at least three staff members could communicate in Spanish. No school program could have matched these results.

Skill teachers are made scarce by the belief in the value of licenses. Certification constitutes a form of market manipulation and is plausible only to a schooled mind. Most teachers of arts and trades are less skillful, less inventive, and less communicative than the best craftsmen and tradesmen. Most high-school teachers of Spanish or French do not speak the language as correctly as their pupils might after half a year of competent drills. Experiments conducted by Angel Quintero in Puerto Rico suggest that many young teen-agers, if given the proper incentives, programs, and access to tools, are better than most schoolteachers at introducing their peers to the scientific exploration of plants, stars, and matter, and to the discovery of how and why a motor or a radio functions.

Opportunities for skill-learning can be vastly multiplied if we open the "market." This depends on matching the right teacher with the right student when he is highly motivated in an intelligent program, without the constraint of curriculum.

Free and competing drill instruction is a subversive blasphemy to the orthodox educator. It dissociates the acquisition of skills from "humane" education, which schools package together, and thus it promotes unlicensed learning no less than unlicensed teaching for unpredictable purposes.

There is currently a proposal on record which seems at first to make a great deal of sense. It has been prepared by Christopher Jencks of the Center for the Study of Public Policy and is sponsored by the Office of Economic Opportunity. It proposes to put educational "entitlements" or tuition grants into the hands of parents and students for expenditure in the schools of their choice. Such individual entitlements could indeed be an important step in the right direction. We need a guarantee of the right of each citizen to an equal share of tax-derived educational resources, the right to verify this share, and the right to sue for it if denied. It is one form of a guarantee against regressive taxation.

The Jencks proposal, however, begins with the ominous statement that "conservatives, liberals, and radicals have all complained at one time or another that the American educational system gives professional educators too little incentive to provide high quality education to most children." The proposal condemns itself by proposing tuition grants which would have to be spent on schooling.

This is like giving a lame man a pair of crutches and stipulating that he use them only if the ends are tied together. As the proposal for tuition grants now stands, it plays into the hands not only of the professional educators but of racists, promoters of religious schools, and others whose interests are socially divisive. Above all, educational entitlements restricted to use within schools play into the hands of all those who want to continue to live in a society in which social advancement is tied not to proven knowledge but to the learning pedigree by which it is supposedly acquired. This discrimination in favor of schools which dominates Jencks's discussion on refinancing education could discredit one of the most critically needed principles for educational reform: the return of initiative and accountability for learning to the learner or his most immediate tutor.

The deschooling of society implies a recognition of the two-faced nature of learning. An insistence on skill drill alone could be a disaster; equal emphasis must be placed on other kinds of learning. But if schools are the wrong places for learning a skill, they are even worse places for getting an education. School does both tasks badly, partly because it does not distinguish between them. School is inefficient in skill instruction especially because it is curricular. In most schools a program which is meant to improve one skill is chained always to another irrelevant task. History is tied to advancement in math, and class attendance to the right to use the playground.

Schools are even less efficient in the arrangement of the circumstances which encourage the open-ended, exploratory use of acquired skills, for which I will reserve the term "liberal education." The main reason for this is that school is obligatory and becomes schooling for schooling's sake: an enforced stay in the company of teachers, which pays off in the doubtful privilege of more such company. Just as skill instruction must be freed from curricular restraints, so must liberal education be dissociated from obligatory attendance. Both skill-learning and education for inventive and creative behavior can be aided by institutional arrangement, but they are of a different, frequently opposed nature.

Most skills can be acquired and improved by drills, because skill implies the mastery of definable and predictable behavior. Skill instruction can rely, therefore, on the simulation of circumstances in which the skill will be used. Education in the exploratory and creative use of skills, however, cannot rely on drills. Education can be the outcome of instruction, though instruction of a kind fundamentally opposed to drill. It relies on the relationship between partners who already have some of the keys which give access to memories stored in and by the community. It relies on the critical intent of all those who use memories creatively. It relies on the surprise of the unexpected question which opens new doors for the inquirer and his partner.

The skill instructor relies on the arrangement of set circumstances which permit the learner to develop standard responses. The educational guide or master is concerned with helping matching partners to meet so that learning can take place. He matches individuals starting from their own, unresolved questions. At the most he helps the pupil to formulate his puzzlement since only a clear statement will give him the power to find his match, moved like him, at the moment, to explore the same issue in the same context.

Matching partners for educational purposes initially seems more difficult to imagine than finding skill instructors and partners for a game. One reason is the deep fear which school has implanted in us, a fear which makes us censorious. The unlicensed exchange of skills—even undesirable skills—is more predictable and therefore seems less dangerous than the unlimited opportunity for meeting among people who share an issue which for them, at the moment, is socially, intellectually, and emotionally important.

The Brazilian teacher Paulo Freire knows this from experience. He discovered that any adult can begin to read in a matter of forty hours if the first words he deciphers are charged with political meaning. Freire trains his teachers to move into a village and to discover the words which designate current important issues, such as the access to a well or the compound interest on the debts owed to the *patron*. In the evening the villagers meet for the discussion of these key words. They begin to realize that each word stays on the blackboard even after its sound has faded. The letters continue to unlock reality and to make it manageable as a problem. I have frequently witnessed how discussants grow in social awareness and how they are impelled to take political action as fast as they learn to read. They seem to take reality into their hands as they write it down.

I remember the man who complained about the weight of pencils: they were difficult to handle because they did not weigh as much as a shovel; and I remember another who on his way to work stopped with his Companions and wrote the word they were discussing with his hoe on the ground: "*agua*." Since 1962 my friend Freire has moved from exile to exile, mainly because he refuses to conduct his sessions around words which are preselected by approved educators, rather than those which his discussants bring to the class.

The educational matchmaking among people who have been successfully schooled is a different task. Those who do not need such assistance are a minority, even among the readers of serious journals. The majority cannot and should not be rallied for discussion around a slogan, a word, or a picture. But the idea remains the same: they should be able to meet around a problem chosen and defined by their own initiative. Creative, exploratory learning requires peers currently puzzled about the same terms or problems. Large universities make the futile attempt to match them by multiplying their courses, and they generally fail since they are bound to curriculum, course structure, and bureaucratic administration. In schools, including universities, most resources are spent to purchase the time and motivation of a limited number of people to take up predetermined problems in a ritually defined setting. The most radical alternative to school would be a network or service which gave each man the same opportunity to share his current concern with others motivated by the same concern.

Let me give, as an example of what I mean, a description of how an intellectual match might work in New York City. Each man, at any given moment and at a minimum price, could identify himself to a computer with his address and telephone number, indicating the book, article, film, or recording on which he seeks a partner for discussion. Within days he could receive by mail the list of others who recently had taken the same initiative. This list would enable him by telephone to arrange for a meeting with persons who initially would be known exclusively by the fact that they requested a dialogue about the same subject.

Matching people according to their interest in a particular title is radically simple. It permits identification only on the basis of a mutual desire to discuss a statement recorded by a third person, and it leaves the initiative of arranging the meeting to the individual. Three objections are usually raised against this skeletal purity. I take them up not only to clarify the theory that I want to illustrate by my proposal for they highlight the deep-seated resistance to deschooling education, to separating learning from social control but also because they may help to suggest existing resources which are not now used for learning purposes.

The first objection is: Why cannot self-identification be based also on an *idea* or an issue? Certainly such subjective terms could also be used in a computer system. Political parties, churches, unions, clubs, neighborhood centers, and professional societies already organize their educational activities in this way and in effect they act as schools. They all match people in order to explore certain "themes"; and these are dealt with in courses, seminars, and curricula in which presumed "common interests" are prepackaged. Such theme-matching is by definition teacher-centered: it requires an authoritarian presence to define for the participants the starting point for their discussion.

By contrast, matching by the title of a book, film, etc., in its pure form leaves it to the author to define the special language, the terms, and the framework within which a given problem or fact is stated; and it enables those who accept this starting point to identify themselves to one another. For instance, matching people around the idea of "cultural revolution" usually leads either to confusion or to demagoguery. On the other hand, matching those interested in helping each other understand a specific article by Mao, Marcuse, Freud, or Goodman stands in the great tradition of liberal learning from Plato's Dialogues, which are built around presumed statements by Socrates, to Aquinas's commentaries on Peter the Lombard. The idea of matching by title is thus radically different from the theory on which the "Great Books" clubs, for example, were built: instead of relying on the selection by some Chicago professors, any two partners can choose any book for further analysis.

The second objection asks: Why not let the identification of match seekers include information on age, background, world view, competence, experience, or other defining characteristics? Again, there is no reason why such discriminatory restrictions could not and should not be built into some of the many universities—with or without walls—which could use title-matching as their basic organizational device. I could conceive of a system designed to encourage meetings of interested persons at which the author of the book chosen would be present or represented; or a system which guaranteed the presence of a competent adviser; or one to which only students registered in a department or school had access; or one which permitted meetings only between people who defined their special approach to the title under discussion. Advantages for achieving specific goals of learning could be found for each of these restrictions. But I fear that, more often than not, the real reason for proposing such restrictions is contempt arising from the presumption that people are ignorant: educators want to avoid the ignorant meeting the ignorant around a text which they may not understand and which they read *only* because they are interested in it.

The third objection: Why not provide match seekers with incidental assistance that will facilitate their meetings—with space, schedules, screening, and protection? This is now done by schools with all the inefficiency characterizing large bureaucracies. If we left the initiative for meetings to the match seekers themselves, organizations which nobody now classifies as educational would probably do the job much better. I think of restaurant owners, publishers, telephone-answering services, department store managers, and even commuter train executives who could promote their services by rendering them attractive for educational meetings.

At a first meeting in a coffee shop, say, the partners might establish their identities by placing the book under discussion next to their cups. People who took the initiative to arrange for such meetings would soon learn what items to quote to meet the people they sought. The risk that the self-chosen discussion with one or several strangers might lead to a loss of time, disappointment, or even unpleasantness is certainly smaller than the same risk taken by a college applicant. A computer arranged meeting to discuss an article in a national magazine, held in a coffee shop off Fourth Avenue, would obligate none of the participants to stay in the company of his new acquaintances for longer than it took to drink a cup of coffee, nor would he have to meet any of them ever again. The chance that it would help to pierce the opaqueness of life in a modern city and further new friendship, self-chosen work, and critical reading is high. (The fact that a record of personal readings and meetings could be obtained thus by the FBI is undeniable; that this should still worry anybody in 1970 is only amusing to a free man, who willy-nilly contributes his share in order to drown snoopers in the irrelevancies they gather.)

Both the exchange of skills and matching of partners are based on the assumption that education for all means education by all. Not the draft into a specialized institution but only the mobilization of the whole population can lead to popular culture. The equal right of each man to exercise his competence to learn and to instruct is now pre-empted by certified teachers. The teachers' competence, in turn, is restricted to what may be done in school. And, further, work and leisure are alienated from each other as a result: the spectator and the worker alike are supposed to arrive at the work place all ready to fit into a routine prepared for them. Adaptation in the form of a product's design, instruction, and publicity shapes them for their role as much as formal education by schooling. A radical alternative to a schooled society requires not only new formal mechanisms for the formal acquisition of skills and their educational use. A deschooled society implies a new approach to incidental or informal education.

Incidental education cannot any longer return to the forms which learning took in the village or the medieval town. Traditional society was more like a set of concentric circles of meaningful structures, while modern man must learn how to find meaning in many structures to which he is only marginally related. In the village, language and architecture and work and religion and family customs were consistent with one another, mutually explanatory and reinforcing. To grow into one implied a growth into the others. Even specialized apprenticeship was a by-product of specialized activities, such as shoemaking or the singing of psalms. If an apprentice never became a master or a scholar, he still contributed to making shoes or to making church services solemn. Education did not compete for time with either work or leisure. Almost all education was complex, lifelong, and unplanned.

Contemporary society is the result of conscious designs, and educational opportunities must be designed into them. Our reliance on specialized, full-time instruction through school will now decrease, and we must find more ways to learn and teach: the educational quality of all institutions must increase again. But this is a very ambiguous forecast. It could mean that men in the modern city will be increasingly the victims of an effective process of total instruction and manipulation once they are deprived of even the tenuous pretense of critical independence which liberal schools now provide for at least some of their pupils.

It could also mean that men will shield themselves less behind certificates acquired in school and thus gain in courage to "talk back" and thereby control and instruct the institutions in which they participate. To ensure the latter we must learn to estimate the social value of work and leisure by the educational give-and-take for which they offer opportunity. Effective participation in the politics of a street, a work place, the library, a news program, or a hospital is therefore the best measuring stick to evaluate their level as educational institutions.

I recently spoke to a group of junior-high-school students in the process of organizing a resistance movement to their obligatory draft into the next class. Their slogan was "participation not simulation." They were disappointed that this was understood as a demand for less rather than for more education, and reminded me of the resistance which Karl Marx put up against a passage in the Gotha program which one hundred years ago wanted to outlaw child labor. He opposed the proposal in the interest of the education of the young, which could happen only at work. If the greatest fruit of man's labor should be the education he receives from it and the opportunity which work gives him to initiate the education of others, then the alienation of modern society in a pedagogical sense is even worse than its economic alienation. . . .

PART IV

Sexuality and Education

In this section, the term *sexuality* refers not only to gender but also to sexual orientation. The approximately 5 to 10 percent of the population who have an alternative sexual orientation are included when we use this term, and not just simply the heterosexual population. This distinction is an important one in that, until the last decade, individuals with an alternative sexual orientation have been largely excluded from discussions about education and schooling.

Including sexual orientation in a book like this is not meant to deemphasize gender as an issue in education. New and more complex approaches that consider the individual as a totality need to be taken. Thus, students, or populations of students, need to be understood not only in terms of their gender, race, ethnicity, and social class but also in terms of their sexual orientation.

Such an approach is essentially postmodern. It argues that the modern classifications used to understand education are too limited to continue to be useful by themselves. Gender or race, for example, are useful concepts, but they are inadequate to describe the complexity of most situations or individuals.

As you read the following selections, keep in mind these questions:

1. What role does sexuality play in the definition of individuals?
2. How do issues of sexual orientation play out in terms of personal and civil rights?
3. How should teachers and schools address issues of sexual orientation?
4. What is the law, and is it adequate to meet the needs of a diverse population?

15

Selection From A Vindication of the Rights of Woman *(1792)*

The idea of coeducation, as well as the equal education of women, is a relatively recent concept. The English feminist Mary Wollstonecraft (1759–1797), in her 1792 treatise *A Vindication of the Rights of Woman,* made one of the first modern cases for educational equality.

As you read this selection, consider the following questions:

1. What are the advantages and potential liabilities of same sex education?
2. What are some of the explanations for gender discrimination playing such an important role in our educational history?
3. What is the relationship between gender discrimination and other types of discrimination?

15

Selection From A Vindication of the Rights of Woman *(1792)*

Mary Wollstonecraft

I have already animadverted on the bad habits which females acquire when they are shut up together; and I think that the observation may fairly be extended to the other sex, till the natural inference is drawn which I have had in view throughout—that to improve both sexes they ought, not only in private families, but in public schools, to be educated together.

If marriage be the cement of society, mankind should all be educated after the same model, or the intercourse of the sexes will never deserve the name of fellowship, nor will women ever fulfill the peculiar duties of their sex, till they become enlightened citizens, till they become free by being enabled to earn their own subsistance, independent of men; in the same manner, I mean, to prevent misconstruction, as one man is independent of another. Nay, marriage will never be held sacred till women, by being brought up with men, are prepared to be their companions rather than their mistresses; for the mean doublings of cunning will ever render them contemptible, whilst oppression renders them timid. So convinced am I of this truth, that I will venture to predict that virtue will never prevail in society till the virtues of both sexes are founded on reason; and, till the affections common to both are allowed to gain their due strength by the discharge of mutual duties.

Were boys and girls permitted to pursue the same studies together, those graceful decencies might early be inculcated which produce modesty without those sexual distinctions that taint the mind. Lessons of politeness, and that formulary of decorum, which treads on the heels of falsehood, would be

Source: Wollstonecraft, Mary. 1891. *A Vindication of the Rights of Woman*, 237–253. London: T. Fisher Unwin.

rendered useless by habitual propriety of behavior. Not indeed put on for visitors, like the courtly robe of politeness, but the sober effect of cleanliness of mind. Would not this simple elegance of sincerity be a chaste homage paid to domestic affections, far surpassing the meretricious compliments that shine with false lustre in the heartless intercourse of fashionable life?

Let an enlightened nation then try what effect reason would have to bring them back to nature, and their duty; and allowing them to share the advantages of education and government with man, see whether they will become better, as they grow wiser and become free. They cannot be injured by the experiment, for it is not in the power of man to render them more insignificant than they are at present.

To render this practicable, day schools for particular ages should be established by Government, in which boys and girls might be educated together. The school for the younger children, from five to nine years of age, ought to be absolutely free and open to all classes. A sufficient number of masters should also be chosen by a select committee in each parish, to whom any complaint of negligence, &c., might be made, if signed by six of the children's parents.

Ushers would then be unnecessary; for I believe experience will ever prove that this kind of subordinate authority is particularly injurious to the morals of youth. What, indeed, can tend to deprave the character more than outward submission and inward contempt? Yet how can boys be expected to treat an usher with respect, when the master seems to consider him in the light of a servant, and almost to countenance the ridicule which becomes the chief amusement of the boys during the play hours?

But nothing of this kind could occur in an elementary day school, where boys and girls, the rich and poor, should meet together. And to prevent any of the distinctions of vanity, they should be dressed alike, and all obliged to submit to the same discipline, or leave the school. The schoolroom ought to be surrounded by a large piece of ground, in which the children might be usefully exercised, for at this age they should not be confined to any sedentary employment for more than an hour at a time. But these relaxations might all be rendered a part of elementary education, for many things improve and amuse the senses, when introduced as a kind of show, to the principles of which, dryly laid down, children would turn a deaf ear. For instance, botany, mechanics, and astronomy; reading, writing, arithmetic, natural history, and some simple experiments in natural philosophy, might fill up the day; but these pursuits should never encroach on gymnastic plays in the open air. The elements of religion, history, the history of man, and politics, might also be taught by conversations in the Socratic form.

After the age of nine, girls and boys, intended for domestic employments, or mechanical trades, ought to be removed to other schools, and receive instruction in some measure appropriated to the destination of each individual, the two sexes being still together in the morning; but in the afternoon the girls should attend a school, where plain work, mantua-making, millinery, &c., would be their employment.

The young people of superior abilities, or fortune, might now be taught, in another school, the dead and living languages, the elements of science, and continue the study of history and politics, on a more extensive scale, which would not exclude polite literature.

Girls and boys still together? I hear some readers ask. Yes. And I should not fear any other consequence than that some early attachment might take place; which, whilst it had the best effect on the moral character of the young people, might not perfectly agree with the views of the parents, for it will be a long time, I fear, before the world will be so far enlightened that parents, only anxious to render their children virtuous, shall allow them to choose companions for life themselves. . . .

* * *

I have already inveighed against the custom of confining girls to their needle, and shutting them out from all political and civil employments; for by thus narrowing their minds they are rendered unfit to fulfil the peculiar duties which nature has assigned them. . . .

Make them free, and they will quickly become wise and virtuous, as men become more so, for the improvement must be mutual, or the injustice which one-half of the human race are obliged to submit to retorting on their oppressors, the virtue of man will be worm-eaten by the insect whom he keeps under his feet.

16

Seneca Falls Declaration (1848)

In 1848, Elizabeth Cady Stanton (1815–1902) and Lucretia Mott (1793–1880) together called the first conference to address women's rights. The meeting in Seneca Falls, New York, and the document excerpted here are considered to be the beginning of the feminist movement in the United States.

Consider the following questions as you read this selection:

1. In light of the fact that the Seneca Falls Declaration draws on the Declaration of Independence as its model, is it therefore a revolutionary document?
2. Under the law, are there legitimate reasons to consider women different from men?

16

Seneca Falls Declaration (1848)

Elizabeth Cady Stanton

When, in the course of human events, it becomes necessary for one portion of the family of man to assume among the people of the earth a position different from that which they have hitherto occupied, but one to which the laws of nature and of nature's God entitle them, a decent respect to the opinions of mankind requires that they should declare the causes that impel them to such a course.

We hold these truths to be self-evident: that all men and women are created equal; that they are endowed by their Creator with certain inalienable rights; that among these are life, liberty, and the pursuit of happiness; that to secure these rights governments are instituted, deriving their just powers from the consent of the governed. Whenever any form of government becomes destructive of these ends, it is the right of those who suffer from it to refuse allegiance to it, and to insist upon the institution of a new government, laying its foundation on such principles, and organizing its powers in such form, as to them shall seem most likely to effect their safety and happiness. Prudence, indeed, will dictate that governments long established should not be changed for light and transient causes; and accordingly all experience hath shown that mankind are more disposed to suffer, while evils are sufferable, than to right themselves by abolishing the forms to which they were accustomed. But when a long train of abuses and usurpations, pursuing invariably the same object, evinces a design to reduce them under absolute despotism, it is their duty to throw off such government, and to provide new guards for their future security. Such has been the patient sufferance of the women under this government, and such is now the necessity which constrains them to demand the equal station to which they are entitled.

Source: Stanton, Elizabeth Cady, Susan B. Anthony, and Matilda Joslyn Gage, eds. 1887. *History of Women's Suffrage.* Vol. 1, 70.

The history of mankind is a history of repeated injuries and usurpations on the part of man toward woman, having in direct object the establishment of an absolute tyranny over her. To prove this, let facts be submitted to a candid world.

He has never permitted her to exercise her inalienable right to the elective franchise.

He has compelled her to submit to laws, in the formation of which she had no voice.

He has withheld from her rights which are given to the most ignorant and degraded men—both natives and foreigners.

Having deprived her of this first right of a citizen, the elective franchise, thereby leaving her without representation in the halls of legislation, he has oppressed her on all sides.

He has made her, if married, in the eye of the law, civilly dead.

He has taken from her all right in property, even to the wages she earns.

He has made her, morally, an irresponsible being, as she can commit many crimes with impunity, provided they be done in the presence of her husband. In the covenant of marriage, she is compelled to promise obedience to her husband, he becoming to all intents and purposes, her master—the law giving him power to deprive her of her liberty, and to administer chastisement.

He has so framed the laws of divorce, as to what shall be the proper causes, and in case of separation, to whom the guardianship of the children shall be given, as to be wholly regardless of the happiness of women—the law, in all cases, going upon a false supposition of the supremacy of man, and giving all power into his hands.

After depriving her of all rights as a married woman, if single, and the owner of property, he has taxed her to support a government which recognizes her only when her property can be made profitable to it.

He has monopolized nearly all the profitable employments, and from those she is permitted to follow, she receives but a scanty remuneration. He closes against her all the avenues to wealth and distinction which he considers most honorable to himself. As a teacher of theology, medicine, or law, she is not known.

He has denied her the facilities for obtaining a thorough education, all colleges being closed against her.

He allows her in Church, as well as State, but a subordinate position, claiming Apostolic authority for her exclusion from the ministry, and, with some exceptions, from any public participation in the affairs of the Church.

He has created a false public sentiment by giving to the world a different code of morals for men and women, by which moral delinquencies which exclude women from society, are not only tolerated, but deemed of little account in man.

He has usurped the prerogative of Jehovah himself, claiming it as his right to assign for her a sphere of action, when that belongs to her conscience and to her God.

He has endeavored, in every way that he could, to destroy her confidence in her own powers, to lessen her self-respect, and to make her willing to lead a dependent and abject life.

Now, in view of this entire disfranchisement of one-half the people of this country, their social and religious degradation—in view of the unjust laws above mentioned, and because women do feel themselves aggrieved, oppressed, and fraudulently deprived of their most sacred rights, we insist that they have immediate admission to all the rights and privileges which belong to them as citizens of the United States.

In entering upon the great work before us, we anticipate no small amount of misconception, misrepresentation, and ridicule; but we shall use every instrumentality within our power to effect our object. We shall employ agents, circulate tracts, petition the State and National legislatures, and endeavor to enlist the pulpit and the press in our behalf. We hope this Convention will be followed by a series of Conventions embracing every part of the country.

17

Equal Rights Amendment (1921)

The Equal Rights Amendment (ERA) to the United States Constitution was first written by the suffragist Alice Paul (1885–1977) in 1921 and introduced in Congress during every session since 1923. It finally passed Congressional approval in 1972 but failed to be ratified by the necessary thirty-eight states as required by law by July 1982. (Thirty-five states ratified the law.) Advocates for the ERA maintain that the amendment is necessary, because the Fourteenth Amendment does not provide adequate protection against sexual discrimination.

Consider the following questions as you read this selection:

1. Should Section 1 of the Equal Rights Amendment be rewritten to read "Equality of Rights under the law shall not be denied or abridged by the United States or any state on account of sexual orientation"?
2. Is there a good reason not to pass the amendment?

17

Equal Rights Amendment (1921)

Alice Paul

SECTION 1

Equality of Rights under the law shall not be denied or abridged by the United States or any state on account of sex.

SECTION 2

The Congress shall have the power to enforce, by appropriate legislation, the provisions of this article.

SECTION 3

This amendment shall take effect two years after the date of ratification.

Source: The Equal Rights Amendment. Web site for the Alice Paul Institute in Collaboration with the ERA Task Force of the National Council of Women's Organizations. Available at http://www.equalrightsamendment.org

18

Title IX (1972)

Title IX was the first comprehensive federal law to prohibit sexual discrimination against students and employees of educational institutions. The law benefits both men and women, making it illegal to discriminate in schools based on gender in recruitment, admissions, activities, course offerings, counseling, financial aid, employment assistance, facilities and housing, athletics, health and insurance benefits, and the like.

As you read this selection, consider the following questions:

1. Since its passage in 1972, how has Title IX affected women's participation in sports?
2. Should men and women be able to participate in all of the same activities in schools?

18

Title IX (1972)

Congress of the United States of America

Section 1681. Sex

(A) PROHIBITION AGAINST DISCRIMINATION; EXCEPTIONS

No person in the United States shall, on the basis of sex, be excluded from participation in, be denied the benefits of, or be subjected to discrimination under any education program or activity receiving Federal financial assistance, except that:

(1) Classes of educational institutions subject to prohibition

in regard to admissions to educational institutions, this section shall apply only to institutions of vocational education, professional education, and graduate higher education, and to public institutions of undergraduate higher education;

(2) Educational institutions commencing planned change in admissions

in regard to admissions to educational institutions, this section shall not apply (A) for one year from June 23, 1972, nor for six years after June 23, 1972, in the case of an educational institution which has begun the process of changing from being an institution which admits only students of one sex to being an institution which admits students of both sexes, but only if it is carrying out a plan for such a change which is approved by the Secretary of Education or

---

Source: United States Congress. Title 20 U.S.C. Sections 1681–1688. Available at http://www.dol.gov/oasam/regs/statutes/titleix.htm

(B) for seven years from the date an educational institution begins the process of changing from being an institution which admits only students of one sex to being an institution which admits students of both sexes, but only if it is carrying out a plan for such a change which is approved by the Secretary of Education, whichever is the later;

(3) Educational institutions of religious organizations with contrary religious tenets

this section shall not apply to any educational institution which is controlled by a religious organization if the application of this subsection would not be consistent with the religious tenants of such organization;

(4) Educational institutions training individuals for military services or merchant marine

this section shall not apply to an educational institution whose primary purpose is the training of individuals for the military services of the United States, or the merchant marine;

(5) Public educational institutions with traditional and continuing admissions policy

in regard to admissions this section shall not apply to any public institution of undergraduate higher education which is an institution that traditionally and continually from its establishment has had a policy of admitting only students of one sex;

(6) Social fraternities or sororities; voluntary youth service organizations

this section shall not apply to membership practices—

(A) of a social fraternity or social sorority which is exempt from taxation under section 501(a) of Title 26, the active membership of which consists primarily of students in attendance at an institution of higher education, or

(B) of the Young Men's Christian Association, Young Women's Christian Association; Girl Scouts, Boy Scouts, Camp Fire Girls, and voluntary youth service organizations which are so exempt, the membership of which has traditionally been limited to persons of one sex and principally to persons of less than nineteen years of age;

(7) Boy or Girl conferences

this section shall not apply to—

(A) any program or activity of the American Legion undertaken in connection with the organization or operation of any Boys State conference, Boys Nation conference, Girls State conference, or Girls Nation conference; or

(B) any program or activity of any secondary school or educational institution specifically for—

- (i) the promotion of any Boys State conference, Boys Nation conference, Girls State conference, or Girls Nation conference; or
- (ii) the selection of students to attend any such conference;

(8) Father-son or mother-daughter activities at educational institutions

this section shall not preclude father-son or mother-daughter activities at an educational institution, but if such activities are provided for students of one sex, opportunities for reasonably comparable activities shall be provided for students of the other sex; and

(9) Institutions of higher education scholarship awards in "beauty" pageants

this section shall not apply with respect to any scholarship or other financial assistance awarded by an institution of higher education to any individual because such individual has received such award in any pageant in which the attainment of such award is based upon a combination of factors related to the personal appearance, poise, and talent of such individual and in which participation is limited to individuals of one sex only, so long as such pageant is in compliance with other nondiscrimination provisions of Federal law.

(B) PREFERENTIAL OR DISPARATE TREATMENT BECAUSE OF IMBALANCE IN PARTICIPATION OR RECEIPT OF FEDERAL BENEFITS; STATISTICAL EVIDENCE OF IMBALANCE

Nothing contained in subsection (a) of this section shall be interpreted to require any educational institution to grant preferential or disparate treatment to the members of one sex on account of an imbalance which may exist with respect to the total number or percentage of persons of that sex participating in or receiving the benefits of any federally supported program or activity, in comparison with the total number or percentage of persons of that sex in any community, State, section, or other area: *Provided,* that this subsection shall not be construed to prevent the consideration in any hearing or proceeding under this chapter of statistical evidence tending to show that such an imbalance exists with respect to the participation in, or receipt of the benefits of, any such program or activity by the members of one sex.

(C) EDUCATIONAL INSTITUTION DEFINED

For the purposes of this chapter an educational institution means any public or private preschool, elementary, or secondary school, or any institution of vocational, professional, or higher education, except that in the case of an educational institution composed of more than one school, college, or department which are administratively separate units, such term means each such school, college or department. . . .

19

"The Absent Presence: Patriarchy, Capitalism, and the Nature of Teacher Work" (1987)

As the following selection argues, gender plays a critical role in shaping institutions such as schools. Likewise, it influences professions dominated by women, such as teaching. Female teachers often perpetuate the process of discrimination as they pass their values from one generation to the next. Understanding the relationship between gender and the teaching profession is essential. Lather argues that "taping the estrangement and sense of relative deprivation that feminism engenders in women is a key to transforming the occupation of public school teaching."

Consider the following questions as you read this work:

1. How is gender a socially constructed phenomenon?
2. How does gender affect the work of teachers?
3. What is meant by the idea that gender can be used as a tool for social analysis?

19

"The Absent Presence: Patriarchy, Capitalism, and the Nature of Teacher Work" (1987)

Patti Lather

Through the questions it poses and the absences it locates, feminism argues the centrality of gender in the shaping of our consciousness, skills, and institutions as well as the distribution of power and privilege. The central premise of feminism is that gender is a basic organizing principle of all known societies and that, along with race, class, and the sheer specificity of historical circumstance, it profoundly shapes/mediates the concrete conditions of our lives.[1]

The last fifteen years of feminist scholarship argues strongly that if what we are about is understanding the intersection of choice and constraint in human experience, the relationship of social structure and consciousness, then gender cannot be ignored. This is especially true in an occupational field as tied to women's social position as is public school teaching. As Michael Apple notes (1983b, 1985), the history of teaching is the history of a gendered work force. Yet Apple calls gender "the absent presence" in most research on teaching (1983b, p. 625). Even within leftist work, where one might expect more attention to the interactive dynamics of all forms of oppression, the marginalization of gender in neo-Marxist sociology of education is well noted (O'Brien, 1984; Connell et al., 1982; Walker & Barton, 1983; McRobbie, 1980; Macdonald, 1981; Clarricoates, 1981).

It is the purpose of this paper to argue the centrality of gender in understanding and changing the work lives of teachers. After sketching the history of

Source: Lather, Patti. 1987. "The Absent Presence: Patriarchy, Capitalism, and the Nature of Teacher Work." *Teacher Education Quarterly* 14 (2): 25–38.

the stormy relationship between feminism and Marxism, I will explore what opens up both theoretically and strategically once we do pay attention to gender in our efforts to understand the nature of teacher work.

The Unhappy Marriage of Feminism and Marxism

> Our subordination to men is not theorized in terms of the benefits that accrue to them and the vested interests they have in maintaining those benefits but in terms of the benefits to capitalism. (Mahony, 1985, p. 66)

> In the case of women, their definition as a group and the subsequent collapsing of the group into the general category of the exploited have more to do with patriarchal astigmatism than with social reality. . . . The highlighting of the economic exploitation of women by capital and the obscuring of their oppression by men is an ideological practice—in life and in research. (O'Brien, 1984, p. 44)

> Traditional Marxists acknowledge the existence of male dominance, but their recognition is not central to their theory or their practice. (Jaggar, 1983, p. 239)

"The feminist project" (Mazza, 1983) has moved from being accused of factionalism and bourgeois selfishness by male Marxists through what Rowbotham terms the "ominous politeness" of the 1970s (1981, p. 101). We are presently witnessing the "and women, of course" phenomenon, which Mary O'Brien terms "the commatization of women": Gender is tacked on to an analysis in a way that makes women's struggles tactically rather than theoretically present in neo-Marxist discourse. O'Brien argues, furthermore, that such marginalization is "not mere patriarchal prejudice but rather a consequence of serious defects in Marxist theory" (1984, p. 43). Bringing women's capacity for dissent to the center of our transformative aspirations has theoretical and tactical implications for neo-Marxist praxis that will be dealt with later in this paper. But first I want to explore the nature of the relationship between feminism and Marxism by looking at the gender blindness of so much neo-Marxist sociology of education.

While I am aware of MacKinnon's warning against the, anxiety that lurks under most efforts to justify women's struggle in Marxist terms, "as if only that would make them legitimate" (1982, p. 524), I argue that Marxist thought is as essential to save feminism from its tendencies toward partiality and privatism as feminism is to save Marxism from its abstraction and dogmatism (Eisenstein, 1979; Smith, 1979; Kuhn & Wolpe, 1978; O'Brien, 1981, 1984; Sargent, 1981; Rowbotham et al., 1981). Feminism that disregards the workings of economic privilege and the force of material circumstance disempowers itself. Marxism that loses connection with concrete individuals living contradictory and phenomenologically dense lives abstracts itself out of the realm of the useful.

A core feminist belief is that patriarchy,[2] the socially sanctioned power of men over women, operates in both the private and public spheres to perpetuate a social order that benefits men at the expense of women (Sokoloff, 1980; O'Brien, 1981; Barrett, 1980). Patriarchy is reproduced through the social construction of gender that reflects and reinforces the splits between nurturance and autonomy, public and private, male and female (Flax, 1980; Grumet, 1981). Which biological sex we are born into makes an immense difference in the material and psychic patterns of our lives. Patriarchal hegemony, however, obscures both male privilege and gender as a cultural construction that profoundly shapes our lives. Such hegemony operates as much in neo-Marxist discourse as it does in any other part of the culture.

There are exceptions. At the token end of the continuum are the sociology of education anthologies that include an essay of gender while in no way viewing as problematic the invisibility of gender in the remaining essays (Apple, 1982; Apple & Weis, 1983; Dale et al., 1981; Barton et al., 1981). Michael Apple's recent work clearly argues that gender is as integral an analytical tool as is class (1983b, 1985), in contrast to his earlier analysis of teacher deskilling where gender is largely invisible (1983a). There is a handful of male reconceptual curriculum theorists who use gender as a key analytic category and seem reasonably familiar with feminist discourse (Sears, 1983; Pinar, 1981, 1983; Pinar & Johnson, 1980; Taubman, 1981). There is the work of Connell et al. in Australia where, after a year's fieldwork, the research team of academics and classroom teachers came to the unexpected realization that the interaction of gender and class is central to understanding what happens in schools (1982, p. 73). Both class and gender were recognized as structures of power that involve control of some over others and the ability of the controllers to organize social life to their own advantage. Class and gender "abrade, inflame, amplify, twist, negate, dampen and complicate one another. In short, they interact vigorously . . . with significant consequences for schooling" (p. 182). But the norm among "neo-Marxist curricularists" (Schubert et al., 1984) is a lack of awareness regarding gender issues, including the wealth of academic scholarship that has developed over the last fifteen years.

Feminism provides a golden opportunity for Marxists to do their part in what Aronowitz calls "the long process by which society learns to make the self-criticism needed to save itself" (1981, p. 53). Grasping the implications for social transformation of women's struggle for self-determination requires an end to the sexism and economism inherent in the refusal to see cultural resistance and revolutionary struggle outside of the "workerism" that permeates the male neo-Marxists search for revolutionary actors (Rowbotham et al., 1981, p. 32; Lather, 1984).

Heidi Hartmann (1981) has termed the relationship of feminism and Marxism an "unhappy marriage": Whether orthodox, neo- or "post-Althusserean,"[3] Marxists cannot see women's experiences and capacities as a motor force in history. So, as in patriarchal marriage, two become one and that one is the husband. Gender considerations become secondary, if acknowledged at all. Class is the ultimate contradiction. To see women's subordination as a central rather than a peripheral feature of society would require a probing of "the epistemological contradictions of using gender analysis as an appendage to an androcentric theoretical perspective" (Tabakin & Densmore, 1985, p. 13). It is, of course, much easier to ignore the whole issue, especially in terms of the philosophically fundamental dimensions of the feminist challenge. The "and women, of course" phenomenon allows male Marxist scholars to feel they have addressed gender issues—without ever asking how a field of inquiry must be reconstructed "if it is genuinely to include women's lives, experiences, work, aspirations" (Martin, 1986).

Habermas has termed feminism a new ideological offensive (1981). As such, it is, I argue, the contemporary social movement taking fullest advantage of the profound crisis of established paradigms in intellectual thought. The charge of feminist scholars is to document the specificity of how gender inequality permeates intellectual frameworks and to generate empowering alternatives. The challenge of such work to neo-Marxist sociology of education is no less than this: to bring women to the center of our transformative aspirations is an opportunity to address the "black holes"[4] that have stymied a Marxist praxis relevant to the conditions of life under advanced monopoly capitalism.

Issues of Praxis

My argument in this section is that if we want to understand and change the work lives of teachers, issues of gender are central. What follows is a sketch of what opens up both theoretically and strategically when we bring gender to the center of our efforts to understand the nature of teacher work. After an overview of the way gender has shaped the social relations of teaching, three problematic areas of Marxism will be touched upon: the public/private split, the failure to come to grips with subjectivity, and the reductionism that still typifies so much of contemporary Marxism and stymies the sustaining of systematic opposition.

Gender and the Shaping of Public School Teaching

The central claim of materialist-feminism[5] is that gender specific forms of oppression are not reducible to the demands of capitalism. There is an interactive reciprocity and interweaving of the needs of patriarchy and capital that must be taken into account in understanding the work lives of teachers. How has gender shaped the nature of teacher work?

To see the family as a "greedy institution for women" (Coser & Rokoff, 1971, p. 545) is to understand that the conditions of maintaining capitalism via the gender system require an analysis of the reproduction of mothering by women both inside and outside the home (Chodorow, 1978: Dinnerstein, 1976; Sokoloff, 1980). Problematizing the feminization of the teaching role provides an exemplary illustration of the way women's labor in the "helping professions" becomes "motherwork": the reproduction of classed, raced, and gendered workers.

Sara Lightfoot writes: "Mothers and teachers are also involved in an alien task. Both are required to raise children in the service of a dominant group whose values and goals they do not determine. . . . to socialize their children to conform to a society that belongs to men" (1978, p. 70). Teaching has come to be formulated as an extension of women's role in the family: to accept male leadership as "natural" and to provide services that reproduce males for jobs and careers, females for wives and mothers and a reserve labor force. Margaret Adams (1971) calls this "the compassion trap": Women feed their skills into social programs they have rarely designed that, while ripe with contradictions, are "fundamentally geared to the maintenance of society's status quo in all its destructive, exploitative aspects" (p. 562).

Women's subordination has been built into the very dynamics of the teaching role. This is not to deny that classroom teachers exert a form of power over their students. But Jean Baker Miller's (1976) distinction between relationships of temporary and permanent inequality is helpful here. Women are dominant in relations of temporary inequality such as parent and teacher, where adult power is used to foster development and eventually removes the initial disparity; they are submissive in permanently unequal relations where power is used both to cement dominant/subordinate dynamics and to rationalize the need for continued inequality (pointed out in Gilligan, 1982, p. 168).

Teachers stand at the juncture of nurturing and sending out, preparing children to go from the private to the public world. To the degree women teachers serve as transmitters of cultural norms rather than cultural transformers, they, like mothers, find themselves caught in the contradiction of perpetuating their own oppression. With training for docility,[6] teaching becomes an extension of women's maternal role as capitalism's "soft cops" (Wasserman, 1974), serving the dual function of both presenting the capitalist-patriarchy's human face and providing social and political containment (Rowbotham, 1973, p. 91).

As "the secular arm of the church" (Howe, 1976, p. 85), dedicated to sacrifice and service, disempowered by the "normal school mentality" fostered by their education (Mattingly, 1975), crowded into an occupation full of structural disincentives, and oversocialized to be "good girls," women teachers have focused on responsive concern for students and worries about job performance at the cost of developing a more critical stance toward their cultural task of passing on a received heritage. The structure of the public schools has grown up around women's subordination. Little wonder, then, that the possibilities for nurturing Giroux's "oppositional teacher" (1983) or Zaret's "the teacher as transition agent" (1975) are directly linked to empowering women.

The Public/Private Split

The public/private split that is the foundation of the capitalist-patriarchy has relegated women's sphere to the periphery of social thought, the realm of the "natural" and hence unchangeable, the biological. Materialist-feminist analysis grows out of the primary female experience with reproduction and reproduction expanded to include nurturing, caretaking, and socializing work—"shadow work" that does not get counted in either the gross national product (Illich, 1982, p. 45) or Marxist theories of the motor forces of history (Jaggar, 1983). The materialist feminist analysis insists that the forces and relations of reproduction be recognized to be as central as production in the social fabric (O'Brien, 1981; Ferguson, 1979; Bridenthal, 1976; Kuhn & Wolpe, 1979). Materialist-feminist theory posits that reproduction stands in dialectical relationship to production as the material base of history; they are, in effect, warp and woof of the social fabric.

Mary O'Brien (1981) argues that to continue dismissing change in the reproductive sector as being of no historical consequence is rooted in a biologism that contradicts Marxism's essential postulate of the dialectical relationship between nature and culture. Other major shifts in social consciousness have been rooted in the public realm. With feminism, "the private realm is where the new action is" (p. 189), as women undertake "a conscious struggle to transform a social reality that in turn will transform consciousness" (p. 208).

Coming to Grips With Subjectivity

Rosalind Coward (1983) argues that just as the great debate of nineteenth century social theory, the relationship between nature and culture, was moved forward by focusing on sexual relations, the position of women holds great hope for theoretical advances in the late twentieth-century quest to understand the relationship between consciousness and social structure. The focus on false consciousness, hegemony, and ideology that characterizes contemporary Marxist thought is rooted in the hidden nature of exploitation under advanced monopoly capitalism (Jaggar, 1983, p. 215); this results in a society where "the very fact of domination has to be proven to most Americans" (Giroux, 1981).

Because as women, we live intimately with our patriarchal oppressors, we have been especially subjected to layers of myths about our own nature and that of the society in which we live. Studying "the extent to which gender is a world-view-structuring experience" (Hartsock, 1983, p. 231) can hence shed much light on the processes of both ideological mystification and coming to critical consciousness.

Western women presently find themselves in an extremely contradictory position. Widespread access to birth control gives women broad-based reproductive control for the first time in history. Aspirations are geometrically advancing in a no-growth era; most women put in "double days" in a culture that in practice cares little for children (Grubb & Lazerson, 1982). Some women experience double and triple oppression due to race, class, and sexual preference; many are part of the feminization of poverty. All receive double messages from our culture with schizophrenic regularity. Women are, collectively, prime candidates for ideological demystification, the probing of contradictions to find out why our ways of looking at the world do not seem to be working in our favor (Eisenstein, 1982).

"Feminism is the first theory to emerge from those whose interest it affirms" (MacKinnon, 1982, p. 543). It is rooted in a deep respect for experience-based knowledge. It is best summarized in the phrase "the personal is political"—a radical extension of the scope of politics that transcends the public/private split. Feminism is premised on an intimate knowledge of the multifaceted and contradictory elements of consciousness and the deeply structured patterns of inequality reinforced through dominant meanings and practices. As we extend the question of consent from the public to the private realm, we find that "because women's consensus shows more signs of erosion than working-class consensus, it is a more promising field for research and political praxis" (O'Brien, 1984, p. 58).

Transcending Reductionism

What a materialist-feminism refuses is to reduce Marxism solely to an analysis of capital; it insists that historical materialism can shed much light on the oppression of women and that Marxism would benefit from a focus on the interactive reciprocity and interweaving of the needs of patriarchy and capital. Perhaps most important, feminism argues the need for Marxism to recognize that revolutionary constituencies shift with historical circumstances. To the degree women's struggle is made invisible by economistic reductionism, Marxism loses touch with the potential that feminism offers for social transformation.

The relationship between the theoretical analysis and political strategies is a long-standing concern within Marxism. Whitty argues that change efforts in the schools must be linked to broader oppositional movements (1985, p. 24). To continue to disallow gender in our analysis of teacher work is to not tap into the potential that feminism offers for bringing about change in our schools. As Zaret wrote in 1975, "For women who are teachers, the starting point is you in your own situation" (p. 47). Until the rebirth of feminism, women had no access to oppositional ideologies that encouraged them to question the gender status quo. Making gender problematic opens one up to the layers of shaping forces and myths in our society with great implications for one's conception of the teaching role. Let us look, for example, at some of the contradictions in the lives of women teachers that a gender analysis illuminates.

- As women teachers, we are simultaneously assumed to place home and family above career and to be dedicated "professionals," which often means "a kind of occupational subservience" (Dreeben, 1970, p. 34; see Darling-Hammond, 1985).
- The "paradox of conformity" (Zaret, 1975, p. 46) makes us complicitors in our own oppression to the extent that we maintain the status quo.
- As women teachers, we are simultaneously in positions of power and powerlessness. Like motherhood, teaching is "responsibility without power" (Rich, 1976). Women's subordination has been built into the very dynamics of the teaching role. Lightfoot writes of the cultural perceptions of the teacher as woman and as child (1978, p. 64). Yet we expect teachers to perform miracles, to overcome our society's most intransigent problems.
- As both teachers and mothers, we daily witness the rhetoric of America as a child-centered society versus the reality of our culture's devaluation of the care and raising of children.
- As married women teachers, we live daily the contradiction of needing the home as a refuge from the alienating dimensions of teaching versus the alienating reality of our double day (Sokoloff, 1980, p. 210; see Pogrebin, 1983, regarding how little household work American men do).

It is the central contention of this paper that taping the estrangement and sense of relative deprivation that feminism engenders in women is a key to transforming the occupation of public school teaching.

Conclusion

Given the androcentrism of Marxist theory, feminism benefits from exposure to this powerful, well-developed body of social theory that continues to dominate revolutionary discourse so long as feminists remain aware of the need to subvert the intellectual ground under our feet. We need to be sure we do not become "good wives" of a Marxist patriarch. What neo-Marxist sociology of education needs right now is a way to transcend its theoreticism, its lack of praxis, its malaise rooted in its long-standing lament regarding "the continuing absence of a movement capable of advancing alternatives" (Genovese, 1967, p. 102).

Given the intimate connection of public school teaching with the social role of women, the continued invisibility of gender in neo-Marxist analysis of public school teaching greatly limits its usefulness in restructuring the work lives of teachers. To the extent male neo-Marxists continue to ignore the forces and relations of patriarchy and to marginalize women as historical protagonists in their theory and strategy building, they are as much a part of the problem as of the solution.

Notes

1. Gender as a social construction is a key assumption of all strands of feminism. Feminism argues that what gender is, what men and women are, and what types of relations they have are not so much the products of biological "givens" as of social and cultural forces. Symbolic and ideological dimensions of culture play especially important roles in creating, reproducing, and transforming gender. See S. Ortner and H. Whitehead (Eds.), *Sexual Meanings: The Cultural Construction of Gender and Sexuality.* New York: Cambridge University Press, 1981.

2. Barrett (1980) and Coward (1983) discuss the analytic problems with the concept of patriarchy in feminist work.

3. In a continuing profusion of "kinds of Marxism," Mary O'Brien defines post-Althusserean Marxism as "attempts to re-socialize the substructural/superstructural model . . . which is problematic in any case" (1984, p. 45).

4. I first heard Jim Sears use this term at the Fifth Curriculum Theorizing Conference, Dayton, 1984.

5. I now call myself a "materialist-feminist," thanks largely to French social theorist, Christine Delphy (1984), but I have also, finally, grasped the essence of the "new French feminists" (Marks & de Courtivon, 1980): that I am a constantly moving subjectivity. To be a materialist means to understand social reality as arising in the lived experiences of concrete individuals under particular historical conditions.

6. For a feminist critique of teacher education, see Lather, "Gender and the Shaping of Public School Teaching: Do Good Girls Make Good Teachers?"; paper presented at the National Women's Studies Association annual meeting, New Brunswick, New Jersey, 1984. See, also, Ava McCall, "Learning to Teach: The Empowering Quality of Nurturance"; paper presented at the Curriculum Theorizing Conference, Dayton, 1986.

References

Adams, M. (1971). The compassion trap. In V. Gornick and B. Moran (Eds.), *Woman in a sexist society: Studies in power and powerlessness.* New York: Basic Books.

Apple, M. (1982). Reproduction and contradiction in education: An introduction. In M. Apple (Ed.), *Cultural and economic reproduction in education: Essays on class, ideology and the state.* Boston: Routledge and Kegan Paul.

——. (1983a). Curricular form and the logic of technical control. In M. Apple and L. Weis (Eds.), *Ideology and practice in schooling* (pp. 143–166). Philadelphia: Temple University Press.

——. (1983b). Work, gender, and teaching. *Teacher's College Record,* 84(3), 611–628.
——. (1985). Teaching and "women's work": A comparative historical and ideological analysis. *Teacher's College Record,* 86(3), 455–473.
Apple M. and L. Weis (Eds.). (1983). *Ideology and practice in schooling.* Philadelphia: Temple University Press.
Aronowitz, S. (1981). *The crisis in historical materialism: Class, politics, and culture in marxist theory.* New York: Praeger.
Barrett, M. (1980). *Women's oppression today: Problems in marxist-feminist analysis.* London: Verso.
Barton, L., R. Meighan, and S. Walker (Eds.). (1981). *Schooling, ideology, and the curriculum.* Barcombe, England: Falmer Press.
Bridenthal, R. (1976). The dialectics of production and reproduction in history. *Radical America,* 10, 3–11.
Chodorow, N. (1978). *The reproduction of mothering: Psychoanalysis and the socialization of gender.* Berkeley: University of California Press.
Clarricoates, K. (1981). The experience of patriarchal schooling. *Interchange,* 12(23), 185–204.
Connell, R. W., D. J. Ashenden, S. Kessler, and G. W. Dowsett (1982). *Making the difference: Schools, families, and social division.* Sydney: George Allen and Unwin.
Coser, R. and G. Rokoff (1971). Women in the occupational world: Social disruption and conflict. *Social Problems,* 18, 535–554.
Coward, R. (1983). *Patriarchal precedents: Sexuality and social relations.* Boston: Routledge and Kegan Paul.
Dale, R., G. Esland, and M. MacDonald (Eds.). (1981). *Education and the state.* Vol. 2. Barcombe, England: Falmer Press.
Darling-Hammond, L. (1985). Valuing teachers: The making of a profession. *Teacher's College Record,* 87(2), 205–218.
Delphy, C. (1984). *Close to home: A materialist analysis of women's oppression.* Amherst: University of Massachusetts Press.
Dinnerstein, D. (1976). *The mermaid and the minotaur: Sexual arrangements and the human malaise.* New York: Harper Colophon.
Dreeban, R. (1970). *The nature of teacher work: Schools and the work of teachers.* Glenview, IL: Scott-Foresman.
Eisenstein, Z. (Ed.). (1979). *Capitalist patriarchy and the case for socialist-feminism.* London: Monthly Review Press.
Eisenstein, Z. (1982). The sexual politics of the new right: Understanding the "crisis of liberalism" for the 1980s. *Signs,* 7(3), 567–588.
Ferguson, A. (1979). Women as a new revolutionary class. In P. Walker (Ed.), *Between labor and class.* Boston: South End Press.
Flax, J. (1980). Mother-daughter relationships. In H. Eisenstein and A. Jardine (Eds.), *The future of difference* (pp. 20–40). Boston: G. K. Hall.
Fox Keller, E. (1985). *Reflections on gender and science.* New Haven, CN: Yale University Press.
Freire, P. (1973). *Pedagogy of the oppressed.* New York: Seabury Press.
Genovese, E. (1967). On Antonio Gramsci. *Studies on the left,* 7(1–2), 83–107.
Gilligan, C. (1982). *In a different voice.* Cambridge, MA: Harvard University Press.
Giroux, H. (1981). *Ideology, culture, and the process of schooling.* Philadelphia: Temple University Press.
——. (1983). *Theory and resistance in education.* New York: J. F. Bergin.

Gray, E. D. (1982). *Patriarchy as a conceptual trap.* Wellesley, Mass.: Roundtable Press.

Grubb, W. and M. Lazerson (1982). *Broken promises: How Americans fail their children.* New York: Basic Books.

Grumet, M. (1981). Pedagogy for patriarchy: The feminization of teaching. *Interchange,* 12(2–3), 165–184.

Habermas, J. (1981). New social movements. *Telos,* 49, 33–38.

Hartmann, H. (1981). The unhappy marriage of marxism and feminism: Towards a more progressive union. In L. Sargent (Ed.), *Women and revolution* (pp. 1–41). Boston: South End Press.

Hartsock, N. (1983). *Money, sex, and power: Toward a feminist historical materialism.* Boston: Northwestern University Press.

Howe, F. (1981). Feminist scholarship-the extent of the revolution. In *Liberal education and the new scholarship on women: Issues and constraints in institutional change* (A report of the Wingspread Conference, October 22–24; pp. 5–21). Washington, DC: Association of American Colleges.

Illich, I. (1982). *Gender.* New York: Pantheon Books.

Jaggar, A. (1983). *Feminist politics and human nature.* Totowa, NJ: Rowman and Allanheld.

Kuhn, A. and A. M. Wolpe (Eds.). (1978). *Feminism and materialism: Women and modes of production.* Boston: Routledge and Kegan Paul.

Lather, P. (1984). Critical theory, curricular transformation, and feminist mainstreaming. *Journal of Education,* 166(1), 49–62.

Lightfoot, S. L. (1978). *Worlds apart: Relationships between families and schools.* New York: Basic Books.

Macdonald, M. (1981). Schooling and the reproduction of class and gender relations. In R. Dale et al. (Eds.), *Education and the state: Politics, patriarchy, and practice.* Vol. 2 (pp. 159–178). Barcombe: Open University Press.

MacKinnon, C. (1982). Feminism, marxism, method, and the state: An agenda for theory. *Signs,* 7(3), 515–544.

Mahony, P. (1985). *Schools for boys? Co-education reassessed.* London: Hutchinson.

Marks, E. and I. de Courtivon (Eds.). (1980). *New french feminisms.* Amherst, MA: University of Massachusetts Press.

Martin, J. (1986). Questioning the question. (Review of S. Harding, *The Science Question in Feminism,* 1986.) *Women's Review of Books,* 4(3), 17–18.

Mattingly, P. (1975). *The classless profession: American schoolmen in the nineteenth century.* New York: University Press.

Mazza, K. (1983, April). *Feminist perspectives and the reconceptualization of the disciplines.* Paper presented at the meeting of the American Educational Research Association, Montreal, Canada.

McRobbie, A. (1980). Settling accounts with subcultures. *Screen Education,* 34, 37–39.

Miller, J. (1976). *Toward a new psychology of women.* Boston: Beacon Press.

O'Brien, M. (1981). *The politics of reproduction.* Boston: Routledge and Kegan Paul.

——. (1984). The commatization of women: Patriarchal fetishism in the sociology of education. *Interchange,* 15(2), 43–60.

Pinar, W. (1981). Gender, sexuality, and curriculum studies: The beginning of the debate. *McGill Journal of Education,* 16(3), 305–316.

——. (1983). Curriculum as gender text: Notes on reproduction, resistance, and male-male relations. *Journal of Curriculum Theorizing,* 5, 26–52.

Pinar, W. and L. Johnson (1980). Aspects of gender analysis in recent feminist psychological thought and their implications for curriculum. *Journal of Education*, 162(4), 113–126.

Pogrebin, L. C. (1983). *Family politics: Love and power on an intimate frontier.* New York: McGraw-Hill.

Rich, A. (1976). *Of woman born: Motherhood as experience and institution.* New York: Bantam Books.

Rowbotham, S. (1973). *Woman's consciousness, man's world.* Middlesex, England: Penguin Books.

Rowbotham, S., L. Segal, and H. Wainwright (1981). *Beyond the fragments: Feminism and the making of socialism.* Boston: Alyson.

Sargent, L. (Ed.). (1981). *Women and revolution: A discussion of the unhappy marriage of marxism and feminism.* Boston: South End Press.

Schubert, W., G. Willis, and E. Short (1984). Curriculum theorizing: An emergent form of curriculum study in the U.S. *Curriculum Perspectives*, 4(1), 69–74.

Sears, J. (1983, June). *Sex equity: An ethnographic account of meaning-making in teacher education.* Paper presented at the meeting of the National Women's Studies Association, Columbus, Ohio.

Smith, D. (1979). A sociology for women. In J. Sherman and E. Beck (Eds.), *The prism of sex: Essays on the sociology of knowledge* (pp. 135–188). Madison, WI: University of Wisconsin Press.

Sokoloff, N. (1980). *Between money and love: The dialectics of women's home and market work.* New York: Praeger.

Tabakin, G. and K. Densmore (1985, April). *Teacher professionalization and gender analysis.* Paper presented at the meeting of the American Educational Research Association, Chicago, IL.

Taubman, P. (1981). Gender and curriculum: Discourse and the politics of sexuality. *Journal of Curriculum Theorizing.*

Walker, S. and L. Barton (1983). *Gender, class, and education.* New York: Falmer Press.

Wasserman, M. (1974). *Demystifying school.* New York: Praeger.

Whitty, G. (1985, April). *Curriculum theory, research, and politics: A rapprochement.* Paper presented at the meeting of the American Educational Research Association, Chicago, IL.

Zaret, E. (1975). Women/school/society. In J. Macdonald and E. Zaret (Eds.), *Schools in search of meaning.* Washington DC: Association for Supervision and Curriculum Development.

20

"A Queer Youth" (1996)

The experience of a queer student coming out is described in the following essay by Paul H. Cottell, Jr. In this essay, he reveals the very real tensions felt by individuals with alternative sexual orientations as they negotiate family and community.

As you read this selection, consider the following questions:

1. What is gained and what is potentially lost as gay students come to terms with who they are sexually?
2. How is discrimination against gay students different from other types of discrimination?
3. What should be the rights of gay students and teachers in the schools?
4. How important is the use of alternative spellings (such as "womyn" for woman) as part of a process of trying to overcome male-dominated models in American culture?

20

"A Queer Youth" (1996)

Paul H. Cottell, Jr.

The two things most central to my identity are my Christian faith and my being Queer. A motley mixture you might say. It took me a long time to be able to affirm myself as a Queer person in the context of being a Christian. I was raised loosely in the Roman Catholic faith. By this I mean that my family never went to church but we followed all the typical Catholic traditions (i.e., baptism, first communion, etc.). When I was in the eighth grade, I entered Catholic school, and I found my faith. My knowledge and belief in Christianity and Catholicism grew tenfold. I went on numerous retreats, including a pilgrimage to Denver, Colorado, to celebrate World Youth Day '93 with Pope John Paul II.

But as time went by, I began to doubt some Roman Catholic teachings. I disagreed with the Church's views on abortion, contraception, female ordination, most teachings on Mary (for example, the Immaculate Conception, which teaches that Mary was conceived free from original sin), and the Dogma of Papal Infallibility (which holds that when the pope speaks about moral and theological issues, he is speaking without error). These irrational viewpoints of the Roman Catholic Church, along with my budding acceptance of my sexuality, eventually led me to leave the Church.

I first came out to my close friend, Marie, in April 1994. Marie was the most understanding person in the world to me, considering that, in the past, I had made extremely homophobic remarks about her friend who is a lesbian. Marie didn't pressure me to talk about my sexuality. Rather, she gave me the time and space I needed to accept myself. Unfortunately, Marie was a foreign exchange student who returned to Belgium two months after I came out to her.

Source: Cottell, Paul H., Jr. 1996. "A Queer Youth." *Harvard Educational Review* 66 (2): 185–188.

I felt as if my world had fallen apart. The only person who knew I was Queer had left me.

It took some time after Marie left for me to face my sexuality again and to face the fact that no matter how much I prayed, I was still going to be Queer. The following poem in some ways explains the way I felt at this point in my life:

Does It Matter?

> My father asked if I am Gay I asked Does it matter? He said No not really I said Yes. He said get out of my life I guess it mattered
>
> My boss asked if I am Gay I asked Does it matter? He said No not really I told him Yes.
>
> He said you're fired Faggot I guess it mattered
>
> My friend asked if I am Gay I said Does it matter? He said No not really I told him Yes. He said don't call me your friend I guess it mattered
>
> My lover asked Do you love me? I asked Does it Matter? He said Yes. I told him I love you He said Let me hold you in my arms For the first time in my life something matters
>
> My God asked me Do you love yourself? I said Does it matter? [She] said YES I said How can I love myself? I am Gay [She] said That is the way I made you Nothing will ever matter again

—An Anonymous High School Student[1]

In August 1994, I finally accepted my sexuality. I worked up enough courage to attend a BAGLY (Boston Alliance of Gay and Lesbian [also bisexual and transgender] Youth) meeting. I finally met people who had struggled with some of the same issues as I. I soon formed a close friendship with a girl named Jill. We both had been deeply involved in youth groups at our churches and knew some of the same people. We talked a lot about the role faith plays in our lives and about the different issues we have with the Roman Catholic Church. Unfortunately, most of my Queer friends are unlike Jill and abhor religion. She remains one of the few Queer people with whom I feel comfortable talking about religion.

After going to BAGLY, I hastily labeled myself as gay. I don't know why I did this because, even at the time, I knew in my heart that I was attracted to both "womyn"[2] and men. This "gay" label stuck for a long time, but in time I gave it up. I realized that both gender and sexuality exist on a continuum, and that my gender identity and my sexual orientation fall just about smack dab in the middle. I also realized that although labels help us identify who we are, they are, in essence, degrading and often leave people feeling trapped. That is why I try not to label myself, but when I must, I choose Queer.

That fall, as my mother was about to leave for work one day, I told her that when she came home from work there was something we needed to talk about. Being a worrisome person, my mother asked me to tell her then. After shouting off a list of possibilities that included "Who did you get pregnant?" and "Are you doing drugs?" my mother then asked, "Are you gay?" She expected me to say no, but what else could I say but "YES." My mother was in shock. It took her a few months to understand who I am. She still struggles to accept me. But she is trying, and that's all I can ask from anybody. My mother did two things to come to terms with the fact that I am Queer. She had a series of telephone conversations with Al Ferreira, coordinator of Project 10 East, the Gay/Straight Alliance (GSA) at Cambridge Rindge and Latin High School. He assured her that my coming out experiences and identity struggles were actually quite typical of a Queer youth. She also talked to a gay cousin, who helped her understand what it is like to come out.

As a result of coming out, I left my Catholic high school that fall. The administration asked me to leave after my theology teacher broke my confidence and told them I was Queer; I gladly submitted to their request. I home-schooled from November 1994 through January 1995. I found a place to live in Cambridge, and entered Cambridge Rindge and Latin as a sophomore at the end of January 1995. The environment there was one of acceptance. It was nothing at all like my old school. I witnessed and experienced what education around issues of homosexuality can do for gay students and the whole school community. I joined Project 10 East, which, like any GSA, is a group of both Queer and straight youth that come together to talk about and fight issues of homophobia and heterosexism. I soon became the student coordinator for Project 10 East. In this capacity I organized meetings, did office work, and spoke around the community. At Cambridge Rindge and Latin we are lucky to have a community that is, for the most part, accepting of Queer people. I continue to do this work in the hope that acceptance for Queer people will be heightened.

In January 1995 I finally left the Roman Catholic rite and began studying to become an Episcopalian. In many ways this was harder on my mother than when I came out. She could not understand that I could no longer stay in a church that called my friends and me sinners. For a long time my self-esteem had suffered because of my church's stand on homosexuality. I had even contemplated suicide. Finally, at the Easter Vigil in 1995, I was confirmed by the Right Reverend Barbara C. Harris (the first female bishop in the world), and my mother was there with me. I did not choose a church that is primarily gay, but one that is primarily straight. I did this because I feel it is dangerous to isolate myself in the "gay" subculture. Unless Queer people are out in both the gay and straight communities, we will not obtain the rights that have been denied us.

A whole year has gone by since I came out. I can't say that everything is going well in the world. As a sexually active teenager, the reality of AIDS is frightening for me and many of my friends. While adults stand around and debate sex education and condom distribution, young adults take unnecessary health risks. Teachers' and parents' puritanical moralistic judgments will only lead to the death of many Queer and straight youth and adults. In the absence of sex education, the epidemic of AIDS/HIV will continue to claim the lives of more people. That is why it is important that youth educate each other and adults about the importance of safer sex practices—knowledge is the best protection against HIV/AIDS.

I worry about my friend Rick, who hustles sometimes, because his parents threw him out of their house at the age of sixteen when he told them he is gay. I worry about my best friend William, who constantly gets harassed in school about his sexuality. I know that harassment is not conducive to his learning. I still have to think about where there are safe places that my boyfriend and I can show affection publicly. Yet, despite all the prejudice and ignorance in the world directed toward Queers, I would never desire anything but to be who I am.

Notes

1. Taken from Bennett L. Singer, ed., *Growing Up Gay, A Literary Anthology* (New York: W. W. Norton, 1993).

2. Feminist spelling of women, one of the many ways I don't bow down to the patriarchy.

21

"How and Why Boys Under-Achieve" (2000)

The underachievement of boys in schools has been perceived as a problem throughout the English-speaking world. The reasons that boys perform less well in school than girls are open to considerable debate. In the following selection from the book *Getting It Right for Boys—and Girls,* the reasons why boys underachieve are examined in detail. Although the book focuses on the situation in the United Kingdom, the issues raised are of equal interest in the United States.

As you read the following selection, consider the following questions:

1. To what extent are the attitudes of boys toward learning a reflection of either genetic qualities or learned dispositions?
2. What social forces are at work that shape the attitudes of boys toward learning and schooling?

21

"How and Why Boys Under-Achieve" (2000)

Wendy Bradford and Colin Noble

Probably the most debatable aspect of the generally controversial issue of boys' achievement is that of the cause of the problem. It is rich territory for the nature versus nurture debaters. Although the arguments normally generate more heat than light it is a valuable one to be had if you are interested in bringing about change. It does capture interest and reflection and forces the different sides to focus on the nature of learning, gender characteristics, and pupils as individuals. The debate can be a catalyst for change.

In some ways it does not matter what the causes of boys' underachievement may be. Teachers and the education establishment in general have to work with the situation before them, and its source—obscure, confused and controversial—may be interesting but hardly useful. It is the practical strategies with which teachers are most concerned. However, unless we have some understanding of the background causes, we may be adopting plans and policies which are wholly inappropriate to the problem. . . .

Boys and the Anti-SWOT Culture

Some teachers have argued with conviction that we are in danger of overcomplicating a very simple fact: Some boys don't work as hard as most girls. They tend to be lazier, less motivated, less organised, poorer presenters, and less

Source: Bradford, Wendy, and Noble, Colin. 2000. "How and Why Boys Under-Achieve." *Getting It Right for Boys—and Girls,* Chap. 2. London: Routledge.

eager to please. In some schools, they positively promote an anti-culture which both justifies their own behaviour and challenges the rights of other boys, and occasionally girls, to try hard. This argument is irrefutable but far too reductionist. It leaves two fundamental questions unanswered: First, why is this culture so prevalent when many boys *do* want to work hard and succeed in doing so; and second, where has this culture come from? The simple diagnosis tends to promote a simple prescription—let's change the culture of boys. This is laudable, but without knowing more about its genesis it is impossible to understand the mechanisms and direction of change. In one school we came across a boy who had hidden a large number of books under his sweater. He was on his way home to get on with his homework but dared not display his willingness to work nor his lack of 'cool' in carrying a bag. This is symptomatic of the complexity of the culture that has to be erased. We are suggesting that there are six main reasons why boys are presently achieving less than girls at school. Not everyone will agree with them or give them the titles we have, but it will help the discussion in your workplace.

The Six Possible Reasons Why Boys Presently Achieve Less Than Girls

1. GENETIC

This will leave female colleagues cheering and alienate the males. Are women really more intelligent than men? Has their natural superiority been oppressed by centuries of male domination? Is their true potential only showing itself now as we enter an age of generally increasing equality? We have no idea. But there is a certain amount of evidence that women may have an intuitive or genetic disposition to be better communicators than men. Research, mainly in the United States, suggests that newborn babies show clear gender differences in their ability to understand and discriminate between sounds. Surrey LEA found 3-year-olds to have marked differences in linguistic abilities between boys and girls; and the Key Stage 1 SATs show a gender gap which is not shortened over the next nine years of schooling.

Darwinists have argued that the reason for this gap, for the large telephone bills which are the rites of passage for teenage girls and for the GCSE differences, goes back to the roles which women and men have played for thousands of years. Women have always been the nurturers, the talkers, the makers of homes and occupiers of kitchens where conversation is not only possible but necessary. Men on the other hand have tended to take on more isolated roles, whether it be hunter-gatherers, tillers, or herdsmen. It is only in fairly recent times in the span of human history that these roles have changed. It will be some time yet before evolution catches up with the needs of the modern male. There are many more strands to this argument—left and right hemispheres, whole brain thinking, spatial awareness, links to dyslexia—about genetic dispositions which we do not intend to explore. It is an interesting debate, but it does not take us very far forward. There is also a danger that those who take a genetic line become defeatist, arguing that whatever we try to do in the classroom we are predestined to fail.

2. CHANGES IN SOCIETY

> And the men shall come singing from the fields, for they have provided for their own. (Old English proverb, apparently, quoted in Heinz tomato soup television advertisement—1998)

Society has changed so quickly over the last three decades that it has sometimes become difficult for us to know exactly how things are different from a generation ago. Most adults, even those in regular contact with young people, often tend to judge present youthful experiences from a twenty- or thirty-year-old perspective. But the environment in which children and young people grow up has changed radically, and looks as if it will continue to do so.

> The social upheavals of the last 25 years—feminist challenges, unemployment, the collapse of the male bread winner and the traditional father as head of the household, the emergence of HIV/AIDS and deindustrialisation—have unsettled the traditional models of dominant, white, heterosexual masculinities. (David Jackson, in Epstein *et al.*, 1998, p. 79)

We have no intention of examining or listing all these changes, but there are some which have had a radical impact upon the life chances of males and affected the way many of them view themselves.

Perhaps the most important change has been in the field of employment. For many boys who were of below average academic ability in the 1960s, there was little difficulty in finding a job, although this may have varied with the economic cycle. Labouring, factory work, the coal-mines, shipyards and steel mills, semi-skilled jobs on the railway, were all available, sometimes through apprenticeship schemes, and they paid wages which enabled workers to make their way and raise a family. Moreover, there were millions of people doing this. It was an expectation, a normality, and the workers from whom the young apprentices learned were other men who often had a respect derived from their experience and skill. There were few problems in identifying a path to follow. It may not have been a particularly exciting or visionary expectation by today's standards, but it was valued by all those involved. This culture pre-dates the revolution of expectation, when the idea that a favourite hobby could be listed as 'shopping' would be incomprehensible. Having a great deal of disposable income, and having the non-essential goods in the shops to purchase, had not yet reached the vast majority of working people.

The shopping, advertising and commercialisation revolutions of the 1970s and 1980s have changed all that. The growth of the importance of image and style has coincided with the demise of millions of engineering, technical, colliery, shipyard, and steel jobs. They, and the communities they supported, were bastions of male values and male hegemony. They have largely disappeared and in some parts of the country, for example, South Yorkshire, one can still feel a sense of mourning because they have not been adequately replaced. A film like *Brassed Off* effectively captured the beginning of that process, while *The Full Monty,* underneath the humour and surrealism, says an awful lot about the breakdown of families, the need to be respected and the importance of male role models for boys. Both films were set in South Yorkshire and both depict a society left behind by technological changes.

What has replaced them are millions of new jobs in the service sector. Insurance, commerce, finance, tourism, clerical and other office-based jobs do not need the sort of strength and skills men once used in the old industries. Instead they need good communication skills and, often, good keyboard skills. They are often seen as 'women's jobs,' and as most of the staff working in them are women, one can see why. Not only do they demand the sort of skills women have, these same skills are ones which men tend to lack. The old certainties and expectations have disappeared with the jobs, and this has had a dramatic effect upon boys and young men. The underachieving 7-year-old is unlikely to blame technological change for his reluctance to try harder but, if pressed gently, he may say that the only people he knows who work hard are women. The girls in his class seem to work, his mother, aunts, and sister work, but the males in his life resemble resting actors. There are some parts of the UK where for some time the women have been the only breadwinners in the family and the men have come to accept long-term unemployment as a way of life. The sons of these men, who may never have worked, have sometimes adopted a culture which is hard to challenge. This could be viewed as a rational adaptation to the real life chances they have (Kress, 1998). What alternative model is offered by the many critics of boys?

If girls are defined by their work ethic, how do boys define themselves? In the absence of anything else, it may be that boys see that to be a boy means that you don't work. As he gets older this view is confirmed by the popular image of success. The television advertisements, many films of modern life, and men's magazines portray successful men as having fast cars, attractive women, designer clothes, and exciting holidays. They are seldom portrayed working (although interestingly women are), and there seems therefore to be a causal connection between success and not working. The young man cannot quite rationalise this, but he buys into the image of success without knowing how it is achieved. Perhaps it is achieved by being cool, by not trying too hard. In this context it is not surprising that some boys have developed the idea of effortless achievement. Schools would be ill-advised to use footballers as role models, unless—like the admirable Barrie Home of Huddersfield Town—they are prepared to talk about the value of their academic qualifications and the possibilities they open up. The age of working smart, not hard, has contributed to the anti-work culture. It is no wonder that the men are no longer singing as they come home from the fields.

3. CHANGES IN FAMILIES

> My mother cries in the middle of the night, too. She says she's worn out nursing and feeding and changing and four boys is too much for her. She wishes she had one little girl all for herself. She'd give anything for a girl. (McCourt, 1997, p. 14)

There are now 1,250,000 single parent families in the United Kingdom, and in the vast majority of cases they are headed by women. Just how much involvement the fathers have with their children, and particularly their sons, varies enormously between families. There is no doubt that there are large numbers of boys who do not have significant adult males in their lives, and who may not see any male teachers at primary school. This is not just a case of a lack of a role model, which is important enough. If a child does not have any form of meaningful relationship with a male adult before the age of 11, and sometimes after that, what does he or she think about men and, if a boy, what does he think he will be growing up to be? They may not actually verbalise the feminist question 'What are men for?' because other forms of information fill the vacuum. Popular culture has a fairly lurid or glamorous view of men which has little connection with real lives, but in the absence of anything more immediate, boys have images and information which do not suggest that being a man is about working hard.

Questions also need to be asked about the role of men when they *do* live with their children. Surveys reveal that men are much less involved with the supervision of homework than women, tend to attend fewer parents' evenings, and hear their children read less than women. Just to compound the crime, fathers are less demanding of their sons than their daughters. Girls are expected to be well behaved, well presented, neat, organised, be keener readers, and clean and conventional. Boys tend to be expected to be less mature, less responsible, more rebellious, dirtier, sportier, irresponsible, and to have lower concentration spans. These expectations are usually met. Many parents feel that there is no need to worry about their sons' learning until they get to secondary school, by which time it is often too late.

4. CURRICULUM REASONS

The curriculum has changed. This should be no surprise. Following the second National Curriculum of 1995, its 'paring back' in 1998 and its full-scale rewriting for 2000, teachers will soon be tired of change, if they are not already. One of the reasons why they could be disillusioned with permanent curriculum revolution has not often been voiced. The new curriculum tends to be more hostile to boys and this has had an effect upon their attitude, behaviour, effort, and achievement.

This is not an argument for changing the curriculum to favour boys, but rather to be aware of the potential effects upon boys—and girls—of changes to the curriculum and assessment methods, and to take account of this in school and classroom management.

> To be fair to both boys and girls it is likely that a variety of assessment modes should be used so that all pupils have opportunities to produce their best performance. (Arnot *et al.*, 1998, p. 39)

5. SCHOOL MANAGEMENT

School managers have had an awful lot to deal with in recent years. Aside from the massive changes to the curriculum, delegation from the LEA, governors, league tables, parental pressure, Ofsted and a school population which mirrors the stresses in society, they also have to manage a revolution in expectation of themselves. They are now monitors of the quality of teaching and learning and managers of change. It is not an easy job. Many also teach, which for some is a blessed relief from meetings, telephones, crises, and reports. It is thus with a sense of guilt that we write that school managers also have a large measure of responsibility for boys' under-achievement.

It is mainly by a neglect of what they could have done, rather than through what they have actually done, that managers should examine themselves. The lack, or lack of use in classrooms, of early data about pupil potential is still a large problem despite the huge amount of paperwork devoted to this area. The publication of bench-mark data in Key Stages 2, 3, and 4 might now help schools to focus on the potential of younger age groups.

The acceptance of, or inability to tackle, the anti-SWOT culture is largely a management responsibility. It will be a recurring theme of this book that schools must be, and must portray themselves as, learning organisations. There should be no place for the anti-SWOT culture. Schools should treat it as they do racism; there should be no tolerance of it. It is an assault upon equal opportunities and results in misery and under-achievement. We shall address the issue of tackling this culture later in the book.

Another recent phenomenon has been the reintroduction of setting and streaming in an increasing number of primary schools, and its spread to more subjects in secondary schools. We deal in detail with setting in Chapter 6, but in synopsis it is evident that there is no perfect way of grouping pupils and students. All methods have advantages and disadvantages, but the most successful have two characteristics: (1) the staff using it believe in it; and (2) the inherent weaknesses in the system are recognised and addressed by intelligent and focused use of resources, time and training. Good teachers can compensate for bad grouping, but why make it hard for everyone? The rush towards setting in the past two years has often been at the expense of boys, as we explore later.

6. CLASSROOM MANAGEMENT

Most teachers in mixed schools are aware that there are two different genders in the classroom with them. They are also aware that these two genders can exhibit distinctly different sorts of behaviours; that they spend more time telling boys off; that boys tend to be less punctual, reliable, motivated, and organised. What is less evident is that teachers realise or accept that there may be two different types of *learner* in the class. Seating policy, display, and teaching and learning styles are addressed in later chapters, but we want to make the point early in the book that teachers have an enormous amount of discretion in their classroom management which can either exacerbate or ameliorate the motivation and underachievement of boys. There is no blueprint for success but there are techniques and strategies which have been tried in a number of schools and have been found to be successful. Our experience of this work has witnessed the teacher reclaiming his or her confidence and skills as a creative professional who is prepared to try things out, sometimes fail, but more often succeed. Whether these strategies work in any particular classroom is the result of a complex equation in which teacher belief, determination, and skill are the most important factors, as well as the nature of the particular group of pupils. Are teachers aware of the need to force boys, in particular, to reflect on their learning—to think about what they have just learned? Do teachers consciously keep lessons divided into clearly delineated, fairly short tasks and attempt to avoid the long term? Is the teacher concentrating on learning—rather than behaviour—as the major reason why he or she gives boys attention? And is the anti-SWOT atmosphere eradicated in culture, language, and action?

References

Arnot, M. et al. (1998). *Recent research on gender and educational performance.* Ofsted.
Epstein, D. et al. (1998). *Failing boys? Issues in gender and achievement.* Open University Press.
Kress, G. (1998). The future still belongs to boys. *The Independent,* 11 June, pp. 4-5.
McCourt, F. (1997). *Angela's ashes.* Flamingo.

PART V

Race, Multiculturalism, and Education

Race and multiculturalism are two of the most important factors that define American culture and education. In the case of race, the importation of the first slaves to Jamestown in 1619 led to outcomes such as the Civil War and the civil rights movement. While race relations and equity have advanced significantly since the 1950s, there is still an underlying tension in American culture over racial issues. The wounds from this conflict, while healing, are nonetheless there.

Along with race, multiculturalism (which can include race) is a second important theme in American culture. We are, and continue to be, a nation of immigrants from wide and diverse backgrounds, not only European but also Asiatic and African. The inclusion of the Education for All Handicapped Children Act (Law 94–142) in this section of the book also recognizes that individuals with special needs represent another aspect of our culture's diversity.

As you read the pieces in this section, consider the following questions:

1. How has race shaped American education? How would American education be different if race were not a factor?
2. How do issues discussed earlier in this book, such as the hidden and null curriculum, have relevance in a racial context to what is, or has been, taught in the schools?

3. What types of issues are raised for the educational system as a result of the widespread diversity found in American culture?
4. How do factors such as gender, race, and ethnicity combine to define students and, in turn, their educational experience?
5. Will American society eventually become such a "blended" culture that issues of race and ethnicity will no longer be relevant?

22

Laws Prohibiting the Education of Slaves (1830–1832)

In the early 1830s, laws were passed throughout the South making it illegal to educate slaves to read and write. Part of the motivation for this movement was a result of several slave rebellions, including the famous Nat Turner rebellion in 1831. In addition, there was a fear that Northern abolitionists would move into the South and foment rebellion among slave populations.

As you read the following excerpts from state laws, ask yourself the following questions:

1. What were the probable reasons for prohibiting literacy among slaves?
2. What were the probable long-term consequences of deliberately keeping slaves from becoming literate?
3. If text literacy was not permitted in slave culture, did other things likely take its place?
4. What is the relationship between literacy and power?

22

Laws Prohibiting the Education of Slaves (1830–1832)

General Assembly of the State of North Carolina

AN ACT TO PREVENT ALL PERSONS FROM TEACHING SLAVES TO READ OR WRITE, THE USE OF FIGURES EXCEPTED

Whereas the teaching of slaves to read and write has a tendency to excite dissatisfaction in their minds, and to produce insurrection and rebellion, to the manifest injury of the citizens of this State: Therefore,

I. *Be it enacted by the General Assembly of the State of North Carolina, and it is hereby enacted by the authority of the same,* That any free person, who shall hereafter teach, or attempt to teach, any slave within the State to read or write, the use of figures excepted, or shall give or sell to such slave or slaves any books or pamphlets, shall be liable to indictment in any court of record in this State having jurisdiction thereof, and upon conviction, shall, at the discretion of the court, if a white man or woman, be fined not less than one hundred dollars, nor more than two hundred dollars, or imprisoned; and if a free person of color, shall be fined, imprisoned, or whipped, at the discretion of the court, not exceeding thirty nine lashes, nor less then twenty lashes.

Sources: Acts Passed by the General Assembly of the State of North Carolina at the Session of 1830–1831 (Raleigh, N.C., 1831), p. 11; Acts Passed at a General Assembly of the Commonwealth of Virginia, 1830–1831 (Richmond, 1831), pp. 107–108; and Acts Passed at the Thirteenth Annual Session of the General Assembly of Alabama, 1831–1832 (Montgomery, Ala, 1832), p. 16.

II. *Be it further enacted,* That if any slave shall hereafter teach, or attempt to teach, any other slave to read or write, the use of figures excepted, he or she may be carried before any justice of the peace, and on conviction thereof, shall be sentenced to receive thirty nine lashes on his or her bare back.

III. *Be it further enacted,* That the judges of the Superior Courts and the justices of the County Courts shall give this act in charge to the grand juries of their respective counties.

General Assembly of the Commonwealth of Virginia

5. *Be it further enacted,* That if any white person or persons assemble with free negroes or mulattoes, at any school-house, church, meeting-house, or other place for the purpose of instructing such free negroes or mulattoes to read or write, such person or persons shall, on conviction thereof, be fined in a sum not exceeding fifty dollars, and moreover may be imprisoned at the discretion of the jury, not exceeding two months.

6. *Be it further enacted,* That if any white person, for pay or compensation, shall assemble with any slaves for the purpose of teaching and shall teach any slave to read or write, such person, or any white person or persons contracting with such teacher, so to act, who shall offend as aforesaid, shall, for such offence, be fined at the discretion of a jury, in a sum not less than ten, not exceeding one hundred dollars, to be recovered on any information or indictment.

General Assembly of Alabama

Sec. 10. *And be it further enacted,* That any person or persons who shall endeavor or attempt to teach any free person of color, or slave to spell, read, or write, shall upon conviction thereof by indictment, be fined in a sum not less than two hundred and fifty dollars nor more than five hundred dollars.

23

"Industrial Education for the Negro" (1903)

By 1900, Booker T. Washington (1856–1915) had become the most prominent black leader in the United States. As head of the Tuskegee Institute in Alabama, he argued for an accomodationist position in which American blacks would gradually achieve greater equality by making themselves indispensable to the economy. His views were in marked contrast to the more radical W. E. B. Du Bois, who called for the development of a black elite, or "Talented Tenth."

As you read this selection, consider the following questions:

1. What should constitute the content of higher education?
2. Who is potentially served by Washington's educational ideas?
3. What does Washington's approach suggest about the creation of a social caste system in American culture?

23

"Industrial Education for the Negro" (1903)

Booker T. Washington

In what I say here I would not by any means have it understood that I would limit or circumscribe the mental development of the Negro student. No race can be lifted until its mind is awakened and strengthened. By the side of industrial training should always go mental and moral training, but the pushing of mere abstract knowledge into the head means little. We want more than the mere performance of mental gymnastics. Our knowledge must be harnessed to the things of real life. I would encourage the Negro to secure all the mental strength, all the mental culture—whether gleaned from science, mathematics, history, language, or literature that his circumstances will allow, but I believe most earnestly that for years to come the education of the people of my race should be so directed that the greatest proportion of the mental strength of the masses will be brought to bear upon the every-day practical things of life, upon something that is needed to be done, and something which they will be permitted to do in the community in which they reside. . . .

I would teach the race that in industry the foundation must be laid—that the very best service which any one can render to what is called the higher education is to teach the present generation to provide a material or industrial foundation. On such a foundation as this will grow habits of thrift, a love of economy, ownership of property, bank accounts. Out of it in the future will grow practical education, professional education, positions of public responsibility. Out of it will grow moral and religious strength. Out of it will grow

---

Source: Washington, Booker T. 1903. "Industrial Education for the Negro." *The Negro Problem: A Series of Articles by Representative American Negroes of Today,* edited by Booker T. Washington et al., 16–23, 28–29. New York: James Pott.

wealth from which alone can come leisure and the opportunity for the enjoyment of literature and the fine arts. . . .

I would set no limits to the attainments of the Negro in arts, in letters or statesmanship, but I believe the surest way to reach those ends is by laying the foundation in the little things of life that lie immediately about one's door. I plead for industrial education and development for the Negro not because I want to cramp him, but because I want to free him. I want to see him enter the all-powerful business and commercial world. . . .

Early in the history of the Tuskegee Institute we began to combine industrial training with mental and moral culture. Our first efforts were in the direction of agriculture, and we began teaching this with no appliances except one hoe and a blind mule. From this small beginning we have grown until now the Institute owns two thousand acres of land, eight hundred of which are cultivated each year by the young men of the school. We began teaching wheel wrighting and blacksmithing in a small way to the men, and laundry work, cooking and sewing and housekeeping to the young women. The fourteen hundred and over young men and women who attended the school during the last school year received instruction—in addition to academic and religious training—in thirty-three trades and industries, including carpentry, blacksmithing, printing, wheelwrighting, harnessmaking, painting, machinery, founding, shoemaking, brickmasonry and brickmaking, plastering, sawmilling, tinsmithing, tailoring, mechanical and architectural drawing, electrical and steam engineering, canning, sewing, dressmaking, millinery, cooking, laundering, housekeeping, mattress making, basketry, nursing, agriculture, dairying and stock raising, horticulture.

Not only do the students receive instruction in these trades, but they do actual work, by means of which more than half of them pay some part or all of their expenses while remaining at the school. Of the sixty buildings belonging to the school all but four were almost wholly erected by the students as a part of their industrial education. Even the bricks which go into the walls are made by students in the school's brick yard, in which, last year, they manufactured two million bricks. . . .

I close, then, as I began, by saying that as a slave the Negro was worked, and that as a freeman he must learn to work. There is still doubt in many quarters as to the ability of the Negro unguided, unsupported, to hew his own path and put into visible, tangible, indisputable form, products and signs of civilization. This doubt cannot be much affected by abstract arguments, no matter how delicately and convincingly woven together. Patiently, quietly, doggedly, persistently, through summer and winter, sunshine and shadow, by self-sacrifice, by foresight, by honesty and industry, we must re-enforce argument with results. One farm bought, one house built, one home sweetly and intelligently kept, one man who is the largest tax payer or has the largest bank account, one school or church maintained, one factory running successfully, one truck garden profitably cultivated, one patient cured by a Negro doctor, one sermon well preached, one office well filled, one life cleanly lived—these will tell more in our favor than all the abstract eloquence that can be summoned to plead our cause. Our pathway must be up through the soil, up through swamps, up through forests, up through the streams, the rocks, up through commerce, education, and religion!

24

"The Talented Tenth" (1903)

"The Talented Tenth" is among the most important early essays of the black social and political activist W. E. B. Du Bois (1869–1963). It was published late in 1903 as the second chapter in a collection of articles titled *The Negro Problem* and in the following year in Du Bois's book, *The Souls of Black Folk.* Du Bois proposed the conscious creation, through education, of a black elite. Interestingly, while he objected to white domination of black people, he does not seem to have considered the possibility that a black elite, or "Talented Tenth," could have had their own class and social biases that did not necessarily conform with the needs and interests of the black "masses."

Du Bois's distance from the black masses is clear. Toward the end of this essay, he asks,

> Can the masses of the Negro people be in any possible way more quickly raised than by the effort and example of this aristocracy of talent and character? Was there ever a nation on God's fair earth civilized from the bottom upward? Never; it is, ever was and ever will be from the top downward that culture filters. The Talented Tenth rises and pulls all that are worth the saving up to their vantage ground. This is the history of human progress.

As you read DuBois's essay, consider the following questions:

1. Socioeconomic class issues are largely ignored in American culture. What are the implications of Du Bois's ideas about the Talented Tenth, in terms of class?
2. What are the advantages and limitations of Du Bois's model?
3. How does Du Bois's model compare with those of a figure such as Booker T. Washington?

24

"The Talented Tenth" (1903)

W. E. B. Du Bois

The Negro race, like all races, is going to be saved by its exceptional men. The problem of education, then, among Negroes must first of all deal with the Talented Tenth; it is the problem of developing the Best of this race that they may guide the Mass away from the contamination and death of the Worst, in their own and other races. Now the training of men is a difficult and intricate task. Its technique is a matter for educational experts, but its object is for the vision of seers. If we make money the object of man-training, we shall develop money-makers but not necessarily men; if we make technical skill the object of education, we may possess artisans but not, in nature, men. Men we shall have only as we make manhood the object of the work of the schools—intelligence, broad sympathy, knowledge of the world that was and is, and of the relation of men to it—this is the curriculum of that Higher Education which must underlie true life. On this foundation we may build bread winning, skill of hand and quickness of brain, with never a fear lest the child and man mistake the means of living for the object of life.

If this be true—and who can deny it—three tasks lay before me; first to show from the past that the Talented Tenth as they have risen among American Negroes have been worthy of leadership; secondly to show how these men may be educated and developed; and thirdly to show their relation to the Negro problem.

You misjudge us because you do not know us. From the very first it has been the educated and intelligent of the Negro people that have led and elevated the mass, and the sole obstacles that nullified and retarded their efforts were slavery and race prejudice; for what is slavery but the legalized survival of

---

Source: Du Bois, W. E. B. 1903. "The Talented Tenth." *The Negro Problem: A Series of Articles by Representative American Negroes of Today,* edited by Booker T. Washington et al., Chap. 2. New York: James Potts.

the unfit and the nullification of the work of natural internal leadership? Negro leadership therefore sought from the first to rid the race of this awful incubus that it might make way for natural selection and the survival of the fittest. . . .

How then shall the leaders of a struggling people be trained and the hands of the risen few strengthened? There can be but one answer: The best and most capable of their youth must be schooled in the colleges and universities of the land. We will not quarrel as to just what the university of the Negro should teach or how it should teach it—I willingly admit that each soul and each race-soul needs its own peculiar curriculum. But this is true: A university is a human invention for the transmission of knowledge and culture from generation to generation, through the training of quick minds and pure hearts, and for this work no other human invention will suffice, not even trade and industrial schools.

All men cannot go to college but some men must; every isolated group or nation must have its yeast, must have for the talented few centers of training where men are not so mystified and befuddled by the hard and necessary toil of earning a living, as to have no aims higher than their bellies, and no God greater than Gold. This is true training, and thus in the beginning were the favored sons of the freedmen trained. Out of the colleges of the North came, after the blood of war, Ware, Cravath, Chase, Andrews, Bumstead, and Spence to build the foundations of knowledge and civilization in the black South. Where ought they to have begun to build? At the bottom, of course, quibbles the mole with his eyes in the earth. Aye! truly at the bottom, at the very bottom; at the bottom of knowledge, down in the very depths of knowledge there where the roots of justice strike into the lowest soil of Truth. And so they did begin; they founded colleges, and up from the colleges shot normal schools, and out from the normal schools went teachers, and around the normal teachers clustered other teachers to teach the public schools; the college trained in Greek and Latin and mathematics, 2,000 men; and these men trained full 50,000 others in morals and manners, and they in turn taught thrift and the alphabet to nine millions of men, who today hold $300,000,000 of property. It was a miracle—the most wonderful peace-battle of the 19th century, and yet today men smile at it, and in fine superiority tell us that it was all a strange mistake; that a proper way to found a system of education is first to gather the children and buy them spelling books and hoes; afterward men may look about for teachers, if haply they may find them; or again they would teach men Work, but as for Life—why, what has Work to do with Life, they ask vacantly. . . .

The problem of training the Negro is today immensely complicated by the fact that the whole question of the efficiency and appropriateness of our present systems of education, for any kind of child, is a matter of active debate, in which final settlement seems still afar off. Consequently it often happens that persons arguing for or against certain systems of education for Negroes have these controversies in mind and miss the real question at issue. The main question, so far as the Southern Negro is concerned, is: What under the present circumstance must a system of education do in order to raise the Negro as quickly as possible in the scale of civilization? The answer to this question seems to me clear: It must strengthen the Negro's character, increase his knowledge, and teach him to earn a living. Now it goes without saying that it is hard to do all these things simultaneously or suddenly and that at the same time it will not do to give all the attention to one and neglect the others; we could give black boys trades, but that alone will not civilize a race of ex-slaves; we might simply increase their knowledge of the world, but this would not necessarily make them wish to use this knowledge honestly; we might seek to strengthen character and purpose, but to what end if these people have nothing to eat or to wear? A system of education is not one thing, nor does it have a single definite object, nor is it a mere matter of schools. Education is that whole system of human training within and without the school house walls, which molds and develops men. If then we start out to train an ignorant and unskilled people with a heritage of bad habits, our system of training must set before itself two great aims—the one dealing with knowledge and character, the other part seeking to give the child the technical knowledge necessary for him to earn a living under the present circumstances. These objects are accomplished in part by the opening of the common schools on the one, and of the industrial schools on the other. But only in part, for there must also be trained those who are to teach these schools—men and women of knowledge and culture and technical skill who understand modern civilization, and have the training and aptitude to impart it to the children under them. There must be teachers, and teachers of teachers, and to attempt to establish any sort of a system of common and industrial school training, without *first* (and I say *first* advisedly) providing for the higher training of the very best teachers, is simply throwing your money to the winds. School houses do not teach themselves—piles of brick and mortar and machinery do not send out *men*. It is the trained, living human soul, cultivated and strengthened by long study and thought, that breathes the real breath of life into boys and girls and makes them human, whether they be black or white, Greek, Russian, or American. Nothing, in these latter days, has so dampened the faith of thinking Negroes in recent educational movements, as the fact that such movements have been accompanied by ridicule and denouncement and decrying of those very institutions of higher training which made the Negro public school possible, and make Negro industrial schools thinkable. It was: Fisk, Atlanta, Howard, and Straight, those colleges born of the faith and sacrifice of the abolitionists, that placed in the black schools of the South the 30,000 teachers and more, which some, who depreciate the work of these higher schools, are using to teach their own new experiments. If Hampton, Tuskegee, and the hundred other industrial schools prove in the future to be as successful as they deserve to be, then their success in training black artisans for the South will be due primarily to the white colleges of the North and the black colleges of the South, which trained the teachers who today conduct these institutions. There was a time when the American people believed pretty devoutly that a log of wood with a boy at one end and Mark Hopkins at the other represented the highest ideal of human training. But in these eager days it would seem that we have changed all that and think it necessary to add a couple of saw-mills and a hammer to this outfit, and, at a pinch, to dispense with the services of Mark Hopkins. I would not deny, or for a moment seem to deny, the paramount necessity of teaching the Negro to work, and to work steadily and skillfully; or seem to depreciate in the slightest degree the important part industrial schools must play in the accomplishment of these ends, but I *do* say, and insist upon it, that it is industrialism drunk with its vision of success to imagine that its own work can be accomplished without providing for the training of broadly cultured men and women to teach its own teachers and to teach the teachers of the public schools.

But I have already said that human education is not simply a matter of schools; it is much more a matter of family and group life—the training of one's home, of one's daily companions, of one's social class. Now the black boy of the South moves in a black world—a world with its own leaders, its own thoughts, its own ideals. In this world he gets by far the larger part of his life training, and through the eyes of this dark world he peers into the veiled world beyond. Who guides and determines the education which he receives in his world? His teachers here are the group-leaders of the Negro people—the physicians and clergymen, the trained fathers and mothers, the influential and forceful men about him of all kinds; here it is, if at all, that the culture of the surrounding world trickles through and is handed on by the graduates of the higher schools. Can such culture training of group leaders be neglected? Can we afford to ignore it? Do you think that if the leaders of thought among Negroes are not trained and educated thinkers, that they will have no leaders? On the contrary a hundred half-trained demagogues will still hold the places they so largely occupy now, and hundreds of vociferous busy-bodies will multiply. You have no choice; either you must help furnish this race from within its own ranks with thoughtful men of trained leadership, or you must suffer the evil consequences of a headless misguided rabble.

I am an earnest advocate of manual training and trade teaching for black boys, and for white boys, too. I believe that next to the founding of Negro colleges the most valuable addition to Negro education since the war has been industrial training for black boys. Nevertheless, I insist that the object of all true education is not to make men carpenters, it is to make carpenters men; there are two means of making the carpenter a man, each equally important: the first is to give the group and community in which he works liberally trained teachers and leaders to teach him and his family what life means; the second is to give him sufficient intelligence and technical skill to make him an efficient workman; the first object demands the Negro college and college-bred men—not a quantity of such colleges, but a few of excellent quality; not too many college-bred men, but enough to leaven the lump, to inspire the masses, to raise the Talented Tenth to leadership; the second object demands a good system of common schools, well-taught, conveniently located and properly equipped. . . .

Men of America, the problem is plain before you. Here is a race transplanted through the criminal foolishness of your fathers. Whether you like it or not the millions are here, and here they will remain. If you do not lift them up, they will pull you down. Education and work are the levers to uplift a people. Work alone will not do it unless inspired by the right ideals and guided by intelligence. Education must not simply teach work—it must teach Life. The Talented Tenth of the Negro race must be made leaders of thought and missionaries of culture among their people. No others can do this work and Negro colleges must train men for it. The Negro race, like all other races, is going to be saved by its exceptional men.

25

"A Talk to Teachers" (1963)

"A Talk to Teachers" was first given as a speech in 1963 by the black novelist and political activist James Baldwin (1924–1987). Baldwin's essay was remarkably prophetic. In it, he brought to light the discrepancy between the United States's heroic vision of itself and the actual treatment of African Americans in the United States.

Baldwin also asks how the educational system can reconcile the racism of the culture and the need of schools to teach its students to question what is around them. He called for black students to develop an understanding of their history and culture, separate, or at least differentiated, from that of the mainstream culture.

As you read this essay, consider the following questions:

1. If schools, to a certain degree, socialize and acculturate students, what responsibility do teachers have to their students if the culture is unjust or discriminatory?
2. How important is it for historically oppressed groups such as African Americans to have access to their history?

25

"A Talk to Teachers" (1963)

James Baldwin

Let's begin by saying that we are living through a very dangerous time. Everyone in this room is in one way or another aware of that. We are in a revolutionary situation, no matter how unpopular that word has become in this country. The society in which we live is desperately menaced, not by Khrushchev, but from within. So any citizen of this country who figures himself as responsible—and particularly those of you who deal with the minds and hearts of young people—must be prepared to "go for broke." Or to put it another way, you must understand that in the attempt to correct so many generations of bad faith and cruelty, when it is operating not only in the classroom but in society, you will meet the most fantastic, the most brutal, and the most determined resistance. There is no point in pretending that this won't happen. Now, since I am talking to schoolteachers and I am not a teacher myself, and in some ways am fairly easily intimidated, I beg you to let me leave that and go back to what I think to be the entire purpose of education in the first place. It would seem to me that when a child is born, if I'm the child's parent, it is my obligation and my high duty to civilize that child. Man is a social animal. He cannot exist without a society. A society, in turn, depends on certain things which everyone within that society takes for granted. Now, the crucial paradox which confronts us here is that the whole process of education occurs within a social framework and is designed to perpetuate the aims of society. Thus, for example, the boys and girls who were born during the era of the Third Reich, when educated to the purpose of the Third Reich, became barbarians. The paradox of education is precisely this; that as one begins to become conscious, one begins to examine the society in which he is being educated. The purpose of education, finally, is to create [in] a person the ability to look at the world

---

Source: Baldwin, James. 1963, December 21. "A Talk to Teachers." *Saturday Review,* 44 (28): 42–44.

for himself, to make his own decisions, to say to himself this is black or white, to decided for himself whether there is a God in heaven or not. To ask questions of the universe, and then learn to live with these questions, is the way he achieves his own identity. But no society is really anxious to have that kind of person around. What societies really, ideally want is a citizenry which will simply obey the rules of society. If a society succeeds in this, that society is about to perish. The obligation of anyone who thinks of himself as responsible is to examine society and try to change it and to fight it—at no matter what risk. This is the only way societies change. Now, if what I have tried to sketch has any validity, it becomes thoroughly clear, at least to me, that any Negro who is born in this country and undergoes the American educational system runs the risk of becoming schizophrenic. On the one hand he is born in the shadow of the stars and stripes, and he is assured it represents a nation which has never lost a war. He pledges allegiance to that flag which guarantees "liberty and justice for all." He is part of a country in which anyone can become President, and so forth. But on the other hand he is also assured by his country and his countrymen that he has never contributed anything to civilization—that his past is nothing more than a record of humiliations gladly endured. He is assured by the republic that he, his father, his mother, and his ancestors were happy shiftless, watermelon-eating darkies who loved Mr. Charlie and Miss Ann, that the value he has as a black man is proven by one thing only—his devotion to white people. If you think I am exaggerating, examine the myths which proliferate in this country about Negroes. Now all this enters the child's consciousness much sooner than we as adults would like to think it does. As adults, we are easily fooled because we are so anxious to be fooled. But children are very difficult. Children, not yet aware that it is dangerous to look too deeply at anything, look at everything, have the vocabulary to express what they see, and we, their elders, know how to intimidate them very easily and very soon. But a black child, looking at the world around him, though he cannot know quite what to make of it, is aware that there is a reason why his mother works so hard, why his father is always on edge. He is aware that there is some reason why, if he sits down in the front of the bus, his father or mother drags him to the back of the bus. He is aware that there is some terrible weight on his parents' shoulders which menaces him. And it isn't long—in fact it begins very early—when he is in school—before he discovers the shape of his oppression. Let us say that the child is seven years old and I am his father, and I decide to take him to the zoo, or to Madison Square Garden, or to the U.N. Building, or to any of the tremendous monuments we find all over New York. We get into the bus and we go from where I live on 131st Street and Seventh Avenue downtown through the park and we get into New York City, which is not Harlem. Now, where the boy lives—even if it is a housing project—is in an undesirable neighborhood. If he lives in one of those housing projects of which everyone in New York is so proud, he has at his front door, if not closer, the pimps, the whores, the junkies—in a word, the danger of life in the ghetto. And the child knows this, though he doesn't know why. I still remember my first sight of New York. It was really another city when I was born—where I was born. . . . The Park Avenue I grew up on, which is still standing, is dark and dirty. No one would dream of opening a Tiffany's on that Park Avenue, and when you go downtown you discover that you are literally in the white world. It is rich or at least it looks rich. It is clean—because they collect garbage downtown. There are doormen. People walk about as though they own the world—and indeed they do. And it's a great shock. It's very hard to relate yourself to this. You don't know what is for you. You know this before you are told. And who it is for and who is paying for it? And why isn't it for you?

Later on when you become a grocery boy or messenger and you try to enter one of those buildings a man says, "Go to the back door." Still later, if you happen to have a friend in one of those buildings, the man says, "Where's your package?" Now this is by no means the core of the matter. What I'm trying to get at is that by the time the Negro child has effectively had almost all the doors of opportunity shut in his face, there are very few things he can do about it. He can more or less accept it with an absolutely inarticulate and dangerous rage inside—all the more dangerous because it is never expressed. It is precisely those silent people whom white people see every day of their lives—I mean your porter and your maid, who never say anything more than "Yes, Sir" and "No, Ma'am." They will tell you it's raining if that is what you want to hear, and they will tell you the sun is shining if that is what you want to hear. They really hate you—really hate you because in their eyes (and they're right) you stand between them and life. I want to come back to that in a moment. It is the most sinister of the facts, I think, which we now face. There is something else the Negro child can do, too. Every street boy—and I was street boy, so I know—looking at the society which has produced him, looking at the standards of that society which are not honored by anybody, looking at your churches and the government and the politicians, understands that this structure is operated for someone else's benefit—not for his. And there's no room in it for him. If he is really cunning, really ruthless, really strong and many of us are—he becomes a kind of criminal. He becomes a criminal because that's the only way that he can live. Harlem and every other ghetto in this city—every ghetto in this country—is full of people who live outside the law. They wouldn't dream of calling a policeman. They wouldn't for a moment listen to any of those professions of which we are so proud of on the Fourth of July. They have turned away from this country totally and forever. They live by their wits and really long to see the day when the entire structure comes down. The point of all this is that black men were brought here as a source of cheap labor. They were indispensable to the economy. In order to justify the fact that men were treated as though they were animals, the white republic had to brainwash itself into believing that they were indeed animals and deserved to be treated like animals. Therefore it is impossible for any Negro child to discover anything about his actual history. The reason is that this "animal," once he starts to suspect his own worth, once he starts believing that he is a man, has begun to attack the entire power structure. This is why America has spent such a long time keeping the Negro in his place. What I am trying to suggest to you is that it was not an accident, it was not an act of God, it was not a well-meaning people muddling into something which they didn't understand. It was a deliberate policy hammered into place in order to make money from black flesh. And now, in 1963, because we have never faced this fact, we are in intolerable trouble. The Reconstruction, as I read the evidence, was a bargain between the North and South to this effect: "We've liberated them from the land—and delivered them to the bosses." When we left Mississippi to come North, we did not come to freedom. We came to the bottom of the labor market, and we are still there. Even the Depression of the 1930s failed to make a dent in Negroes' relationship to white workers in the labor unions. Even today, so brainwashed is this republic that people seriously ask in what they suppose to be good faith, "What does the Negro want?" I've heard a great many asinine questions in my life, but that is perhaps the most insulting. But the point here is that people who ask that question, thinking that they ask it in good faith, are really the victims of this conspiracy to make Negroes believe that they are less than human. In order for me to live, I decided very early that some mistake had been made somewhere. I was not a "nigger" even though you called me one. But if I was a "nigger" in your eyes, there was something about you—there was something you needed. I had to realize when I was very young that I was none of those things I was told I was. I was not, for example, happy. I never touched a watermelon for all kinds of reasons. I had been invented by white people, and I knew enough life by this time to understand that whatever you invent, whatever you project is you! So where we are now is that a whole country of people believe I'm a "nigger," and I *don't,* and the battle's on! Because if I am not what I've been told that I am, then it means that you are not what you thought you were either! And that is the crisis.

It is not really a "Negro" revolution that is upsetting this country. What is upsetting the country is a sense of its own identity. If, for example, one managed to change the curriculum in all the schools so that Negroes learned more about themselves and their real contributions to this culture, you would be liberating not only Negroes, you'd be liberating white people who know nothing about their own history. And the reason is that if you are compelled to lie about one aspect of anybody's history, you must lie about all. If you have to lie about my real role here, if you have to pretend that I hoed all that cotton just because I loved you, then you have done something to yourself. You are mad.

Now let's go back a minute. I talked earlier about those silent people—the porter and the maid—who, as I said, don't look up at the sky if you ask them if it is raining, but look into your face. My ancestors and I were very well trained. We understood very early that this was not a Christian nation. It didn't matter what you said or how often you went to church. My father and my mother and my grandfather and my grandmother knew that Christians didn't act this way. It was as simple as that. And if that were so there was no point in dealing with white people in terms of their own moral professions, for they were not going to honor them. What one did was to turn away, smiling all the time, and tell white people what they wanted to hear. But people always accuse you of reckless talk when you talk like this. All this means that there are in this country tremendous reservoirs of bitterness which have never been able to find an outlet, but may find an outlet soon. It means that well meaning white liberals place themselves in great danger when they try to deal with Negroes as though they were missionaries. It means, in brief, that a great price is demanded to liberate all those silent people so that they can breathe for the first time and tell you what they think of you. And a price is demanded to liberate all those white children—some of them near forty—who have never grown up, and who never will grow up, because they have no sense of their identity.

What passes for identity in America is a series of myths about one's heroic ancestors. It's astounding to me, for example, that so many people really appear to believe that the country was founded by a band of heroes who wanted to be free. That happens not to be true. What happened was that some people left Europe because they couldn't stay any longer and had to go someplace else to make it. That's all. They were hungry, they were poor, they were convicts. Those who were making it in England, for example, did not get on the Mayflower. That's how the country was settled. Not by Gary Cooper. Yet we have a whole race of people, a whole republic who believe the myths to the point where even today they select political representatives, as far as I can tell, by how closely they resemble Gary Cooper. Now this is dangerously infantile, and it shows in every level of national life. When I was living in Europe, for example, one of the worst revelations to me was the way Americans walked around Europe buying this and buying that and insulting everybody—not even out of malice, just because they didn't know any better. Well, that is the way they have always treated me. They weren't cruel, they just didn't know that you were alive. They didn't know you had any feelings. What I am trying to suggest here is that in the doing of all this for 100 years or more, it is the white American man who has long since lost his grip on reality. In some peculiar way having created this myth about Negroes, and the myth about his own history, he created myths about the world so that for example he was astounded by the fact that some people could prefer Castro, astounded that there are people in the world who don't go into hiding when they hear the word "Communism," astounded that Communism is one of the realities of the twentieth century which we will not overcome by pretending that it does not exist. The political level in this country now, on the part of people who should know better, is abysmal. The Bible says somewhere that where there is no vision the people perish. I don't think anyone can doubt that in this country today we are menaced—intolerably menaced—by a lack of vision.

It is inconceivable that a sovereign people should continue, as we do so abjectly, to say, "I can't do anything about it. It's the government." The government is the creation of the people. It is responsible to the people. And the people are responsible for it. No American has the right to allow the present government to say, when Negro children are being bombed and hosed and shot and beaten all over the deep South, that there is nothing we can do about it. There must have been a day in this country's life when the bombing of four children in Sunday School would have created a public uproar and endangered the life of Governor Wallace. It happened here and there was no public uproar.

I began by saying that one of the paradoxes of education was that precisely at the point when you begin to develop a conscience, you must find yourself at war with your society. It is your responsibility to change society if you think of yourself as an educated person. And on the basis of the evidence—the moral and political evidence—one is compelled to say that this is a backward society. Now if I were a teacher in this school, or any Negro school, and I were dealing with Negro children, who were in my care only a few hours of every day and would then return to their homes and to the streets, children who have an apprehension of their future which every hour grows darker and grimmer, I would try to teach them—I would try to make them know—that those streets, those houses, those dangers, those agonies by which they are surrounded, are criminal. I would try to make each child know that these things are the result of a criminal conspiracy to destroy them. I would teach him that if he intends to get to be a man, he must at once decide that he is stronger than this conspiracy and that he must never make his peace with it. And that one of his weapons for destroying it depends on what he thinks he is worth. I would teach him that there are currently few standards in this country which are worth a man's respect. That it is up to him to begin to change these standards for the sake of the life of this country. I would suggest to him that the popular culture—as represented, for example, on television and in comic books and in movies—is based on fantasies created by very ill people, and he must be aware that these are fantasies and they have nothing to do with reality. I would teach him that the press he reads is not as free as it says it is—and that he can do something about that, too. I would try to make him know that just as

American history is longer, larger, more various, more beautiful, and more terrible than anything anyone has every said about it, so is the world larger, more daring, more beautiful and more terrible, but principally larger—and that it belongs to him. I would teach him that he doesn't have to be bound by the experiences of any given policy, any given time—that he has the right and the necessity to examine everything. I would try to show him that one has not learned anything about Castro when one says, "He is a Communist." This is a way of not learning something about Castro, something about Cuba, something in fact about the world. I would suggest to him that he is living, at the moment, in an enormous province. America is not the world and if America is going to become a nation, she must find a way—and this child must help her to find a way—to use the tremendous potential and tremendous energy that this child represents. If this country does not find a way to use that energy, it will be destroyed by that energy.

26

Education for All Handicapped Children Act

(Public Law 94–142, November 29, 1975)

The Education for All Handicapped Children Act of 1975, now known as the Individuals With Disabilities Education Act (IDEA), represents a radical redefinition of the federal government's role in providing equal educational opportunity for students with special needs. The most important section of the legislation is that which requires that students with special needs be taught "to the maximum extent appropriate" in the same classrooms with mainstream students and that every student with special needs be provided an individualized education program.

As you read this selection, consider the following questions:

1. How does the work of the average classroom teacher change as a result of the implementation of public laws such as 94–142?
2. What does the passage of a law like 94–142 suggest about changing attitudes toward individuals with special needs and the ways they should be educated?

26

Education for All Handicapped Children Act

(Public Law 94–142, November 29, 1975)

Congress of the United States of America

The Congress finds that—

1. there are more than eight million handicapped children in the United States today;

2. the special educational needs of such children are not being fully met;

3. more than half of the handicapped children in the United States do not receive appropriate educational services which would enable them to have full equality of opportunity;

4. one million of the handicapped children in the United States are excluded entirely from the public school system and will not go through the educational process with their peers;

5. there are many handicapped children throughout the United States participating in regular school programs whose handicaps prevent them from having a successful educational experience because their handicaps are undetected;

Source: Education for All Handicapped Children Act, Public Law 94–142. November 29, 1975. Available at http://asclepius.com/angel/special.html

6. because of the lack of adequate services within the public school system, families are often forced to find services outside of the public school system, often at great distance from their residence and at their own expense;

7. developments in the training of teachers and in diagnostic and instructional procedures and methods have advanced to the point that, given appropriate funding, State and local educational agencies can and will provide effective special education and related services to meet the needs of handicapped children;

8. State and local educational agencies have a responsibility to provide education for all handicapped children, but present financial resources are inadequate to meet the special educational needs of handicapped children; and

9. it is in the national interest that the Federal Government assist State and local efforts to provide programs to meet the educational needs of handicapped children in order to assure equal protection of the law.

It is the purpose of this Act to assure that all handicapped children have available to them . . . a free appropriate public education which emphasizes special education and related services designed to meet their unique needs, to assure that the rights of handicapped children and their parents or guardians are protected, to assist States and localities to provide for the education of all handicapped children, and to assess and assure the effectiveness of efforts to educate handicapped children. . . .

The State has established . . . procedures to assure that, to the maximum extent appropriate, handicapped children, including children in public or private institutions or other care facilities, are educated with children who are not handicapped, and that special classes, separate schooling, or other removal of handicapped children from the regular educational environment occurs only when the nature of severity of the handicap is such that education in regular classes with the use of supplementary aids and services cannot be achieved satisfactorily, and procedures to assure that testing and evaluation materials and procedures utilized for the purposes of evaluation and placement of handicapped children will be selected and administered so as not to be racially or culturally discriminatory. Such materials or procedures shall be provided and administered in the child's native language or mode of communication, unless it clearly is not feasible to do so, and no single procedure shall be the sole criterion for determining an appropriate educational program for a child.

27

"Border Pedagogy in the Age of Postmodernism" (1988)

In "Border Pedagogy in the Age of Postmodernism," Henry Giroux (1943–) argues for the need to teach students to read the different "cultural codes, experiences and languages" that make up American culture. According to Giroux, border pedagogy suggests a model of teaching and learning

> which does more than provide students with a language and context by which to critically engage the plurality of habits, practices, experiences, and desires that define them as part of a particular social formation within ongoing relations of domination and resistance. Border pedagogy provides opportunities for teachers to deepen their own understanding of the discourse of various others in order to effect a more dialectical understanding of their own politics, values, and pedagogy.

Giroux's model clearly calls for teachers to become more critically and politically engaged in their work.

As you read the following article, consider these questions:

1. What are the implications of border pedagogy for the work teachers do in classrooms?
2. To what extent is teaching a cultural act?
3. To what extent is teaching a political act?
4. From a cultural point of view, can teaching be neutral?

27

"Border Pedagogy in the Age of Postmodernism" (1988)

Henry Giroux

Border pedagogy offers the opportunity for students to engage the multiple references that constitute different cultural codes, experiences, and languages. This means educating students not only to read these codes critically but also to learn the limits of such codes, including the ones they use to construct their own narratives and histories. Partiality becomes, in this case, the basis for recognizing the limits built into all discourses and necessitates taking a critical view of authority. Within this discourse, a student must engage knowledge as a border-crosser, as a person moving in and out of borders constructed around coordinates of difference and power (Hicks, 1988). These are not only physical borders, they are cultural borders historically constructed and socially organized within maps of rules and regulations that limit and enable particular identities, individual capacities, and social forms. In this case, students cross over into borders of meaning, maps of knowledge, social relations, and values that are increasingly being negotiated and rewritten as the codes and regulations which organize them become destabilized and reshaped. Border pedagogy decenters as it remaps. The terrain of learning becomes inextricably linked to the shifting parameters of place, identity, history, and power.

Within critical social theory, it has become commonplace to argue that knowledge and power are related, though the weight of the argument has often overemphasized how domination works through the intricacies of this relationship (Foucault, 1977b). Border pedagogy offers a crucial theoretical and political corrective to this insight. It does so by shifting the emphasis of the

Source: Giroux, Henry. 1988. "Border Pedagogy in the Age of Postmodernism." *Journal of Education,* 170, 162–181.

knowledge/power relationship away from the limited emphasis on the mapping of domination to the politically strategic issue of engaging the ways in which knowledge can be remapped, reterritorialized, and decentered in the wider interests of rewriting the borders and coordinates of an oppositional cultural politics. This is not an abandonment of critique as much as it is an extension of its possibilities. In this case, border pedagogy not only incorporates the postmodern emphasis on criticizing official texts and using alternative modes of representation (mixing video, photography, and print), it also incorporates popular culture as a serious object of politics and analysis and makes central to its project the recovery of those forms of knowledge and history that characterize alternative and oppositional Others (Said, 1983). How these cultural practices might be taken up as pedagogical practices has been demonstrated by a number of theorists (Brodkey & Fine, 1988; Cherryholmes, 1988; Giroux & Simon, 1988; Scholes, 1985).

For example, Robert Scholes (1985) develops elements of a "border pedagogy" around the notion of textual power. According to Scholes, texts have to be seen in historical and temporal terms and not treated as a sacred vehicle for producing eternal truths. Instead of simply imparting information to students, Scholes argues that teachers should replace teaching texts with what he calls textuality. What this refers to pedagogically is a process of textual study that can be identified by three forms of practice: reading, interpretation, and criticism, which roughly correspond to what Scholes calls reading within, upon, and against a text. In brief, reading within a text means identifying the cultural codes that structure an author's work. But it also has the pedagogical value of illuminating further how such codes function as part of a student's own attempt "to produce written texts that are 'within' the world constructed by their reading" (p. 27). This is particularly important, Scholes adds, in giving students the opportunity to "retell the story, to summarize it, and to expand it." Interpretation means reading a text along with a variety of diverse interpretations that represent a second commentary on the text. At issue here is the pedagogical task of helping students to analyze texts within "a network of relations with other texts and institutional practices" so as to make available to students "the whole intertextual system of relations that connects one text to others—a system that will finally include the student's own writing" (Scholes, 1985, p. 30). The first two stages of Scholes's pedagogical practice are very important because they demonstrate the need for students to sufficiently engage and disrupt the text. He wants students to read the text in terms that the author might have intended so as not to make the text merely a mirror image of the student's own subjective position, but at the same time he wants students to open the text up to a wide variety of readings so it can be "sufficiently other for us to interpret it and, especially to criticize it" (Scholes, 1985, p. 39). Finally, Scholes wants students to explode the cultural codes of the text through the assertion of the reader's own textual power, to analyze the text in terms of its absences, to free "ourselves from [the] text [by] finding a position outside the assumptions upon which the text is based" (p. 62). Scholes combines the best of postmodern criticism with a notion of modernity in his notion of pedagogy. He wants, on the one hand, to engage texts as semiotic objects, but on the other hand he employs a modernist concern for history by arguing that the point of such an interrogation is to "liberate us from the empirical object—whether institution, even, or individual work—by displacing our attention to its constitution as an object and its relationship to the other objects constituted" (Scholes, 1985, p. 84).

Another example of how a postmodern pedagogy of resistance might inform the notion of border pedagogy can be found in some of the recent work being done on educational theory and popular culture (Giroux & Simon, 1988, 1989). Two important issues are being worked out. First, there is a central concern for understanding how the production of meaning is tied to emotional investments and the production of pleasure. In this view, it is necessary for teachers to incorporate into their pedagogies a theoretical understanding of how the production of meaning and pleasure become mutually constitutive of who students are, how they view themselves, and how they construct a particular vision of their future. Second, rethinking the nature of how students make semantic and emotional investments needs to be theorized within a number of important pedagogical considerations. One such consideration is that the production and regulation of desire must be seen as a crucial aspect of how students mediate, relate, resist, and create particular cultural forms and forms of knowing. Another concern is that popular culture be seen as a legitimate aspect of the everyday lives of students and be analyzed as a primary force in shaping the various and often contradictory subject positions that students take up. Finally, popular culture needs to become a serious object of study in the official curriculum. This can be done by treating popular culture either as a distinct object of study within particular academic disciplines such as media studies or by drawing upon the resources it produces for engaging various aspects of the official curriculum (Giroux & Simon, 1988).

In both of these examples, important elements of a border pedagogy informed by postmodern criticism point to ways in which those master narratives based on white, patriarchal, and class-specific versions of the world can be challenged critically and effectively deterritorialized. That is, by offering a theoretical language for establishing new boundaries with respect to knowledge most often associated with the margins and the periphery of the cultural dominant, postmodern discourses open up the possibility for incorporating into the curriculum a notion of border pedagogy in which cultural and social practices need no longer be mapped or referenced solely on the basis of the dominant models of Western culture. In this case, knowledge forms emanating from the margins can be used to redefine the complex, multiple, heterogeneous realities that constitute those relations of difference that make up the experiences of students who often find it impossible to define their identities through the cultural and political codes of a single, unitary culture.

The sensibility which informs this view of knowledge emphasizes a pedagogy in which students need to develop a relationship of non-identity with respect to their own subject positions and the multiple cultural, political, and social codes which constitute established boundaries of power, dependency, and possibility. In other words, such a pedagogy emphasizes the non-synchronous relationship between one's social position and the multiple ways in which culture is constructed and read. That is, there is no single, predetermined relationship between a cultural code and the subject position that a student occupies. One's class, racial, gender, or ethnic position may influence but does not irrevocably predetermine how one takes up a particular ideology, reads a particular text, or responds to particular forms of oppression. Border pedagogy recognizes that teachers, students, and others often "read and write culture on multiple levels" (Kaplan, 1987, p. 187). Of course, the different subject positions and forms of subjugation that are constituted within these various levels and relations of culture have the potential to isolate and alienate instead of opening up the possibility for criticism and struggle. What is at stake here is developing a border pedagogy that can fruitfully work to break down those ideologies, cultural codes, and social practices that prevent students from recognizing how social forms at particular historical conjunctures operate to repress alternative readings of their own experiences, society, and the world.

Border Pedagogy as Counter-Memory

Postmodernism charts the process of deterritorialization as part of the breakdown of master narratives. It celebrates, in part, the loss of certainty and experience of defamiliarization even as it produces alienation and the displacement of identities (Deleuze & Guattari, 1986). In opposition to conservative readings of this shifting destabilizing process, I believe that such a disruption of traditional meaning offers important insights for developing a theory of border pedagogy based on a postmodernism of resistance. But this language runs the risk of undercutting its own political possibilities by ignoring how a language of difference can be articulated with critical modernist concerns for developing a discourse of public life. It also ignores the possibilities for developing, through the process of counter-memory, new and emancipatory forms of political identity. In what follows, I address some of the important work being done in radical public philosophy and feminist theory, paying particular attention to the issues of identity and counter-memory. The brief final section of this paper will offer some considerations of how the critical insights of a postmodernism of resistance can be deepened within a theory of border pedagogy.

Postmodernism has launched a major attack on the modernist notion of political universality (Ross, 1988). By insisting on the multiplicity of social positions, it has seriously challenged the political closure of modernity with its divisions between the center and the margins and in doing so has made room for those groups generally defined as the excluded others. In effect, postmodernism has reasserted the importance of the partial, the local, and the contingent, and in doing so it has given general expression to the demands of a wide variety of social movements. Postmodernism has also effectively challenged the ways in which written history has embodied a number of assumptions that inform the discourse of Eurocentrism. More specifically, it has rejected such Eurocentric assumptions as the pretentious claim to "speak" for all of mankind (sic) and the epistemological claims to foundationalism.

Laclau (1988) rightfully argues that an adequate approximation of the postmodern experience needs to be seen as part of a challenge to the discourses of modernity, with their "pretension to intellectually dominate the foundation of the social, to give a rational context to the notion of the totality of history, and to base in the latter the project of global human emancipation" (pp. 71–72). But Laclau also points out that the postmodern challenge to modernity does not represent the abandonment of its emancipatory values so much as it opens them up to a plurality of contexts and an indeterminacy "that redefines them in an unpredictable way" (p. 72). Chantal Mouffe (1988) extends this insight and argues, that modernity has two contradictory aspects: Its political project is rooted in a conception of the struggle for democracy, while its social project is tied to a foundationalism which fuels the process of social modernization under "the growing domination of relations of capitalist production" (p. 32). For Mouffe, the modernist project of democracy must be coupled with an understanding of the various social movements and the new politics that have emerged with the postmodern age. At the heart of this position is the need to rearticulate the tradition of liberty and justice with a notion of radical democracy; similarly, there is a need to articulate the concept of difference as more than a replay of liberal pluralism or a pastiche of diverse strands of interests with no common ground to hold them together.

This is not a liberal call to harmonize and resolve differences, as critics like Elizabeth Ellsworth (1988) wrongly argue, but an attempt to understand differences in terms of the historical and social grounds on which they are organized. By locating differences in a particular historical and social location, it becomes possible to understand how they are organized and constructed within maps of rules and regulations and located within dominant social forms which either enable or disable such differences. Differences only exist relative to the social forms in which they are enunciated, that is, in relation to schools, workplaces, families, as well as in relationship to the discourses of history, citizenship, sex, race, gender, and ethnicity. To detach them from the discourse of democracy and freedom is to remove the possibility of either articulating their particular interests as part of a wider struggle for power or understanding how their individual contradictory interests are developed with historically specific conjunctures. At stake here is the need for educators to fashion a critical politics of difference not outside but within a tradition of radical democracy. Similarly, it is imperative for critical educators to develop a discourse of counter-memory, not as an essentialist and closed narrative, but as part of a utopian project that recognizes "the composite, heterogeneous, open, and ultimately indeterminate character of the democratic tradition" (Mouffe, 1988, p. 41). The pedagogical issue here is the need to articulate difference as part of the construction of a new type of subject, one which would be both multiple and democratic. Chantal Mouffe (1988) is worth quoting at length on this issue:

> If the task of radical democracy is indeed to deepen the democratic revolution and to link together diverse democratic struggles, such a task requires the creation of new subject-positions that would allow the common articulation, for example, of antiracism, antisexism, and anticapitalism. These struggles do not spontaneously converge, and in order to establish democratic equivalences, a new "common sense" is necessary, which would transform the identity of different groups so that the demands of each group could be articulated with those of others according to the principle of democratic equivalence. For it is not a matter of establishing a mere alliance between given interests but of actually modifying the very identity of these forces. In order that the defense of workers' interests is not pursued at the cost of the rights of women, immigrants, or consumers, it is necessary to establish an equivalence between these different struggles. It is only under these circumstances that struggles against [authoritarian] power become truly democratic. (p. 42)

How might the issue of democracy and difference be taken up as part of a border pedagogy informed by a project of possibility? I want to argue that the discourses of democracy and difference can be taken up as pedagogical practices through what Foucault calls the notion of counter-memory. For Foucault (1977a), counter-memory is a practice which "transforms history from a judgment on the past in the name of the present truth to a 'counter-memory' that combats our current modes of truth and justice, helping us to understand and change the present by placing it in a new relation to the past" (pp. 160, 163–164). Counter-memory represents a critical reading of not only how the past informs the present but how the present reads the past. Counter-memory provides a theoretical tool to restore the connection between the language of public life and the discourse of difference. It represents an attempt to rewrite the language of resistance in terms that connect human beings within forms of remembrance that dignify public life while at the same time allowing people to speak from their particular histories and voices. Counter-memory refuses to treat democracy as merely inherited knowledge; it attempts, instead, to link democracy to notions of public life that "afford both agency and sources of power or empowering investments" (De Lauretis, 1987, p. 25). It also reasserts as a pedagogical practice the rewriting of history through the power of student voice. This points to the practice of counter-memory as a means of constructing democratic social forms that enable and disable particular subjectivities and identities; put another way, democracy in this instance becomes a referent for understanding how public life organizes differences and what this means for the ways in which schools, teachers, and students define themselves as political subjects, as citizens who operate within particular configurations of power.

In effect, the language of radical democracy provides the basis for educators not only to understand how differences are organized but also how the ground for such difference might be constructed within a political identity rooted in a respect for democratic public life (Giroux, 1988b). What is being suggested here is the construction of a project of possibility in pedagogical terms which is connected to a notion of democracy capable of mobilizing a variety of groups to develop and struggle for what Linda Alcoff (1988) calls a positive alternative vision. She writes, "As the Left should by now have learned, you cannot mobilize a movement that is only and always against: you must have a positive alternative, a vision of a better future that can motivate people to sacrifice their time and energy toward its realization" (Alcoff, 1988, pp. 418–419). If the notion of radical democracy is to function as a pedagogical practice, educators need to allow students to comprehend democracy as a way of life that consistently has to be fought for, has to be struggled over, and has to be rewritten as part of an oppositional politics. This means that democracy has to be viewed as a historical and social construction rooted in the tension between what Bruce James Smith (1985) calls remembrance and custom. I want to extend Smith's argument by developing remembrance as a form of counter-memory and custom as a form of reactionary nostalgia rooted in the loss of memory.

Custom, as Smith (1985) argues, constructs subjects within a discourse of continuity in which knowledge and practice are viewed as a matter of inheritance and transmission. Custom is the complex of ideologies and social practices that views counter-memory as subversive and critical teaching as unpatriotic. It is the ideological basis for forms of knowledge and pedagogy which refuse to interrogate public forms and which deny difference as a fundamental referent for a democratic society. According to Smith (1985), custom can be characterized in the following manner:

> The affection it enjoys and the authority it commands are prescriptive. The behavior of the person of custom is, by and large, habitual. To the question "why?" he [sic] is apt to respond simply, "This is the way it has always been done." . . . A creature of habit, the person of custom does not reflect upon his condition. To the

> extent that a customary society "conceives" of its practice, it is likely to see it, says Pocock, as "an indefinite series of repetitions." If the customary society is, in reality, a fluid order always in the process of adaptation, its continuity and incrementalism give rise to perceptions of changelessness and of the simple repetition of familiar motions.... Indeed... custom operates as if it were a second nature.... Custom is at once both more and less inclusive than remembrance. It includes things that are remembered and things that are forgotten. It is almost a definition of custom that its beginnings are lost. (pp. 15–16)

Remembrance is directed more toward specificity and struggle, it resurrects the legacies of actions and happenings, it points to the multitude of voices that constitute the struggle over history and power. Its focus is not on the ordinary but the extraordinary. Its language presents the unrepresentable, not merely as an isolated voice, but as a subversive interruption, a discursive space, that moves "against the grain" as it occupies "a view... carved in the interstices of institutions and in the chinks and cracks of the power-knowledge apparati" (De Lauretis, 1987, p. 25). Remembrance is part of a language of public life that promotes an ongoing dialogue between the past, present, and future. It is a vision of optimism rooted in the need to bear witness to history, to reclaim that which must not be forgotten. It is a vision of public life which calls for an ongoing interrogation of the past that allows different groups to locate themselves in history while simultaneously struggling to make it.

Counter-memory provides the ethical and epistemological grounds for a politics of solidarity within difference. At one level, it situates the notion of difference and the primacy of the political firmly within the wider struggle for broadening and revitalizing democratic public life. At the same time, it strips reason of its universal pretensions and recognizes the partiality of all points of view. In this perspective, the positing of a monolithic tradition that exists simply to be revered, reaffirmed, reproduced, or resisted is unequivocally rejected. Instead, counter-memory attempts to recover communities of memory and narratives of struggle that provide a sense of location, place, and identity to various dominant and subordinate groups. Counter-memory as a form of pedagogical practice is not concerned with simply marking difference as a historical construct; rather, it is concerned with providing the grounds for self-representation and the struggle for justice and a democratic society. Counter-memory resists comparison to either a humanist notion of pluralism or a celebration of diversity for its own sake. As both a pedagogical and political practice, it attempts to alter oppressive relations of power and to educate both teachers and students to the ways in which they might be complicitous with dominant power relations, victimized by them, and how they might be able to transform such relations. Abdul JanMohamed and David Lloyd (1987) are instructive on what counter-memory might mean as part of discourse of critique and transformation:

> Ethnic or gender difference must be perceived as one among a number of residual cultural elements which retain the memory of practices which have had to be and still have to be repressed in order that the capitalist economic subject may be more easily produced. . . ."Becoming minor" is not a question of essence but a question of positions-a subject-position that can only be defined, in the final analysis, in "political" terms, that is, in terms of the effects of economic exploitation, political disfranchisement, social manipulation, and ideological domination on the cultural formation of minority subjects and discourses. It is one of the central tasks of the theory of minority discourse to define that subject-position and explore the strengths and weaknesses, the affirmations and negations that inhere in it. (p. 11)

Remembrance as a form of counter-memory attempts to create for students the limits of any story that makes claims to predetermined endings and to expose how the transgressions in those stories cause particular forms of suffering and hardship. At the same time, remembrance as counter-memory opens up the past not as nostalgia but as the invention of stories, some of which deserve a retelling, and which speak to a very different future—one in which democratic community makes room for a politics of both difference and solidarity, for otherness stripped of subjugation, and for others fighting to embrace their own interests in opposition to sexism, racism, ethnocentrism, and class exploitation. Counter-memory is tied in this sense to a vision of public life that both resurrects the ongoing struggle for difference and situates difference within the broader struggle for cultural and social justice.

Counter-memory provides the basis and rationale for a particular kind of pedagogy but it cannot on its own articulate the specific classroom practices that can be constructed on the basis of such a rationale.

The formation of democratic citizens demands forms of political identity which radically extend the principles of justice, liberty, and dignity to public spheres constituted by difference and multiple forms of community. Such identities have to be constructed as part of a pedagogy in which difference becomes a basis for solidarity and unity rather than for hierarchy, denigration, competition, and discrimination. It is to that issue that I will now turn.

Border Pedagogy and the Politics of Difference

If the concept of border pedagogy is to be linked to the imperatives of a critical democracy, as it must, it is important that educators possess a theoretical grasp of the ways in which difference is constructed through various representations and practices that name, legitimate, marginalize, and exclude the cultural capital and voices of subordinate groups in American society.

As part of this theoretical project, a theory of border pedagogy needs to address the important question of how representations and practices that name, marginalize, and define difference as the devalued Other are actively learned, interiorized, challenged, or transformed. In addition, such a pedagogy needs to address how an understanding of these differences can be used in order to change the prevailing relations of power that sustain them. It is also imperative that such a pedagogy acknowledge and critically interrogate how the colonizing of differences by dominant groups is expressed and sustained through representations: in which Others are seen as a deficit, in which the humanity of the Others is either cynically posited as problematic or ruthlessly denied. At the same time, it is important to understand how the experience of marginality at the level of everyday life lends itself to forms of oppositional and transformative consciousness. This is an understanding based on the need for those designated as Others to both reclaim and remake their histories, voices, and visions as part of a wider struggle to change those material and social relations that deny radical pluralism as the basis of democratic political community. For it is only through such an understanding that teachers can develop a border pedagogy, one which is characterized by what Teresa De Lauretis (1987) calls "an ongoing effort to create new spaces of discourse, to rewrite cultural narratives, and to define the terms of another perspective—a view from 'elsewhere'" (p. 25). This suggests a pedagogy in which occurs a critical questioning of the omissions and tensions that exist between the master narratives and hegemonic discourses that make up the official curriculum and the self-representations of subordinate groups as they might appear in "forgotten" or erased histories, texts, memories, experiences, and community narratives.

Border pedagogy both confirms and critically engages the knowledge and experience through which students author their own voices and construct social identities. This suggests taking seriously the knowledge and experiences that constitute the individual and collective voices by which students identify and give meaning to themselves and others and drawing upon what they know about their own lives as a basis for criticizing the dominant culture. In this case, student experience has to be first understood and recognized as the accumulation of collective memories and stories that provide students with a sense of familiarity, identity, and practical knowledge. Such experience has to be both affirmed and critically interrogated. In addition, the social and historical construction of such experience has to be affirmed and understood as part of a wider struggle for voice. But it must also be understood that while past experiences can never be denied, their most debilitating dimensions can be engaged through a critical understanding of what was at work in their construction. It is in their critical engagement that such experiences can be remade, reterritorialized in the interest of a social imagery that dignifies the best traditions and possibilities of those groups who are learning to speak from a discourse of dignity and self-governance. In her analysis of the deterritorialization of women as Other, Caren Kaplan (1987) astutely articulates this position:

> Recognizing the minor cannot erase the aspects of the major, but as a mode of understanding it enables us to see the fissures in our identities, to unravel the seams of our totalities. . . . We must leave home, as it were, since our homes are often sites of racism, sexism, and other damaging social practices. Where we come to locate ourselves in terms of our specific histories and differences must be a place with room for what can be salvaged from the past and made anew. What we gain is a reterritorialization; we reinhabit a world of our making (here "our" is expanded to a coalition of identities—neither universal nor particular). (pp. 187–188)

Furthermore, it is important to extend the possibilities of the often contradictory values that give meaning to students' lives by making them the object, of critical inquiry and by appropriating in a similarly critical fashion, when necessary, the codes and knowledges that constitute broader and less familiar historical and cultural traditions. At issue here is the development of a pedagogy that replaces the authoritative language of recitation with an approach that allows students to speak from their own histories, collective memories, and voices while simultaneously challenging the grounds on which knowledge and power are constructed and legitimated. Such a pedagogy contributes to making possible a variety of social forms and human capacities which expand the range of social identities that students may carry and become. It points to the importance of understanding in both pedagogical and political terms how subjectivities are produced within those social forms in which people move but of which they are often only partially conscious. Similarly, it raises fundamental questions regarding how students make particular investments of meaning and affect, how they are constituted within a triad of relationships of knowledge, power, and pleasure, and why students should be indifferent to the forms of authority, knowledge, and values that we produce and legitimate within our classrooms and university. It is worth noting that such a pedagogy not only articulates a respect for a diversity of student voices, it also provides a referent for developing a public language rooted in a commitment to social transformation.

Central to the notion of border pedagogy are a number of important pedagogical issues regarding the role that teachers might play within the interface of modern and postmodern concerns that have been taken up in this essay. Clearly, the concept of border pedagogy suggests that teachers exist within social, political, and cultural boundaries that are both multiple and historical in nature and that place particular demands on a recognition and pedagogical appropriation of differences. As part of the process of developing a pedagogy of difference, teachers need to deal with the plethora of voices, and the specificity and organization of differences that constitute any course, class, or curriculum so as to make problematic not only the stories that give meanings to the lives of their students, but also the ethical and political lineaments that inform their students' subjectivities and identities.

In part this suggests a pedagogy which does more than provide students with a language and context by which to critically engage the plurality of habits, practices, experiences, and desires that define them as part of a particular social formation within ongoing relations of domination and resistance. Border pedagogy provides opportunities for teachers to deepen their own understanding of the discourse of various others in order to effect a more dialectical understanding of their own politics, values, and pedagogy. What border pedagogy makes undeniable is the relational nature of one's own politics and personal investments. But at the same time, border pedagogy emphasizes the primacy of a politics in which teachers assert rather than retreat from the pedagogies they utilize in dealing with the various differences represented by the students who come into their classes. For example, it is not enough for teachers to merely affirm uncritically their students' histories, experiences, and stories. To take student voices at face value is to run the risk of idealizing and romanticizing them. The contradictory and complex histories and stories that give meaning to the lives of students are never innocent, and it is important that they be recognized for their contradictions as well as for their possibilities. Of course, it is crucial that critical educators provide the pedagogical conditions for students to give voice to how their past and present experiences place them within existing relations of domination and resistance. Central to this pedagogical process is the important task of affirming the voices that students bring to school and challenging the separation of school knowledge from the experience of everyday life (Fine, 1987). But it is crucial that critical educators do more than allow such stories to be heard. It is equally important for teachers to help students find a language for critically examining the historically and socially constructed forms by which they live. Such a process involves more than "speaking" one's history and social formation, it also involves engaging collectively with others within a pedagogical framework that helps to reterritorialize and rewrite the complex narratives that make up one's life. This is more than a matter of rewriting stories as counter-memories, it is what Frigga Haug (1987) and her colleagues call memory-work, a crucial example of how the pedagogical functions to interrogate and retrieve rather than to merely celebrate one's voice. She writes:

> By excavating traces of the motives for our past actions, and comparing these with our present lives, we are able to expand the range of our demands and competences. Admittedly, this is not as easy as it sounds. Our stories are expressed in the language we use today. Buried or abandoned memories do not speak loudly; on the contrary we can expect them to meet us with obdurate silence. In recognition of this, we must adopt some method of analysis suited to the resolution of a key question for women; a method that seeks out the unnamed, the silent and the absent. Here too, our experience of education maps out a ready-made path of analysis; we have been taught to content ourselves with decoding texts, with search for truth in textual analysis, complemented at best by the author's own analysis. "Re-learning" in this context means seeing what is not

> said as interesting, and the fact that it was not said as important; it involves a huge methodological leap, and demands more than a little imagination. (p. 65)

The different stories that students from all groups bring to class need to be interrogated for their absences as well as their contradictions, but they also need to be understood as more than simply a myriad of different stories. They have to be recognized as being forged in relations of opposition to the dominant structures of power. At the same time, differences among students are not merely antagonistic as Liz Ellsworth (1988) has argued. She suggests not only that there is little common ground for addressing these differences, but that separatism is the only valid political option for any kind of pedagogical and political action. Regrettably, this represents less an insight than a crippling form of political disengagement. It reduces one to paralysis in the face of such differences. It ignores the necessity of exploring differences for the specific, irreducible interests they represent, for the excesses and reactionary positions they may produce, and for the pedagogical possibilities they contain for helping students to work with other groups as part of a collective attempt at developing a radical language of democratic public life. Moreover, Ellsworth's attempt to delegitimate the work of other critical educators by claiming rather self-righteously the primacy and singularity of her own ideological reading of what constitutes a political project appears to ignore both the multiplicity of contexts and projects that characterize critical educational work and the tension that haunts all forms of teacher authority, a tension marked by the potential contradiction between being theoretically or ideologically correct and pedagogically wrong. By ignoring the dynamics of such a tension and the variety of struggles being waged under historically specific educational conditions, she degrades the rich complexity of theoretical and pedagogical processes that characterize the diverse discourses in the field of critical pedagogy. In doing so, she succumbs to the familiar academic strategy of dismissing others through the use of strawman tactics and excessive simplifications which undermine not only the strengths of her own work, but also the very nature of social criticism itself. This is "theorizing" as a form of "bad faith," a discourse imbued with the type of careerism that has become all too characteristic of many left academics.

At stake here is an important theoretical issue that is worth repeating. Knowledge and power come together not merely to reaffirm difference but also to interrogate it, to open up broader theoretical considerations, to tease out its limitations, and to engage a vision of community in which student voices define themselves in terms of their distinct social formations and their broader collective hopes. As teachers we can never inclusively speak *as* the Other (though we may be the Other with respect to issues of race, class, or gender), but we can certainly work *with* diverse Others to deepen their understanding of the complexity of the traditions, histories, knowledges, and politics that they bring to the schools. This means, as Abdul JanMohamed and David Lloyd (1987) point out, that educators need to recognize the importance of developing a theory of minority discourse which not only explores the strengths and weaknesses, affirmations and negations that inhere in the subject positions of subordinate groups but also "involves drawing our solidarities in the form of similarities between modes of repression and modes of struggle which all minorities separately experience, and experience precisely as minorities" (JanMohamed & Lloyd, 1987, p. 11). To assume such a position is not to practice forms of gender, racial, or class-specific imperialism as Ellsworth suggests; rather, it is to create conditions within particular institutions that allow students to locate themselves and others in histories that mobilize rather than destroy their hopes for the future.

The theoretical sweep may be broad, the sentiment utopian, but it is better than wallowing in guilt or refusing to fight for the possibility of a better world. Sentimentality is no excuse for the absence of any vision for the future. Like Klee's angel in the painting 'Angelus Novus," modernity provides a faith in human agency while recognizing that the past is often built on the suffering of others. In the best of the Enlightenment tradition, reason at least offers the assumption and hope that men and women can change the world in which they live. Postmodernism frays the boundaries of that world and makes visible what has often been seen as unrepresentable. The task of modernity with its faith in reason and emancipation can perhaps renew its urgency in a postmodern world, a world where difference, contingency, and power can reassert, redefine, and in some instances collapse the monolithic boundaries of nationalism, sexism, racism, and class oppression. In a world whose borders have become chipped and porous, new challenges present themselves not only to educators but to all those for whom contingency and loss of certainty do not mean the inevitable triumph of nihilism and despair but rather a state of possibility in which destiny and hope can be snatched from the weakening grasp of modernity. We live in a postmodern world that no longer has any firm—but has ever flexing—boundaries. It is a time when reason is in crisis and new political and ideological conditions exist for fashioning forms of struggle defined in a radically different conception of politics. For educators, this is as much a pedagogical issue as it is a political one. At best, it points to the importance of rewriting the relationship between knowledge, power, and desire. It points as well to the necessity of redefining the importance of difference while at the same time seeking articulations among subordinate groups and historically privileged groups committed to social transformations that deepen the possibility for radical democracy and human survival.

References

Alcoff, L. (1988). Cultural feminism vs. poststructuralism: The identity crisis in feminist theory. *Signs,* 13, 405–436.

Apple, M., & Beyer, L. (Eds.). (1988). *The curriculum: Problems, politics and possibilities.* Albany: State University of New York Press.

Brodkey, L., & Fine, M. (1988). *Presence of mind in the absence of body.* Boston University Journal of Education 170(3), 84–99.

Cherryholmes, C. (1988). *Power and criticism: Poststructural investigations in education.* New York: Teachers College Press.

Deleuze, G., & Guattari, E. (1986). *Toward a minor literature.* Minneapolis: University of Minnesota Press.

De Lauretis, T. (1987). *Technologies of gender.* Bloomington: Indiana University Press.

Dews, P. (1987). *Logics of disintegration.* London: Verso Books.

Dienske, I. (1988). Narrative knowledge and science. *Journal of Learning About Learning,* 1(1), 19–27.

Ellsworth, E. (1988). *Why doesn't this feel empowering? Working through the repressive myths of critical pedagogy.* Paper presented at the Tenth Conference on Curriculum Theory and Classroom Practice, Bergamo Conference Center, Dayton, Ohio, October 26–29, 1988.

Fine, M. (1987). Silencing in the public schools. *Language Arts,* 64(2), 157–174.

Foucault, M. (1977a). *Language, counter-memory, practice: Selected essays and interviews* (D. Bouchard, Ed.). Ithaca: Cornell University Press.

Foucault, M. (1977b). *Power and knowledge: Selected interviews and other writings* (G. Gordon, Ed.). NewYork: Pantheon.

Giroux, H. (1988a). *Schooling and the struggle for public life.* Minneapolis: University of Minnesota Press.

Giroux, H. (1988b). *Teachers as intellectuals.* Granby, MA: Bergin & Garvey.

Giroux, H., & McLaren, P. (1989). Introduction. In H. Giroux & P. McLaren (Eds.), *Critical pedagogy, the state, and cultural struggle.* Albany: State University of New York Press.

Giroux, H., & Simon, R. (1988). Critical pedagogy and the politics of popular culture. *Cultural Studies,* 2, 294–320.

Giroux, H., & Simon, R. (1989). *Popular culture, schooling, and everyday life.* South Hadley, MA: Bergin & Garvey Press.

Haug, F. et al. (1987). *Female sexualization: A collective work of memory.* London: Verso Press.

Hicks, E. (1988). Deterritorialization and border writing. In R. Merrill (Ed.), *Ethics/aesthetics: Post-modern positions* (pp. 47–58). Washington, DC: Maisonneuve Press.

Jameson, E. (1984). Postmodernism or the cultural logic of late capitalism. *New Left Review,* No. 146, pp. 53–93.

JanMohamed, A. (1987). Introduction: Toward a theory of minority discourse. *Cultural Critique,* No. 6, pp. 5–11.

JanMohamed, A., & Lloyd, D. (1987). Introduction: Minority discourse—What is to be done? *Cultural Critique,* No. 7, 5–17.

Kaplan, C. (1987). Deterritorialisations: The rewriting of home and exile in western feminist discourse. *Cultural Critique,* No. 6, 187–198.

Kellner, D. (1988). Postmodernism as social theory: Some challenges and problems. *Theory, Culture and Society,* 5(2 & 3), 239–269.

Kellner, D. (n.d.). Boundaries and borderlines: Reflections on Jean Baudriilard and critical theory.

Kolb, D. (1986). *The critique of pure modernity: Hegel, Heidegger, and after.* Chicago: University of Chicago Press.

Laclau, E. (1988). Politics and the limits of modernity. In A. Ross (Ed.), *Universal abandon? The politics of postmodernism* (pp. 63–82). Minneapolis: University of Minnesota Press.

Laclau, E., & Mouffe, C. (1985). *Hegemony and socialist strategy.* London: Verso Books.

Lash, S., & Urry, J. (1987). *The end of organized capitalism.* Madison: University of Wisconsin Press.

Lunn, E. (1982). *Marxism and modernism.* Berkeley: University of California Press.

Lyotard, J. (1984). *The postmodern condition.* Minneapolis: University of Minnesota Press.

McLaren, P. (1986). Postmodernism and the death of politics: A Brazilian reprieve. *Educational Theory, 36,* 389–401.

McLaren, P. (1988). *Life in schools.* New York: Longman.

Morris, M. (1988). *The pirate's fiancee: Feminism, reading, postmodernism.* London: Verso Press.

Mouffe, C. (1988). Radical democracy: Modern or postmodern? In A. Ross (Ed.), *Universal abandon? The politics of postmodernism* (pp. 31–45). Minneapolis: University of Minnesota Press.

Peller, G. (1987). Reason and the mob: The politics of representation. *Tikkun, 2*(3), 28–31,92–95.

Pinar, W. (Ed.). (1988). *Contemporary curriculum discourses.* Scottsdale, AZ: Gorsuch Scarisbrick.

Pinon, N. (1982). La contaminacion de La Languaje: Interview with Nelida Pinon. *13th Moon,* No. 6(1 & 2), 72–76.

Richard, N. (1987/1988). Postmodernism and periphery. *Third Text,* No. 2, pp. 5–12.

Ross, A. (Ed.). (1988). *Universal abandon? The politics of postmodernism.* Minneapolis: University of Minnesota Press.

Said, E. (1983). Opponents, audiences, constituencies, and community. In H. Foster (Ed.), *The anti-aesthetic: Essays on postmodern culture* (pp. 135–139). Port Townsend, WA: Bay Press.

Scholes, R. (1985). *Textual power.* New Haven: Yale University Press.

Shor, I. (1979). *Critical teaching and everyday life.* Boston: South End Press.

Smith, B. J. (1985). *Politics and remembrance.* Princeton: Princeton University Press.

28

"Multicultural Education and School Reform" (2001)

Sonia Nieto is among the United States' most distinguished multicultural educators. In the following selection from her book *Language, Culture, and Teaching: Critical Perspectives for a New Century,* Nieto defines the meaning of *multicultural education.* In doing so, she calls for a model of multicultural education that is critical and addresses questions of social justice. For her, multicultural education is more than just the celebration of diversity; it also involves the careful examination of American culture and its values concerning race and ethnicity.

Specifically, Nieto argues that multicultural education is (a) antiracist education, (b) basic education, (c) important for all students, (d) pervasive, (e) education for social justice, (f) a process, and (g) critical pedagogy.

As you read the following selection, consider the following questions:

1. What defines multicultural education? Are some types of multicultural education more political than others?
2. Should multicultural education be part of the basic curriculum of schools? What does this mean?
3. What are the implications of marginalizing multicultural education?
4. Is multicultural education appropriate for all people? If so, why?

28

"Multicultural Education and School Reform" (2001)

Sonia Nieto

A Definition Of Multicultural Education

I define *multicultural education* in a sociopolitical context as follows:

> Multicultural education is a process of comprehensive school reform and basic education for all students. It challenges and rejects racism and other forms of discrimination in schools and society and accepts and affirms the pluralism (ethnic, racial, linguistic, religious, economic, and gender, among others) that students, their communities, and teachers reflect. Multicultural education permeates the schools' curriculum and instructional strategies, as well as the interactions among teachers, students, and families, and the very way that schools conceptualize the nature of teaching and learning. Because it uses critical pedagogy as its underlying philosophy and focuses on knowledge, reflection, and action (praxis) as the basis for social change, multicultural education promotes democratic principles of social justice.[1]

The seven basic characteristics of multicultural education in this definition are:

> Multicultural education is antiracist education.
>
> Multicultural education is basic education.
>
> Multicultural education is important for all students.

Source: Nieto, Sonia. (2001). "Multicultural Education and School Reform." In *Language, Culture, and Teaching: Critical Perspectives for a New Century*, Chap. 1. Mahwah, N.J.: Lawrence Erlbaum.

Multicultural education is pervasive.

Multicultural education is education for social justice.

Multicultural education is a process.

Multicultural education is critical pedagogy.

Multicultural Education Is Antiracist Education

Antiracism, indeed antidiscrimination in general, is at the very core of a multicultural perspective. It is essential to keep the antiracist nature of multicultural education in mind because in many schools, even some that espouse a multicultural philosophy, only superficial aspects of multicultural education are apparent. Celebrations of ethnic festivals are as far as it goes in some places. In others, sincere attempts to decorate bulletin boards or purchase materials with what is thought to be a multicultural perspective end up perpetuating the worst kind of stereotypes. And even where there are serious attempts to develop a truly pluralistic environment, it is not unusual to find incongruencies. In some schools, for instance, the highest academic tracks are overwhelmingly White and the lowest are populated primarily by students of color, or girls are invisible in calculus and physics classes. These are examples of multicultural education *without* an explicitly antiracist and antidiscrimination perspective.

I stress multicultural education as antiracist because many people believe that a multicultural program *automatically* takes care of racism. Unfortunately this is not always true. Writing about multicultural education almost two decades ago, Meyer Weinberg asserted,

> Most multicultural materials deal wholly with the cultural distinctiveness of various groups and little more. Almost never is there any sustained attention to the ugly realities of systematic discrimination against the same group that also happens to utilize quaint clothing, fascinating toys, delightful fairy tales, and delicious food. Responding to racist attacks and defamation is also part of the culture of the group under study.[2]

Being antiracist and antidiscriminatory means paying attention to all areas in which some students are favored over others: the curriculum, choice of materials, sorting policies, and teachers' interactions and relationships with students and their families.

To be more inclusive and balanced, multicultural curriculum must by definition be antiracist. Teaching does not become more honest and critical simply by becoming more inclusive, but this is an important first step in ensuring that students have access to a wide variety of viewpoints. Although the beautiful and heroic aspects of our history should be taught, so must the ugly and exclusionary. Rather than viewing the world through rose-colored glasses, antiracist multicultural education forces teachers and students to take a long, hard look at everything as it was and is, instead of just how we wish it were.

Too many schools avoid confronting in an honest and direct way both the positive and the negative aspects of history, the arts, and science. Michelle Fine calls this the "fear of naming," and it is part of the system of silencing in public schools.[3] To name might become too messy, or so the thinking goes. Teachers often refuse to engage their students in discussions about racism because it might "demoralize" them. Too dangerous a topic, it is best left untouched.

Related to the fear of naming is the insistence of schools on sanitizing the curriculum, or what Jonathan Kozol many years ago called "tailoring" important men and women for school use. Kozol described how schools manage to take the most exciting and memorable heroes and bleed the life and spirit completely out of them. It is dangerous, he wrote, to teach a history "studded with so many bold, and revolutionary, and subversive, and exhilarating men and women." Instead, he described how schools drain these heroes of their passions, glaze them over with an implausible veneer, place them on lofty pedestals, and then tell "incredibly dull stories" about them.[4]

The process of "sanitizing" is nowhere more evident than in current depictions of Martin Luther King, Jr. In attempting to make him palatable to the mainstream, schools have made Martin Luther King a Milquetoast. The only thing most children know about him is that he kept having a dream. Bulletin boards are full of ethereal pictures of Dr. King surrounded by clouds. If children get to read or hear any of his speeches at all, it is his "I Have a Dream" speech. As inspirational as this speech is, it is only one of his notable accomplishments. Rare indeed are allusions to his early and consistent opposition to the Vietnam War; his strong criticism of unbridled capitalism; and the connections he made near the end of his life among racism, capitalism, and war. Martin Luther King, a man full of passion and life, becomes lifeless. He becomes a "safe hero."

Most of the heroes we present to our children are either those in the mainstream or those who have become safe by the process of "tailoring." Others who have fought for social justice are often downplayed, maligned, or ignored. For example, although John Brown's actions in defense of the liberation of enslaved people are considered noble by many, in our history books he is presented, if at all, as somewhat of a crazed idealist. Nat Turner is another example. The slave revolt that he led deserves a larger place in our history, if only to acknowledge that enslaved people fought against their own oppression and were not simply passive victims. Yet his name is usually overlooked, and Abraham Lincoln is presented as the "great emancipator," with little acknowledgment of his own inconsistent ideas about race and equality. Nat Turner is not safe; Abraham Lincoln is.

To be antiracist also means to work affirmatively to combat racism. It means making antiracism and antidiscrimination explicit parts of the curriculum and teaching young people skills in confronting racism. It also means that we must not isolate or punish students for naming racism when they see it, but instead respect them for doing so. If developing productive and critical citizens for a democratic society is one of the fundamental goals of public education, antiracist behaviors can help to meet that objective.

Racism is seldom mentioned in school (it is bad, a dirty word) and therefore is not dealt with. Unfortunately, many teachers think that simply having lessons in getting along or celebrating Human Relations Week will make students nonracist or nondiscriminatory in general. But it is impossible to be untouched by racism, sexism, linguicism, heterosexism, ageism, anti-Semitism, classism, and ethnocentrism in a society characterized by all of them. To expect schools to be an oasis of sensitivity and understanding in the midst of this stratification is unrealistic. Therefore, part of the mission of the school becomes creating the space and encouragement that legitimates talk about racism and discrimination and makes it a source of dialogue. This includes learning the missing or fragmented parts of our history.

The dilemma becomes how to challenge the silence about race and racism so that teachers and students can enter into meaningful and constructive dialogue. In the words of Marilyn Cochran-Smith,

> How can we open up the unsettling discourse of race without making people afraid to speak for fear of being naive, offensive, or using the wrong language? Without making people of color do all the work, feeling called upon to expose themselves for the edification of others? Without eliminating conflict to the point of flatness, thus reducing the conversation to platitudes or superficial rhetoric?[5]

A helpful answer to this dilemma, in terms of students, is offered by Henry Giroux. He suggests that although White students may become traumatized by these discussions, bringing race and racism out into full view can become a useful pedagogical tool to help them locate themselves and their responsibilities concerning racism.[6] Beverly Tatum has proposed that discussing racism within the framework of racial and cultural identity theory can help focus on how racism negatively affects all people and provide a sense of hope that it can be changed.[7]

What about teachers? Many teachers have had little experience with diversity. Discussions of racism threaten to disrupt their deeply held ideals of fair play and equality. Since most teachers are uneasy with these topics, fruitful classroom discussions about discrimination rarely happen. If this is the case, neither unfair individual behaviors nor institutional policies and practices in schools will change. Students of disempowered groups will continue to bear the brunt of these kinds of inequities.

Multicultural education needs to prepare teachers to confront discrimination of all kinds, and this needs to happen not just in college classrooms but also through inservice education. In one example of the powerful impact that this preparation can have, Sandra Lawrence and Beverly Daniel Tatum described the impact of antiracist professional development on teachers' classroom practice. In their research, they found that many White teachers were apprehensive about engaging in discussions about race with their students because they thought they would degenerate into angry shouting matches. Yet, according to Lawrence and Tatum, after the teachers had participated in an inservice course, most of them took concrete actions in their classrooms and schools that challenged unfair policies and practices, and they were more comfortable in confronting racist behaviors and comments.[8]

The focus on policies and practices makes it evident that multicultural education is about more than the perceptions and beliefs of individual teachers and other educators. Multicultural education is antiracist because it exposes the racist and discriminatory practices in schools discussed in preceding chapters. A school truly committed to a multicultural philosophy will closely examine its policies and the attitudes and behaviors of its staff to determine how these might discriminate against some students. How teachers react to their students, whether native language use is permitted in the school, how sorting takes place, and the way in which classroom organization might hurt some students and help others are questions to be considered. In addition, individual teachers will reflect on their own attitudes and practices in the classroom and how they are influenced by their background as well as by their ignorance of students' backgrounds. This soul searching is difficult, but it is a needed step in developing an antiracist multicultural philosophy.

But being antiracist does not mean flailing about in guilt or remorse. One of the reasons schools are reluctant to tackle racism and discrimination is that these are disturbing topics for those who have traditionally benefited by their race, gender, and social class, among other differences. Because such topics place people in the role of either the victimizer or the victimized, an initial and understandable reaction of many White teachers and students is to feel guilty. Although this reaction probably serves a useful purpose initially, it needs to be understood as only one step in the process of becoming multiculturally literate and empowered. If one remains at this level, then guilt only immobilizes. Teachers and students need to move beyond guilt to a stage of energy and confidence, where they take action rather than hide behind feelings of remorse.

Although the primary victims of racism and discrimination are those who suffer its immediate consequences, racism and discrimination are destructive and demeaning to everyone. Keeping this in mind, it is easier for all teachers and students to face these issues. Although not everyone is directly guilty of racism and discrimination, we are all responsible for it. Given this perspective, students and teachers can focus on discrimination as something everyone has a responsibility to change.

In discussing slavery in the United States, for example, it can be presented not simply as slave owners against enslaved Africans. There were many and diverse roles among a great variety of people during this period: enslaved Africans and free Africans, slave owners and poor White farmers, Black abolitionists and White abolitionists, White and Black feminists who fought for both abolition and women's liberation, people of Native American heritage who stood on the side of freedom, and so on. Each of these perspectives should be taught so that children, regardless of ethnic background or gender, see themselves in history in ways that are not simply degrading or guilt-provoking.

I clearly remember the incident told to me by the father of the only Black child in a class whose teacher asked all the students to draw themselves as a character during the Civil War. This child drew a horse, preferring to see himself as an animal rather than as an enslaved man. We can only imagine the deep sense of pain and emptiness that this child felt. I have also heard teachers talk about White students who, after learning about slavery or the internment of the Japanese in our country during World War II, feel tremendous guilt. No child should be made to feel guilt or shame about their background. Providing alternative and empowering roles for all students is another aspect of an antiracist perspective because it creates a sense of hope and purpose.

Multicultural Education Is Basic Education

Given the recurring concern for the "basics" in education, multicultural education must be understood as basic education. Multicultural literacy is as indispensable for living in today's world as are reading, writing, arithmetic, and computer literacy.

When multicultural education is peripheral to the core curriculum, it is perceived as irrelevant to basic education. One of the major stumbling blocks to implementing a broadly conceptualized multicultural education is the ossification of the "canon" in our schools. The canon, as understood in contemporary U.S. education, assumes that the knowledge that is most worthwhile is already in place. According to this rather narrow view, the basics have in effect already been defined, and knowledge is inevitably European, male, and upper class in origin and conception. This idea is especially evident in the arts and social sciences. For instance, art history classes rarely leave France, Italy, and sometimes England in considering the "great masters." "Classical music" is another example: What is called classical music is actually *European* classical music. Africa, Asia, and Latin America define their classical music in different ways. This same ethnocentrism is found in our history books, which place

Europeans and European Americans as the actors and all others as the recipients, bystanders, or bit players of history. But the canon as it currently stands is unrealistic and incomplete because history is never as one-sided as it appears in most of our schools' curricula. We need to expand what we mean by "basic" by opening up the curriculum to a variety of perspectives and experiences.

The problem that a canon tries to address is a genuine one: Modern-day knowledge is so dispersed and compartmentalized that our young people learn very little that is common. There is no core to the knowledge to which they are exposed. But proposing a static list of terms, almost exclusively with European and European American referents, does little to expand our actual common culture.

At the same time, it is unrealistic, for a number of reasons, to expect a perfectly "equal treatment" for all people in the curriculum. A force-fit, which tries to equalize the number of African Americans, women, Jewish Americans, and so on in the curriculum, is not what multicultural education is all about. A great many groups have been denied access in the actual making of history. Their participation has not been equal, at least if we consider history in the traditional sense of great movers and shakers, monarchs and despots, and makers of war and peace. But the participation of diverse groups, even within this somewhat narrow view of history, has been appreciable. It therefore deserves to be included. The point is that those who have been present in our history, arts, literature, and science should be made visible. Recent literature anthologies are a good example of the inclusion of more voices and perspectives than ever before. Did they become "great writers" overnight, or was it simply that they had been buried for too long?

We are not talking here simply of the "contributions" approach to history, literature, and the arts.[9] Such an approach can easily become patronizing by simply adding bits and pieces to a preconceived canon. Rather, missing from most curricula is a consideration of how generally excluded groups have made history and affected the arts, literature, geography, science, and philosophy on their own terms.

The alternative to multicultural education is monocultural education. Education reflective of only one reality and biased toward the dominant group, monocultural education is the order of the day in most of our schools. What students learn represents only a fraction of what is available knowledge, and those who decide what is most important make choices that are of necessity influenced by their own limited background, education, and experiences. Because the viewpoints of so many are left out, monocultural education is at best a partial education. It deprives all students of the diversity that is part of our world.

No school can consider that it is doing a proper or complete job unless its students develop multicultural literacy. What such a conception might mean in practice would no doubt differ from school to school. At the very least, we would expect all students to be fluent in a language other than their own; aware of the literature and arts of many different peoples; and conversant with the history and geography not only of the United States but also of African, Asian, Latin American, and European countries. Through such an education, we would expect students to develop social and intellectual skills that would help them understand and empathize with a wide diversity of people. Nothing can be more basic than this.

Multicultural Education Is Important for All Students

There is a widespread perception that multicultural education is only for students of color, or for urban students, or for so-called disadvantaged students. This belief is probably based on the roots of multicultural education, which grew out of the civil rights and equal education movements of the 1960s. The primary objective of multicultural education was to address the needs of students who historically had been most neglected or miseducated by the schools, especially students of color. Those who promoted multicultural education thought that education should strike more of a balance, and that attention needed to be given to developing curriculum and materials that reflect these students' histories, cultures, and experiences. This thinking was historically necessary and is understandable even today, given the great curricular imbalance that continues to exist in most schools.

More recently a broader conceptualization of multicultural education has gained acceptance. It is that all students are miseducated to the extent that they receive only a partial and biased education. The primary victims of biased education are those who are invisible in the curriculum. Females, for example, are absent in most curricula, except in special courses on women's history that are few and far between. Working-class history is also absent in virtually all U.S. curricula. The children of the working class are deprived not only of a more forthright education but, more important, of a place in history, and students of all social class backgrounds are deprived of a more honest and complete view of our history. Likewise, there is a pervasive and inpenetrable silence concerning gays and lesbians in most schools, not just in the curriculum but also in extracurricular activities. The result is that gay and lesbian students are placed at risk in terms of social well being and academic achievement.[10]

Although the primary victims of biased education continue to be those who are invisible in the curriculum, those who figure prominently are victims as well. They receive only a partial education, which legitimates their cultural blinders. European American children, seeing only themselves, learn that they are the norm; everyone else is secondary. The same is true of males. The children of the wealthy learn that the wealthy and the powerful are the real makers of history, the ones who have left their mark on civilization. Heterosexual students receive the message that gay and lesbian students should be ostracized because they are deviant and immoral. The humanity of all students is jeopardized as a result.

Multicultural education is by definition inclusive. Because it is about all people, it is also for all people, regardless of their ethnicity, language, sexual orientation, religion, gender, race, class, or other difference. It can even be convincingly argued that students from the dominant culture need multicultural education more than others because they are generally the most miseducated about diversity. For example, European American youths often think that they do not even have a culture, at least not in the same sense that clearly culturally identifiable youths do. At the same time, they feel that their ways of living, doing things, believing, and acting are the only acceptable ways. Anything else is ethnic and exotic.

Feeling as they do, these young people are prone to develop an unrealistic view of the world and of their place in it. They learn to think of themselves and their group as the norm and of all others as a deviation. These are the children who learn not to question, for example, the name of "flesh-colored" adhesive strips even though they are not the flesh color of three-quarters of humanity. They do not even have to think about the fact that everyone, Christian or not, gets holidays at Christmas and Easter and that other religious holidays are given little attention in our calendars and school schedules. Whereas children from dominated groups may develop feelings of inferiority based on their schooling, dominant group children may develop feelings of superiority. Both responses are based on incomplete and inaccurate information about the complexity and diversity of the world, and both are harmful.

Despite this, multicultural education continues to be thought of by many educators as education for the "culturally different" or the "disadvantaged." Teachers in predominantly European American schools, for example, may feel it is not important or necessary to teach their students anything about the civil rights movement. Likewise, only in scattered bilingual programs in Mexican American communities are students exposed to literature by Mexican and Mexican American authors, and it is generally just at high schools with a high percentage of students of color that ethnic studies classes are offered. These are ethnocentric interpretations of multicultural education.

The thinking behind these actions is paternalistic as well as misinformed. Because anything remotely digressing from the "regular" (European American) curriculum is automatically considered soft by some educators, the usual response to making a curriculum multicultural is to water it down. Poor pedagogical decisions are then based on the premise that so-called disadvantaged students need a watered-down version of the "real" curriculum, whereas more privileged children can handle the "regular" or more academically challenging curriculum. But rather than dilute it, making a curriculum multicultural makes it more inclusive, inevitably enriching it. All students would be enriched by reading the poetry of Langston Hughes or the stories of Gary Soto, or by being fluent in a second language, or by understanding the history of Islam.

Multicultural Education Is Pervasive

Multicultural education is not something that happens at a set period of the day, or another subject area to be covered. In some school systems, there is even a "multicultural teacher" who goes from class to class in the same way as the music or art teacher. Although the intent of this approach may be to formalize a multicultural perspective in the standard curriculum, it is in the long run self-defeating because it isolates the multicultural philosophy from everything else that happens in the classroom. Having specialists take complete responsibility for multicultural education gives the impression that a multicultural perspective is separate from all other knowledge. The schism between "regular" and "multicultural" education widens. In this kind of arrangement, multicultural education becomes exotic knowledge that is external to the real work that goes on in classrooms. Given this conception of multicultural education, it is little wonder that teachers sometimes decide that it is a frill they cannot afford.

A true multicultural approach is pervasive. It permeates everything: the school's climate, physical environment, curriculum, and relationships among teachers and students and community.[11] It is apparent in every lesson, curriculum guide, unit, bulletin board, and letter that is sent home; it can be seen in the process by which books and audiovisual aids are acquired for the library, in the games played during recess, and in the lunch that is served. *Multicultural education is a philosophy, a way of looking at the world, not simply a program or a class or a teacher.* In this comprehensive way, multicultural education helps us rethink school reform.

What might a multicultural philosophy mean in the way that schools are organized? For one, it would probably mean the end of tracking, which inevitably favors some students over others. It would also mean that the complexion of the school, both literally and figuratively, would change. That is, there would be an effort to have the entire school staff be more representative of our nation's diversity. Pervasiveness probably would also be apparent in the great variety and creativity of instructional strategies, so that students from all cultural groups, and females as well as males, would benefit from methods other than the traditional. The curriculum would be completely overhauled and would include the histories, viewpoints, and insights of many different peoples and both males and females. Topics usually considered "dangerous" could be talked about in classes, and students would be encouraged to become critical thinkers. Textbooks and other instructional materials would also reflect a pluralistic perspective. Families and other community people would be visible in the schools because they would offer a unique and helpful viewpoint. Teachers, families, and students would have the opportunity to work together to design motivating and multiculturally appropriate curricula.

In other less global but no less important ways, the multicultural school would probably look vastly different as well. For example, the lunchroom might offer a variety of international meals, not because they are exotic delights but because they are the foods people in the community eat daily. Sports and games from all over the world might be played, and not all would be competitive. Letters would be sent home in the languages that parents understand. Children would not be punished for speaking their native language; on the contrary, they would be encouraged to do so and it would be used in their instruction as well. In summary, the school would be a learning environment in which curriculum, pedagogy, and outreach are all consistent with a broadly conceptualized multicultural philosophy.

Multicultural Education Is Education for Social Justice

All good education connects theory with reflection and action, which is what Paulo Freire defined as praxis.[12] Developing a multicultural perspective means learning how to think in more inclusive and expansive ways, reflecting on what we learn, and applying that learning to real situations. In this regard, John Dewey maintained that "information severed from thoughtful action is dead, a mind-crushing load."[13] Multicultural education invites students and teachers to put their learning into action for social justice. Whether debating a difficult issue, developing a community newspaper, starting a collaborative program at a local senior center, or organizing a petition for the removal of a potentially dangerous waste treatment plant in the neighborhood, students learn that they have power, collectively and individually, to make change.

This aspect of multicultural education fits in particularly well with the developmental level of young people who, starting in the middle elementary grades, are very conscious of what is fair and what is unfair. When their pronounced sense of justice is not channeled appropriately, the result can be anger, resentment, alienation, or dropping out of school physically or psychologically.

Preparing students for active membership in a democracy is the basis of Deweyan philosophy, and it has often been cited by schools as a major educational goal. But few schools serve as a site of apprenticeship for democracy. Policies and practices such as rigid ability grouping, inequitable testing, monocultural curricula, and unimaginative pedagogy mitigate against this lofty aim.

The result is that students in many schools perceive the claim of democracy to be a hollow and irrelevant issue. Henry Giroux, for example, has suggested that what he calls "the discourse of democracy" has been trivialized to mean such things as uncritical patriotism and mandatory pledges to the flag.[14] In some schools, democratic practices are found only in textbooks and confined to discussions of the American Revolution, but the chance for students to practice day-to-day democracy is minimal. Social justice becomes an empty concept in this situation.

The fact that power and inequality are rarely discussed in schools should come as no surprise. As institutions, schools are charged with maintaining the status quo, but they are also expected to wipe out inequality. Exposing the contradictions between democratic ideals and actual manifestations of inequality makes many people uncomfortable, and this includes educators. Still, such issues are at the heart of a broadly conceptualized multicultural perspective because the subject matter of schooling is society, with all its wrinkles and warts and contradictions. Ethics and the distribution of power, status, and rewards are basic societal concerns. Education must address them as well.

Although the connection of multicultural education with students' rights and responsibilities in a democracy is unmistakable, many young people do not learn about these responsibilities, the challenges of democracy, or the central role of citizens in ensuring and maintaining the privileges of democracy. Multicultural education can have a great impact in this respect. A multicultural perspective presumes that classrooms should not simply allow discussions that focus on social justice, but in fact welcome them. These discussions might center on concerns that affect culturally diverse communities—poverty, discrimination, war, the national budget and what students can do to change them. Because all of these concerns are pluralistic, education must of necessity be multicultural.

Multicultural Education Is a Process

Curriculum and materials represent the content of multicultural education, but multicultural education is above all a process. First, it is ongoing and dynamic. No one ever stops becoming a multicultural person, and knowledge is never complete. This means that there is no established canon that is frozen in cement. Second, multicultural education is a process because it involves primarily relationships among people. The sensitivity and understanding teachers show their students are more crucial in promoting student learning than the facts and figures they may know about different ethnic and cultural groups. Also, multicultural education is a process because it concerns such intangibles as expectations of student achievement, learning environments, students' learning preferences, and other cultural variables that are absolutely essential for schools to understand if they are to become successful with all students.

The dimension of multicultural education as a process is too often relegated to a secondary position, because content is easier to handle and has speedier results. For instance, developing an assembly program on Black History Month is easier than eliminating tracking. Changing a basal reader is easier than developing higher expectations for all students. The first involves changing one book for another; the other involves changing perceptions, behaviors, and knowledge, not an easy task. As a result, the processes of multicultural education are generally more complex, more politically volatile, and more threatening to vested interests than even controversial content.

Multicultural education must be accompanied by unlearning conventional wisdom as well as dismantling policies and practices that are disadvantageous for some students at the expense of others. Teacher education programs, for example, need to be reconceptualized to include awareness of the influence of culture and language on learning, the persistence of racism and discrimination in schools and society, and instructional and curricular strategies that encourage learning among a wide variety of students. Teachers' roles in the school also need to be redefined, because empowered teachers help to empower students. The role of families needs to be expanded so that the insights and values of the community can be more faithfully reflected in the school. Nothing short of a complete restructuring of curriculum and of the organization of schools is called for. The process is complex, problematic, controversial, and time consuming, but it is one in which teachers and schools must engage to make their schools truly multicultural.

Multicultural Education Is Critical Pedagogy

Knowledge is neither neutral nor apolitical, yet it is generally treated by teachers and schools as if it were. Consequently, school knowledge tends to reflect the lowest common denominator: that which is sure to offend the fewest (and the most powerful) and is least controversial. Students may leave school with the impression that all major conflicts have already been resolved. But history, including educational history, is full of great debates, controversies, and ideological struggles. These controversies and conflicts are often left at the schoolhouse door.

Every educational decision made at any level, whether by a teacher or by an entire school system, reflects the political ideology and worldview of the decision maker. Decisions to dismantle tracking, discontinue standardized tests, lengthen the school day, use one textbook rather than another, study the

Harlem Renaissance, or use learning centers rather than rows of chairs—all reflect a particular view of learners and of education.

As educators, all the decisions we make, no matter how neutral they may seem, have an impact on the lives and experiences of our students. This is true of the curriculum, books, and other materials we provide for them. State and local guidelines and mandates may limit what particular schools and teachers choose to teach, and this too is a political decision. What is excluded is often as telling as what is included. Much of the literature taught at the high school level, for instance, is still heavily male, European, and European American. The significance of women, people of color, and those who write in other languages is diminished, unintentionally or not.

A major problem with a monocultural curriculum is that it gives students only one way of seeing the world. When reality is presented as static, finished, and flat, the underlying tensions, controversies, passions, and problems faced by people throughout history and today disappear. But to be informed and active participants in a democratic society, students need to understand the complexity of the world and the many perspectives involved. Using a critical perspective, students learn that there is not just one way of seeing things, or even two or three. I use the number 17 facetiously to explain this: There are at least 17 ways of understanding reality, and until we have learned to do that, we have only part of the truth.

What do I mean by "17 ways of understanding reality"? I mean that there are multiple perspectives on every issue. But most of us have learned only the "safe" or standard way of interpreting events and issues. Textbooks in all subject areas exclude information about unpopular perspectives, or the perspectives of disempowered groups in our society. These are the "lies my teacher told me" to which James Loewen refers in his powerful critique of U.S. history textbooks.[15] For instance, there are few U.S. history texts that assume the perspective of working-class people, although they were and are the backbone of our country. Likewise, the immigrant experience is generally treated as a romantic and successful odyssey rather than the traumatic, wrenching, and often less-than-idyllic situation it was and continues to be for so many. The experiences of non-European immigrants or those forcibly incorporated into the United States are usually presented as if they were identical to the experiences of Europeans, which they have not at all been. We can also be sure that if the perspectives of women were taken seriously, the school curriculum would be altered dramatically. Unless all students develop the skill to see reality from multiple perspectives, not only the perspective of dominant groups, they will continue to think of it as linear and fixed and to think of themselves as passive in making any changes.

According to James Banks, the main goal of a multicultural curriculum is to help students develop decision-making and social action skills.[16] By doing so, students learn to view events and situations from a variety of perspectives. A multicultural approach values diversity and encourages critical thinking, reflection, and action. Through this process, students can be empowered as well. This is the basis of critical pedagogy. Its opposite is what Paulo Freire called "domesticating education," education that emphasizes passivity, acceptance, and submissiveness.[17] According to Freire, education for domestication is a process of "transferring knowledge," whereas education for liberation is one of "transforming action."[18] Liberating education encourages students to take risks, to be curious, and to question. Rather than expecting students to repeat teachers' words, it expects them to seek their own answers.

How are critical pedagogy and multicultural education connected? They are what Geneva Gay has called "mirror images."[19] That is, they work together, according to Christine Sleeter, as "a form of resistance to dominant modes of schooling."[20] Critical pedagogy acknowledges rather than suppresses cultural and linguistic diversity. It is not simply the transfer of knowledge from teacher to students, even though that knowledge may challenge what students had learned before. For instance, learning about the internment of Japanese Americans during World War II is not in itself critical pedagogy. It only becomes so when students critically analyze different perspectives and use them to understand and act on the inconsistencies they uncover.

A multicultural perspective does not simply operate on the principle of substituting one "truth" or perspective for another. Rather, it reflects on multiple and contradictory perspectives to understand reality more fully. In addition, it uses the understanding gained from reflection to make changes. Teachers and students sometimes need to learn to respect even those viewpoints with which they may disagree, not to teach what is "politically correct" but to have students develop a critical perspective about what they hear, read, or see.

Consider the hypothetical English literature book previously mentioned. Let us say that students and their teacher have decided to review the textbook to determine whether it fairly represents the voices and perspectives of a number of groups. Finding that it does not is in itself a valuable learning experience. But if nothing more is done with this analysis, it remains academic; it becomes more meaningful if used as the basis for further action. Ira Shor has proposed that critical pedagogy is more difficult precisely because it moves beyond academic discourse: "Testing the limits by practicing theory and theorizing practice in a real context is harder and more risky than theorizing theory without a context."[21] In this sense, critical pedagogy takes courage.

In the example of the English textbooks, students might propose that the English department order a more culturally inclusive anthology for the coming year. They might decide to put together their own book, based on literature with a variety of perspectives. Or they might decide to write a letter to the publisher with their suggestions. Critical pedagogy, however, does not mean that there is a linear process from knowledge to reflection to action. If this were the case, it would become yet another mechanistic strategy.

A few examples of how the typical curriculum discourages students from thinking critically, and what this has to do with a multicultural perspective, are in order. In most schools, students learn that Columbus discovered America; that the United States was involved in a heroic westward expansion until the twentieth century; that Puerto Ricans were granted U.S. citizenship in 1917; that enslaved Africans were freed by the Emancipation Proclamation in 1863; that the people who made our country great were the financial barons of the previous century; and if they learn anything about it at all, that Japanese Americans were housed in detention camps during World War II for security reasons.

History, as we know, is generally written by the conquerors, not by the vanquished or by those who benefit least in society. The result is history books skewed in the direction of dominant groups in a society. When American Indian people write history books, they generally say that Columbus invaded rather than discovered this land, and that there was no heroic westward expansion but rather an eastern encroachment. Mexican Americans often include references to Aztlan, the legendary land that was overrun by Europeans during this encroachment. Puerto Ricans usually remove the gratuitous word granted that appears in so many textbooks and explain that citizenship was instead imposed, and it was opposed by even the two houses of the legislature that existed in Puerto Rico in 1917. African Americans tend to describe the active participation of enslaved Africans in their own liberation, and they may include such accounts as slave narratives to describe the rebellion and resistance of their people. Working-class people who know their history usually credit laborers rather than Andrew Carnegie with building the country and the economy. And Japanese Americans frequently cite racist hysteria, economic exploitation, and propaganda as major reasons for their evacuation to concentration camps during World War II.

Critical pedagogy is also an exploder of myths. It helps to expose and demystify as well as demythologize some of the truths that we take for granted and to analyze them critically and carefully. Justice for all, equal treatment under the law, and equal educational opportunity, although certainly ideals worth believing in and striving for, are not always a reality. The problem is that we teach them as if they were always real, always true, with no exceptions. Critical pedagogy allows us to have faith in these ideals without uncritically accepting their reality.

Because critical pedagogy is based on the experiences and viewpoints of students, it is by its very nature multicultural. The most successful education is that which begins with the learner and, when using a multicultural perspective, students themselves become the foundation for the curriculum. But a liberating education also takes students beyond their own particular and therefore limited experiences, no matter what their background. . . .

Notes

1. See James A. Banks, "Multicultural Education: Historical Development, Dimensions, and Practice." In *Handbook of Research on Multicultural Education,* edited by James A. Banks and Cherry A. McGee Banks (New York: Macmillan, 1995).

2. Meyer Weinberg, "Notes from the Editor." *A Chronicle of Equal Education,* 4, 3 (November, 1982), 7.

3. Michelle Fine, *Framing dropouts: Notes on the politics of an urban public high school* (Albany, NY: State University of New York Press, 1991).

4. Jonathan Kozol, "Great Men and Women (Tailored for School Use)." *Learning Magazine* (December, 1975), 16–20.

5. Marilyn Cochran-Smith, "Uncertain allies: Understanding the boundaries of race and teaching." *Harvard Educational Review,* 65, 4 (Winter, 1995), 541–570.

6. Henry Giroux, "Rewriting the discourse of racial identity: Towards a pedagogy and politics of whiteness." *Harvard Educational Review,* 67, 2 (Summer, 1997), 285–320.

7. Beverly Daniel Tatum, *Why are all the black kids sitting together in the cafeteria? and other conversations about race* (New York: Basic Books, 1997).

8. Sandra M. Lawrence and Beverly Daniel Tatum, "Teachers in transition: The impact of antiracist professional development on classroom practice." *Teachers College Record,* 99, 1 (1997), 162–178.

9. For a discussion of different levels of curriculum integration in multicultural education, see James A. Banks, *Teaching strategies for ethnic studies,* 6th ed. (Boston: Allyn & Bacon, 1997).

10. Cathy A. Pohan and Norma J. Bailey, "Opening the closet: Multiculturalism that is truly inclusive." *Multicultural Education,* 5, 1 (Fall, 1997), 12–15.

11. A good example of how a multicultural approach can include educators, students, and families is found in *Teaching and learning in a diverse world: Multicultural education for young children,* 2nd ed., by Patricia G. Ramsey (New York: Teachers College Press, 1998).

12. Paulo Freire, *Pedagogy of the oppressed* (New York: Seabury Press, 1970).

13. John Dewey, *Democracy and education* (New York: Free Press, 1966; first published 1916), 153.

14. Henry A. Giroux, "Educational leadership and the crisis of democratic government." *Educational Researcher,* 21, 4 (May 1992), 4–11.

15. James W. Loewen, *Lies my teacher told me: Everything your American history textbook got wrong* (New York: New Press, 1995).

16. James A. Banks, *Teaching strategies for ethnic studies,* 6th ed. (Boston: Allyn & Bacon, 1997).

17. Paulo Freire, *The politics of education: Culture, power, and liberation* (South Hadley, MA: Bergin & Garvey, 1985).

18. Paulo Freire, *Pedagogy of the oppressed.*

19. Geneva Gay, "Mirror Images on Common Issues: Parallels Between Multicultural Education and Critical Pedagogy." In *Multicultural education, critical pedagogy, and the politics of difference,* edited by Christine E. Sleeter and Peter L. McLaren (Albany, NY: State University of New York Press, 1995), 155–189.

20. Christine E. Sleeter, *Multicultural education and social activism* (Albany, NY: State University of New York Press), 2.

21. Ira Shor, *When students have power: Negotiating authority in a critical pedagogy* (Chicago: University of Chicago Press, 1996), 3.

PART VI

Social Class and Education

Social class is an important topic that is often ignored in American education. Sociologists define social class as social distinctions based on the unequal distribution of wealth, power, and prestige. Social class is much more visible in other cultures than it is in the United States. Because of the democratic traditions in the United States, it is assumed that social class is less of an issue here than it is in a country such as Great Britain or France.

In fact, as the selections included in this section demonstrate, social class is very much at work in American culture, providing privilege and resources to some, while denying the same advantages to others. How social class works in the educational system in the United States is a particularly interesting topic.

As you read the following selections, keep in mind these questions:

1. How does one get assigned to a social class (working class, middle class, elite class)?
2. How does one move from one social class to another?
3. What types of power does one gain from belonging to a specific social class?
4. Do different social classes define personal success differently?

29

Selection From Pygmalion in the Classroom *(1968)*

In the late 1960s, Robert Rosenthal and Lenore Jacobson made a very important discovery about teaching. They called it the "Pygmalion Effect." Simply stated, the Pygmalion Effect says that when teachers have high expectations of their students in terms of intellectual growth and achievement, the students tend to fulfill the expectations they are given. When they are not encouraged or seen as having potential, then students tend, in turn, to perform at a lower level.

Rosenthal and Jacobson's research points to the importance of teachers not entering the classroom with preconceived notions and prejudices, which may cause them to expect less of their students than what they can actually do. Such attitudes not only affect student performance but are inherently unfair and discriminatory.

As you read the following selection, consider the following questions:

1. How do I deal with people who are the same or different than I along dimensions of race, ethnicity, religion, and social class? Whom am I more comfortable with and why?
2. If I teach, how will I approach students who are culturally and socially different from myself?

29

Selection From Pygmalion in the Classroom *(1968)*

Robert Rosenthal and Lenore Jacobson

People, more often than not, do what is expected of them. Much of our behavior is governed by widely shared norms or expectations that make it possible to prophesy how a person will behave in a given situation, even if we have never met that person and know little of how he differs from others. At the same time, however, there is considerable variability of behavior so that often we can more accurately prophesy the behavior of a person we know well than we can prophesy the behavior of a stranger. To a great extent, our expectations for another person's behavior are accurate because we know his past behavior. But there is now good reason to believe that another factor increases our accuracy of interpersonal predictions or prophecies. Our prediction or prophecy may in itself be a factor in determining the behavior of other people. When we are led to expect that we are about to meet a pleasant person, our treatment of him at first meeting may, in fact, make him a more pleasant person. If we are led to expect that we shall encounter an unpleasant person, we may approach him so defensively that we make him into an unpleasant person. That, in general, is the concern of this selection. It is about interpersonal self-fulfilling prophecies: how one person's expectation for another person's behavior can quite unwittingly become a more accurate prediction simply for its having been made.

The existing evidence for the effects of these interpersonal self-fulfilling prophecies will be summarized and, in greater detail, new evidence will be

---

Source: Rosenthal, Robert, and Lenore Jacobson. 1968. *Pygmalion in the Classroom*, vii–viii, 180–182. New York: Holt, Rinehart and Winston.

presented. This new evidence is from an educational context, and it is addressed to the question of whether a teacher's expectation for her pupils' intellectual competence can come to serve as an educational self-fulfilling prophecy.

To anticipate briefly the nature of this new evidence it is enough to say that 20 percent of the children in a certain elementary school were reported to their teachers as showing unusual potential for intellectual growth. The names of these 20 percent of the children were drawn by means of a table of random numbers, which is to say that the names were drawn out of a hat. Eight months later these unusual or "magic" children showed significantly greater gains in IQ than did the remaining children who had not been singled out for the teachers' attention. The change in the teachers' expectations regarding the intellectual performance of these allegedly "special" children had led to an actual change in the intellectual performance of these randomly selected children.

There are many determinants of a teacher's expectation of her pupils' intellectual ability. Even before a teacher has seen a pupil deal with academic tasks she is likely to have some expectation for his behavior. If she is to teach a "slow group," or children of darker skin color, or children whose mothers are "on welfare," she will have different expectations for her pupils' performance than if she is to teach a "fast group," or children of an upper-middle-class community. Before she has seen a child perform, she may have seen his score on an achievement or ability test or his last year's grades, or she may have access to the less formal information that constitutes the child's reputation. There have been theoretical formulations, and there has been some evidence, most of it anecdotal, that the teacher's expectation, however derived, can come to serve as an educational self-fulfilling prophecy. After a consideration of the new experimental evidence bearing on these formulations, the implications for educational research and practice will be considered.

* * *

On the basis of other experiments on interpersonal self-fulfilling prophecies, we can only speculate as to how teachers brought about intellectual competence simply by expecting it. Teachers may have treated their children in a more pleasant, friendly, and encouraging fashion when they expected greater intellectual gains of them. Such behavior has been shown to improve intellectual performance, probably by its favorable effect on pupil motivation.

Teachers probably watched their special children more closely, and this greater attentiveness may have led to more rapid reinforcement of correct responses with a consequent increase in pupils' learning. Teachers may also have become more reflective in their evaluation of the special children's intellectual performance. Such an increase in teachers' reflectiveness may have led to an increase in their special pupils' reflectiveness, and such a change in cognitive style would be helpful to the performance of the nonverbal skills required by the IQ test employed.

To summarize our speculations, we may say that by what she said, by how and when she said it, by her facial expressions, postures, and perhaps by her touch, the teacher may have communicated to the children of the experimental group that she expected improved intellectual performance. Such communications together with possible changes in teaching techniques may have helped the child learn by changing his self-concept, his expectations of his own behavior, and his motivation, as well as his cognitive style and skills.

It is self-evident that further research is needed to narrow down the range of possible mechanisms whereby a teacher's expectations become translated into a pupil's intellectual growth. It would be valuable, for example, to have sound films of teachers interacting with their pupils. We might then look for differences in the way teachers interact with those children from whom they expect intellectual growth compared to those from whom they expect less. On the basis of films of psychological experimenters interacting with subjects from whom different responses are expected, we know that even in such highly standardized situations, unintentional communications can be incredibly subtle and complex (Rosenthal, 1966). Much more subtle and much more complex may be the communications between children and their teachers, teachers not constrained by the demands of the experimental laboratory to treat everyone equally to the extent that it is possible to do so.

The implications of the research described herein are of several kinds. There are methodological implications for the conduct of educational research, and these were discussed in the last chapter. There are implications for the further investigation of unintentional influence processes especially when these processes result in inter-personally self-fulfilling prophecies, and some of these have been discussed. Finally, there are some possible implications for the educational enterprise, and some of these will be suggested briefly.

Over time, our educational policy question has changed from "who ought to be educated?" to "who is capable of being educated?" The ethical question has been traded in for the scientific question. For those children whose educability is in doubt there is a label. They are the educationally, or culturally, or socioeconomically, deprived children and, as things stand now, they appear not to be able to learn as do those who are more advantaged. The advantaged and the disadvantaged differ in parental income, in parental values, in scores on various tests of achievement and ability, and often in skin color and other phenotypic expressions of genetic heritage. Quite inseparable from these differences between the advantages and the disadvantaged are the differences in their teachers' expectations for what they can achieve in school. There are no experiments to show that a change in pupils' skin color will lead to improved intellectual performance. There is, however, the experiment described in this book to show that change in teacher expectation can lead to improved intellectual performance.

Nothing was done directly for the disadvantaged child at Oak School. There was no crash program to improve his reading ability, no special lesson plan, no extra time for tutoring, no trips to museums or art galleries. There was only the belief that the children bore watching, that they had intellectual competencies that would in due course be revealed. What was done in our program of educational change was done directly for the teacher, only indirectly for her pupils. Perhaps, then, it is the teacher to whom we should direct more of our research attention. If we could learn how she is able to effect dramatic improvement in her pupils' competence without formal changes in her teaching methods, then we could teach other teachers to do the same. If further research shows that it is possible to select teachers whose untrained interactional style does for most of her pupils what our teachers did for the special children, it may be possible to combine sophisticated teacher selection and placement with teacher training to optimize the learning of all pupils.

As teacher-training institutions begin to teach the possibility that teachers' expectations of their pupils' performance may serve as self-fulfilling prophecies, there may be a new expectancy created. The new expectancy may be that children can learn more than had been believed possible, an expectation held by many educational theorists, though for quite different reasons (for example, Bruner, 1960). The new expectancy, at the very least, will make it more difficult when they encounter the educationally disadvantaged for teachers to think, "Well, after all, what can you expect?" The man on the street may be permitted his opinions and prophecies of the unkempt children loitering in a dreary schoolyard. The teacher in the schoolroom may need to learn that those same prophecies within her may be fulfilled; she is no casual passer-by. Perhaps Pygmalion in the classroom is more her role.

References

Bruner, J. S. (1960). *The process of education.* Cambridge, MA: Harvard University Press.
Rosenthal, R. (1966). *Experimenter effects in behavioral research.* New York: Appleton.

30

"Social Class and the Hidden Curriculum of Work" (1980)

Jean Anyon is a political economist and educational theorist who studies issues of social class in schools. The following selection, first published as an article in the *Journal of Education*, examines social class as an issue in five different elementary school settings. Her research reveals that there is a hidden curriculum at work, based on the social economics of the school, which determines not only what is taught to students but how it is taught. In addition, she demonstrates that students are tracked into different job and career paths based on the schools they attend.

As you read this piece, consider the following questions:

1. How do Anyon's findings challenge the myth that public schools in the United States provide equal education for all students?
2. How is it determined which schools provide which types of education for their students?
3. Can you think of examples of socioeconomic class issues at work in your personal experience in schools? Are socioeconomic class issues at work in the college or university that you attend?

30

"Social Class and the Hidden Curriculum of Work" (1980)

Jean Anyon

Scholars in political economy and the sociology of knowledge recently argued that public schools in complex industrial societies like our own make available different types of educational experience and curriculum knowledge to students in different social classes. Bowles and Gintis,[1] for example, have argued that students in different social-class backgrounds are rewarded for classroom behaviors that correspond to personality traits allegedly rewarded in the different occupational strata—the working classes for docility and obedience, the managerial classes for initiative and personal assertiveness. Basil Bernstein, Pierre Bourdieu, and Michael W. Apple,[2] focusing on school knowledge, have argued that knowledge and skills leading to social power and regard (medical, legal, managerial) are made available to the advantaged social groups but are withheld from the working classes, to whom a more "practical" curriculum is offered (manual skills, clerical knowledge). While there has been considerable argumentation of these points regarding education in England, France, and North America, there has been little or no attempt to investigate these ideas empirically in elementary or secondary schools and classrooms in this country.[3]

This article offers tentative empirical support (and qualification) of the above arguments by providing illustrative examples of differences in student work in classrooms in contrasting social class communities. The examples were gathered as part of an ethnographical[4] study of curricular, pedagogical, and

Source: Anyon, Jean. 1980. "Social Class and the Hidden Curriculum of Work." *Journal of Education*, 162 (1): 67–92.

pupil evaluation practices in five elementary schools. The article attempts a theoretical contribution as well and assesses student work in the light of a theoretical approach to social-class analysis. . . . It will be suggested that there is a "hidden curriculum" in schoolwork that has profound implications for the theory and consequence of everyday activity in education. . . .

The social-class designation of each of the five schools will be identified, and the income, occupation, and other relevant available social characteristics of the students and their parents will be described. The first three schools are in a medium-sized city district in northern New Jersey, and the other two are in a nearby New Jersey suburb.

The first two schools I will call working-class schools. Most of the parents have blue-collar jobs. Less than a third of the fathers are skilled, while the majority are in unskilled or semiskilled jobs. During the period of the study (1978–1979), approximately 15 percent of the fathers were unemployed. The large majority (85 percent) of the families are white. The following occupations are typical: platform, storeroom, and stockroom workers; foundrymen, pipe welders, and boilermakers; semiskilled and unskilled assembly-line operatives; gas station attendants, auto mechanics, maintenance workers, and security guards. Less than 30 percent of the women work, some part-time and some full-time, on assembly lines, in storerooms and stockrooms, as waitresses, barmaids, or sales clerks. Of the fifth-grade parents, none of the wives of the skilled workers had jobs. Approximately 15 percent of the families in each school are at or below the federal "poverty" level;[5] most of the rest of the family incomes are at or below $12,000, except some of the skilled workers whose incomes are higher. The incomes of the majority of the families in these two schools (at or below $12,000) are typical of 38.6 percent of the families in the United States.[6]

The third school is called the middle-class school, although because of neighborhood residence patterns, the population is a mixture of several social classes. The parents' occupations can be divided into three groups: a small group of blue-collar "rich," who are skilled, well-paid workers such as printers, carpenters, plumbers, and construction workers. The second group is composed of parents in working-class and middle-class white-collar jobs: women in office jobs, technicians, supervisors in industry, and parents employed by the city (such as firemen, policemen, and several of the school's teachers). The third group is composed of occupations such as personnel directors in local firms, accountants, "middle management," and a few small capitalists (owners of shops in the area). The children of several local doctors attend this school. Most family incomes are between $13,000 and $25,000, with a few higher. This income range is typical of 38.9 percent of the families in the United States.[7]

The fourth school has a parent population that is at the upper income level of the upper middle class and is predominantly professional. This school will be called the affluent professional school. Typical jobs are: cardiologist, interior designer, corporate lawyer or engineer, executive in advertising or television. There are some families who are not as affluent as the majority (the family of the superintendent of the district's schools, and the one or two families in which the fathers are skilled workers). In addition, a few of the families are more affluent than the majority and can be classified in the capitalist class (a partner in a prestigious Wall Street stock brokerage firm). Approximately 90 percent of the children in this school are white. Most family incomes are between $40,000 and $80,000. This income span represents approximately 7 percent of the families in the United States.[8]

In the fifth school the majority of the families belong to the capitalist class. This school will be called the executive elite school because most of the fathers are top executives (for example, presidents and vice-presidents) in major United States-based multinational corporations, for example, ATT, RCA, City Bank, American Express, U.S. Steel. A sizable group of fathers are top executives in financial firms in Wall Street. There are also a number of fathers who list their occupations as "general counsel" to a particular corporation, and these corporations are also among the large multinationals. Many of the mothers do volunteer work in the Junior League, Junior Fortnightly, or other service groups; some are intricately involved in town politics; and some are themselves in well-paid occupations. There are no minority children in the school. Almost all the family incomes are over $100,000, with some in the $500,000 range. The incomes in this school represent less than 1 percent of the families in the United States.[9]

Since each of the five schools is only one instance of elementary education in a particular social class context, I will not generalize beyond the sample. However, the examples of schoolwork which follow will suggest characteristics of education in each social setting that appear to have theoretical and social significance and to be worth investigation in a larger number of schools.

The Working-Class Schools

In the two working-class schools, work is following the steps of a procedure. The procedure is usually mechanical, involving rote behavior and very little decision making or choice. The teachers rarely explain why the work is being assigned, how it might connect to other assignments, or what the idea is that lies behind the procedure or gives it coherence and perhaps meaning or significance. Available textbooks are not always used, and the teachers often prepare their own dittos or put work examples on the board. Most of the rules regarding work are designations of what the children are to do; the rules are steps to follow. These steps are told to the children by the teachers and are often written on the board. The children are usually told to copy the steps as notes. These notes are to be studied. Work is often evaluated not according to whether it is right or wrong but according to whether the children followed the right steps.

The following examples illustrate these points. In math, when two-digit division was introduced, the teacher in one school gave a four-minute lecture on what the terms are called (which number is the division, dividend, quotient, and remainder). The children were told to copy these names in their notebooks. Then the teacher told them the steps to follow to do the problems, saying, "This is how you do them." The teacher listed the steps on the board, and they appeared several days later as a chart hung in the middle of the front wall: "Divide, Multiply, Subtract, Bring Down." The children often did examples of two-digit division. When the teacher went over the examples with them, he told them what the procedure was for each problem, rarely asking them to conceptualize or explain it themselves: "Three into twenty-two is seven; do your subtraction and one is left over." During the week that two-digit division was introduced (or at any other time), the investigator did not observe any discussion of the idea of grouping involved in division, any use of manipulables, or any attempt to relate two-digit division to any other mathematical process. Nor was there any attempt to relate the steps to an actual or possible thought process of the children. The observer did not hear the terms dividend, quotient, and so on, used again. The math teacher in the other working-class school followed similar procedures regarding two-digit division and at one point her class seemed confused. She said, "You're confusing yourselves. You're tensing up. Remember, when you do this, it's the same steps over and over again—and that's the way division always is." Several weeks later, after a test, a group of her children "still didn't get it," and she made no attempt to explain the concept of dividing things into groups or to give them manipulables for their own investigation. Rather, she went over the steps with them again and told them that they "needed more practice."

In other areas of math, work is also carrying out often unexplained fragmented procedures. For example, one of the teachers led the children through a series of steps to make a 1-inch grid on their paper without telling them that they were making a 1-inch grid or that it would be used to study scale. She said, "Take your ruler. Put it across the top. Make a mark at every number. Then move your ruler down to the bottom. No, put it across the bottom. Now make a mark on top of every number. Now draw a line from . . ." At this point a girl said that she had a faster way to do it and the teacher said, "No, you don't; you don't even know what I'm making yet. Do it this way or it's wrong." After they had made the lines up and down and across, the teacher told them she wanted them to make a figure by connecting some dots and to measure that, using the scale of 1 inch equals 1 mile. Then they were to cut it out. She said, "Don't cut it until I check it."

In both working-class schools, work in language arts is mechanics of punctuation (commas, periods, question marks, exclamation points), capitalization, and the four kinds of sentences. One teacher explained to me, "Simple punctuation is all they'll ever use." Regarding punctuation, either a teacher or a ditto stated the rules for where, for example, to put commas. The investigator heard no classroom discussion of the aural context of punctuation (which, of course, is what gives each mark its meaning). Nor did the investigator hear any statement or inference that placing a punctuation mark could be a decision-making process, depending, for example, on one's intended meaning. Rather, the children were told to follow the rules. Language arts did not involve creative writing. There were several writing assignments throughout the year, but in each instance the children were given a ditto, and they wrote answers to questions on the sheet. For example, they wrote their "autobiography" by answering such questions as "Where were you born?" "What is your favorite animal?" on a sheet entitled "All About Me."

In one of the working-class schools, the class had a science period several times a week. On the three occasions observed, the children were not called upon to set up experiments or to give explanations for facts or concepts. Rather, on each occasion the teacher told them in his own words what the book said. The children copied the teacher's sentences from the board. Each day that preceded the day they were to do a science experiment, the teacher told them to copy the directions from the book for the procedure they would carry out the next day and to study the list at home that night. The day after each experiment, the teacher went over what they had "found" (they did the experiments as a class, and each was actually a class demonstration led by the teacher). Then the teacher wrote what they "found" on the board, and the children copied that in their notebooks. Once or twice a year there are science projects. The project is chosen and assigned by the teacher from a box of 3-by-5-inch cards. On the card the teacher has written the question to be answered, the books to use, and how much to write. Explaining the cards to the observer, the teacher said, "It tells them exactly what to do, or they couldn't do it."

Social studies in the working-class schools is also largely mechanical, rote work that was given little explanation or connection to larger contexts. In one school, for example, although there was a book available, social studies work was to copy the teacher's notes from the board. Several times a week for a period of several months the children copied these notes. The fifth grades in the district were to study United States history. The teacher used a booklet she had purchased called "The Fabulous Fifty States." Each day she put information from the booklet in outline form on the board and the children copied it. The type of information did not vary: the name of the state, its abbreviation, state capital, nickname of the state, its main products, main business, and a "Fabulous Fact" ("Idaho grew twenty-seven billion potatoes in one year. That's enough potatoes for each man, woman, and . . .). As the children finished copying the sentences, the teacher erased them and wrote more. Children would occasionally go to the front to pull down the wall map in order to locate the states they were copying, and the teacher did not dissuade them. But the observer never saw her refer to the map; nor did the observer ever hear her make other than perfunctory remarks concerning the information the children were copying. Occasionally the children colored in a ditto and cut it out to make a stand-up figure (representing, for example, a man roping a cow in the Southwest). These were referred to by the teacher as their social studies "projects."

Rote behavior was often called for in classroom work. When going over math and language art skills sheets, for example, as the teacher asked for the answer to each problem, he fired the questions rapidly, staccato, and the scene reminded the observer of a sergeant drilling recruits: above all, the questions demanded that you stay at attention: "The next one? What do I put here?. . . . Here? Give us the next." Or "How many commas in this sentence? Where do I put them. . . . The next one?"

The four fifth-grade teachers observed in the working-class schools attempted to control classroom time and space by making decisions without consulting the children and without explaining the basis for their decisions. The teacher's control thus often seemed capricious. Teachers, for instance, very often ignored the bells to switch classes—deciding among themselves to keep the children after the period was officially over to continue with the work or for disciplinary reasons or so they (the teachers) could stand in the hall and talk. There were no clocks in the rooms in either school, and the children often asked, "What period is this?" "When do we go to gym?" The children had no access to materials. These were handed out by teachers and closely guarded. Things in the room "belonged" to the teacher: "Bob, bring me my garbage can." The teachers continually gave the children orders. Only three times did the investigator hear a teacher in either working-class school preface a directive with an unsarcastic "please," or "let's" or "would you." Instead, the teachers said, "Shut up," "Shut your mouth," "Open your books," "Throw your gum away—if you want to rot your teeth, do it on your own time." Teachers made every effort to control the movement of the children, and often shouted, "Why are you out of your seat??!" If the children got permission to leave the room, they had to take a written pass with the date and time.

Middle-Class School

In the middle-class school, work is getting the right answer. If one accumulates enough right answers, one gets a good grade. One must follow the directions in order to get the right answers, but the directions often call for some figuring, some choice, some decision making. For example, the children must often figure out by themselves what the directions ask them to do and how to get the answer: what do you do first, second, and perhaps third? Answers are usually found in books or by listening to the teacher. Answers are usually words, sentences, numbers, or facts and dates; one writes them on paper, and one should be neat. Answers must be given in the right order, and one cannot make them up.

The following activities are illustrative. Math involves some choice: one may do two-digit division the long way or the short way, and there are some math problems that can be done "in your head." When the teacher explains how to do two-digit division, there is recognition that a cognitive process is involved; she gives you several ways and says, "I want to make sure you understand what you're doing so you get it right"; and, when they go over the homework, she asks the children to tell how they did the problem and what answer they got.

In social studies the daily work is to read the assigned pages in the textbook and to answer the teacher's questions. The questions are almost always designed to check on whether the students have read the assignment and understood it: who did so-and-so; what happened after that; when did it happen, where, and sometimes, why did it happen? The answers are in the book and in one's understanding of the book; the teacher's hints when one doesn't know the answers are to "read it again" or to look at the picture or at the rest of the paragraph. One is to search for the answer in the "context," in what is given.

Language arts is "simple grammar, what they need for everyday life." The language arts teacher says, "They should learn to speak properly, to write business letters and thank-you letters, and to understand what nouns and verbs and simple subjects are." Here, as well, actual work is to choose the right answers, to understand what is given. The teacher often says, "Please read the next sentence and then I'll question you about it." One teacher said in some exasperation to a boy who was fooling around in class, "If you don't know the answers to the questions I ask, then you can't stay in this class! You never know the answers to the questions I ask, and it's not fair to me—and certainly not to you!"

Most lessons are based on the textbook. This does not involve a critical perspective on what is given there. For example, a critical perspective in social studies is perceived as dangerous by these teachers because it may lead to controversial topics; the parents might complain. The children, however, are often curious, especially in social studies. Their questions are tolerated and usually answered perfunctorily. But after a few minutes the teacher will say, "All right, we're not going any farther. Please open your social studies workbook." While the teachers spend a lot of time explaining and expanding on what the textbooks say, there is little attempt to analyze how or why things happen, or to give thought to how pieces of a culture, or, say, a system of numbers or elements of a language fit together or can be analyzed. What has happened in the past and what exists now may not be equitable or fair, but (shrug) that is the way things are and one does not confront such matters in school. For example, in social studies after a child is called on to read a passage about the pilgrims, the teacher summarizes the paragraph and then says, "So you can see how strict they were about everything." A child asks, "Why?" "Well, because they felt that if you weren't busy you'd get into trouble." Another child asks, "Is it true that they burned women at the stake?" The teacher says, "Yes, if a woman did anything strange, they hanged them. [sic] What would a woman do, do you think, to make them burn them? [sic] See if you can come up with better answers than my other [social studies] class." Several children offer suggestions, to which the teacher nods but does not comment. Then she says, "Okay, good," and calls on the next child to read.

Work tasks do not usually request creativity. Serious attention is rarely given in school work on how the children develop or express their own feelings and ideas, either linguistically or in graphic form. On the occasions when creativity or self-expression is requested, it is peripheral to the main activity or it is "enrichment" or "for fun." During a lesson on what similes are, for example, the teacher explains what they are, puts several on the board, gives some other examples herself, and then asks the children if they can "make some up." She calls on three children who give similes, two of which are actually in the book they have open before them. The teacher does not comment on this and then asks several others to choose similes from the list of phrases in the book. Several do so correctly, and she says, "Oh good! You're picking them out! See how good we are?" Their homework is to pick out the rest of the similes from the list.

Creativity is not often requested in social studies and science projects, either. Social studies projects, for example, are given with directions to "find information on your topic" and write it up. The children are not supposed to copy but to "put it in your own words." Although a number of the projects subsequently went beyond the teacher's direction to find information and had quite expressive covers and inside illustrations, the teacher's evaluative comments had to do with the amount of information, whether they had "copied," and if their work was neat.

The style of control of the three fifth-grade teachers observed in this school varied from somewhat easygoing to strict, but in contrast to the working-class schools, the teachers' decisions were usually based on external rules and regulations, for example, on criteria that were known or available to the children. Thus, the teachers always honor the bells for changing classes, and they usually evaluate children's work by what is in the textbooks and answer booklets.

There is little excitement in schoolwork for the children, and the assignments are perceived as having little to do with their interests and feelings. As one child said, what you do is "store facts up in your head like cold storage until you need it later for a test or your job." Thus, doing well is important because there are thought to be other likely rewards: a good job or college.[10]

Affluent Professional School

In the affluent professional school, work is creative activity carried out independently. The students are continually asked to express and apply ideas and concepts. Work involves individual thought and expressiveness, expansion and illustration of ideas, and choice of appropriate method and material. (The class is not considered an open classroom, and the principal explained that because of the large number of discipline problems in the fifth grade this year they did not departmentalize. The teacher who agreed to take part in the study said she is "more structured" this year than she usually is.) The products of work in this class are often written stories, editorials and essays, or representations of ideas in mural, graph, or craft form. The products of work should not be like everybody else's and should show individuality. They should exhibit good design, and (this is important) they must also fit empirical reality. Moreover, one's work should attempt to interpret or "make sense" of reality. The relatively few rules to be followed regarding work are usually criteria for, or limits on, individual activity. One's product is usually evaluated for the quality of its expression and for the appropriateness of its conception to the task. In many cases, one's own satisfaction with the product is an important criterion for its evaluation. When right answers are called for, as in commercial materials like SRA (Science Research Associates) and math, it is important that the children decide on an answer as a result of thinking about the idea involved in what they're being asked to do. Teacher's hints are to "think about it some more."

The following activities are illustrative. The class takes home a sheet requesting each child's parents to fill in the number of cars they have, the number of television sets, refrigerators, games, or rooms in the house, and so on. Each child is to figure the average number of a type of possession owned by the fifth grade. Each child must compile the "data" from all the sheets. A calculator is available in the classroom to do the mechanics of finding the average. Some children decide to send sheets to the fourth-grade families for comparison. Their work should be "verified" by a classmate before it is handed in.

Each child and his or her family has made a geoboard. The teacher asks the class to get their geoboards from the side cabinet, to take a handful of rubber bands, and then to listen to what she would like them to do. She says, "I would like you to design a figure and then find the perimeter and area. When you have it, check with your neighbor. After you've done that, please transfer it to graph paper and tomorrow I'll ask you to make up a question about it for someone. When you hand it in, please let me know whose it is and who verified it. Then I have something else for you to do that's really fun. [pause] Find the average number of chocolate chips in three cookies. I'll give you three cookies, and you'll have to eat your way through, I'm afraid!" Then she goes around the room and gives help, suggestions, praise, and admonitions that they are getting noisy. They work sitting, or standing up at their desks, at benches in the back, or on the floor. A child hands the teacher his paper and she comments, "I'm not accepting this paper. Do a better design." To another child she says, "That's fantastic! But you'll never find the area. Why don't you draw a figure inside [the big one] and subtract to get the area?"

The school district requires the fifth grade to study ancient civilization (in particular, Egypt, Athens, and Sumer). In this classroom, the emphasis is on illustrating and re-creating the culture of the people of ancient times. The following are typical activities: the children made an 8mm film on Egypt, which one of the parents edited. A girl in the class wrote the script, and the class acted it out. They put the sound on themselves. They read stories of those days. They wrote essays and stories depicting the lives of the people and the societal and occupational divisions. They chose from a list of projects, all of which involved graphic representations of ideas: for example, "Make a mural depicting the division of labor in Egyptian society."

Each child wrote and exchanged a letter in hieroglyphics with a fifth grader in another class, and they also exchanged stories they wrote in cuneiform. They made a scroll and singed the edges so it looked authentic. They each chose an occupation and made an Egyptian plaque representing that occupation, simulating the appropriate Egyptian design. They carved their design on a cylinder of wax, pressed the wax into clay, and then baked the clay. Although one girl did not choose an occupation but carved instead a series of gods and slaves, the teacher said, "That's all right, Amber, it's beautiful." As they were working the teacher said, "Don't cut into your clay until you're satisfied with your design."

Social studies also involves almost daily presentation by the children of some event from the news. The teacher's questions ask the children to expand what they say, to give more details, and to be more specific. Occasionally she adds some remarks to help them see connections between events.

The emphasis on expressing and illustrating ideas in social studies is accompanied in language arts by an emphasis on creative writing. Each child wrote a rhebus story for a first grader whom they had interviewed to see what kind of story the child liked best. They wrote editorials on pending decisions by the school board and radio plays, some of which were read over the school intercom from the office and one of which was performed in the auditorium. There is no language arts textbook because, the teacher said, "The principal wants us to be creative." There is not much grammar, but there is punctuation. One morning when the observer arrived, the class was doing a punctuation ditto. The teacher later apologized for using the ditto. "It's just for review," she said. "I don't teach punctuation that way. We use their language." The ditto had three unambiguous rules for where to put commas in a sentence. As the teacher was going around to help the children with the ditto, she repeated several times, "Where you put commas depends on how you say the sentence; it depends on the situation and what you want to say." Several weeks later the observer saw another punctuation activity. The teacher had printed a five-paragraph story on an oak tag and then cut it into phrases. She read the whole story to the class from the book, then passed out the phrases. The group had to decide how the phrases could best be put together again. (They arranged the phrases on the floor.) The point was not to replicate the story, although that was not irrelevant, but to "decide what you think the best way is." Punctuation marks on cardboard pieces were then handed out, and the children discussed and then decided what mark was best at each place they thought one was needed. At the end of each paragraph the teacher asked, "Are you satisfied with the way the paragraphs are now? Read it to yourself and see how it sounds." Then she read the original story again, and they compared the two.

Describing her goals in science to the investigator, the teacher said, "We use ESS (Elementary Science Study). It's very good because it gives a hands-on-experience—so they can make sense out of it. It doesn't matter whether it [what they find] is right or wrong. I bring them together and there's value in discussing their ideas."

The products of work in this class are often highly valued by the children and the teacher. In fact, this was the only school in which the investigator was not allowed to take original pieces of the children's work for her files. If the work was small enough, however, and was on paper, the investigator could duplicate it on the copying machine in the office.

The teacher's attempt to control the class involves constant negotiation. She does not give direct orders unless she is angry because the children have been too noisy. Normally, she tries to get them to foresee the consequences of their actions and to decide accordingly. For example, lining them up to go see a play written by the sixth graders, she says, "I presume you're lined up by someone with whom you want to sit. I hope you're lined up by someone you won't get in trouble with."

One of the few rules governing the children's movement is that no more than three children may be out of the room at once. There is a school rule that anyone can go to the library at any time to get a book. In the fifth grade I observed, they sign their name on the chalkboard and leave. There are no passes. Finally, the children have a fair amount of officially sanctioned say over what happens in the class. For example, they often negotiate what work is to be done. If the teacher wants to move on to the next subject, but the children say they are not ready, they want to work on their present projects some more, she very often lets them do it.

Executive Elite School

In the executive elite school, work is developing one's analytical intellectual powers. Children are continually asked to reason through a problem, to produce intellectual products that are both logically sound and of top academic quality. A primary goal of thought is to conceptualize rules by which elements may fit together in systems and then to apply these rules in solving a problem. Schoolwork helps one to achieve, to excel, to prepare for life.

The following are illustrative. The math teacher teaches area and perimeter by having the children derive formulas for each. First she helps them, through discussion at the board, to arrive at $A = W \times L$ as a formula (not the formula) for area. After discussing several, she says, "Can anyone make up a formula for perimeter? Can you figure that out yourselves? [pause] Knowing what we know, can we think of a formula?" She works out three children's suggestions at the board, saying to two, "Yes, that's a good one," and then asks the class if they can think of any more. No one volunteers. To prod them, she says, "If you use rules and good reasoning, you get many ways. Chris, can you think up a formula?"

She discusses two-digit division with the children as a decision-making process. Presenting a new type of problem to them, she asks, "What's the first decision you'd make if presented with this kind of example? What is the first thing you'd think? Craig?" Craig says, "To find my first partial quotient." She responds, "Yes, that would be your first decision. How would you do that?" Craig explains, and then the teacher says, "OK, we'll see how that works for you." The class tries his way. Subsequently, she comments on the merits and shortcomings of several other children's decisions. Later, she tells the investigator that her goals in math are to develop their reasoning and mathematical thinking and that, unfortunately, "there's no time for manipulables."

While right answers are important in math, they are not "given" by the book or by the teacher but may be challenged by the children.

Going over some problems in late September the teacher says, "Raise your hand if you do not agree." A child says, "I don't agree with sixty-four." The teacher responds, "OK, there's a question about sixty-four. [to class] Please check it. Owen, they're disagreeing with you. Kristen, they're checking yours." The teacher emphasized this repeatedly during September and October with statements like, "Don't be afraid to say you disagree. In the last [math] class, somebody disagreed, and they were right. Before you disagree, check yours, and if you still think we're wrong, then we'll check it out." By Thanksgiving, the children did not often speak in terms of right and wrong math problems but of whether they agreed with the answer that had been given.

There are complicated math mimeos with many word problems. Whenever they go over the examples, they discuss how each child has set up the problem. The children must explain it precisely. On one occasion the teacher said, "I'm more—just as interested in how you set up the problem as in what answer you find. If you set up a problem in a good way, the answer is easy to find."

Social studies work is most often reading and discussion of concepts and independent research. There are only occasional artistic, expressive, or illustrative projects. Ancient Athens and Sumer are, rather, societies to analyze. The following questions are typical of those that guide the children's independent research. "What mistakes did Pericles make after the war?" "What mistakes did the citizens of Athens make?" "What are the elements of a civilization?" "How did Greece build an economic empire?" "Compare the way Athens chose its leaders with the way we choose ours." Occasionally the children are asked to make up sample questions for their social studies tests. On an occasion when the investigator was present, the social studies teacher rejected a child's question by saying, "That's just fact. If I asked you that question on a test, you'd complain it was just memory! Good questions ask for concepts."

In social studies—but also in reading, science, and health—the teachers initiate classroom discussions of current social issues and problems. These discussions occurred on every one of the investigator's visits, and a teacher told me, "These children's opinions are important—it's important that they learn to reason things through." The classroom discussions always struck the observer as quite realistic and analytical, dealing with concrete social issues like the following: "Why do workers strike?" "Is that right or wrong?" "Why do we have inflation, and what can be done to stop it?" "Why do companies put chemicals in food when the natural ingredients are available?" and so on. Usually the children did not have to be prodded to give their opinions. In fact, their statements and the interchanges between them struck the observer as quite sophisticated conceptually and verbally, and well-informed. Occasionally the teachers would prod with statements such as, "Even if you don't know [the answers], if you think logically about it, you can figure it out." And "I'm asking you [these] questions to help you think this through."

Language arts emphasizes language as a complex system, one that should be mastered. The children are asked to diagram sentences of complex grammatical construction, to memorize irregular verb conjugations (he lay, he has lain, and so on . . .), and to use the proper participles, conjunctions, and interjections in their speech. The teacher (the same one who teaches social studies) told them, "It is not enough to get these right on tests; you must use what you learn [in grammar classes] in your written and oral work. I will grade you on that."

Most writing assignments are either research reports and essays for social studies or experiment analyses and write-ups for science. There is only an occasional story or other "creative writing" assignment. On the occasion observed by the investigator (the writing of a Halloween story), the points the teacher stressed in preparing the children to write involved the structural aspects of a story rather than the expression of feelings or other ideas. The teacher showed them a filmstrip, "The Seven Parts of a Story," and lectured them on plot development, mood setting, character development, consistency, and the use of a logical or appropriate ending. The stories they subsequently wrote were, in fact, well-structured, but many were also personal and expressive. The teacher's evaluative comments, however, did not refer to the expressiveness or artistry but were all directed toward whether they had "developed" the story well.

Language arts work also involved a large amount of practice in presentation of the self and in managing situations where the child was expected to be in charge. For example, there was a series of assignments in which each child had to be a "student teacher." The child had to plan a lesson in grammar, outlining, punctuation, or other language arts topic and explain the concept to the class. Each child was to prepare a worksheet or game and a homework assignment as well. After each presentation, the teacher and other children gave a critical appraisal of the "student teacher's" performance. Their criteria were: whether the student spoke clearly, whether the lesson was interesting, whether the student made any mistakes, and whether he or she kept control of the class. On an occasion when a child did not maintain control, the teacher said, "When you're up there, you have authority and you have to use it. I'll back you up."

The executive elite school is the only school where bells do not demarcate the periods of time. The two fifth-grade teachers were very strict about changing classes on schedule, however, as specific plans for each session had been made. The teachers attempted to keep tight control over the children during lessons, and the children were sometimes flippant, boisterous, and occasionally rude. However, the children may be brought into line by reminding them that "It is up to you," "You must control yourself," "You are responsible for your work," "You must set your own priorities." One teacher told a child, "You are the only driver of your car—and only you can regulate your speed." A new teacher complained to the observer that she had thought "these children" would have more control.

While strict attention to the lesson at hand is required, the teachers make relatively little attempt to regulate the movement of the children at other times. For example, except for the kindergartners, the children in this school do not have to wait for the bell to ring in the morning; they may go to their classroom when they arrive at school. Fifth graders often came early to read, to finish work, or to catch up. After the first two months of school, the fifth-grade teachers did not line the children up to change classes or to go to gym, and so on but, when the children were ready and quiet, they were told they could go—sometimes without the teachers.

In the classroom, the children could get materials when they needed them and took what they needed from closets and from the teacher's desk. They were in charge of the office at lunchtime. During class they did not have to sign out or ask permission to leave the room; they just got up and left. Because of the pressure to get work done, however, they did not leave the room very often. The teachers were very polite to the children, and the investigator heard no sarcasm, no nasty remarks, and few direct orders. The teachers never called the children "honey" or "dear" but always called them by name. The teachers were expected to be available before school, after school, and for part of their lunchtime to provide extra help if needed.

The foregoing analysis of differences in schoolwork in contrasting social class contexts suggests the following conclusion: the "hidden curriculum" of schoolwork is tacit preparation for relating to the process of production in a particular way. Differing curricular, pedagogical, and pupil evaluation practices emphasize different cognitive and behavioral skills in each social setting and thus contribute to the development in the children of certain potential relationships to physical and symbolic capital,[11] to authority, and to the process of work. School experience, in the sample of schools discussed here, differed qualitatively by social class. These differences may not only contribute to the development in the children in each social class of certain types of economically significant relationships and not others but would thereby help to reproduce this system of relations in society. In the contribution to the reproduction of unequal social relations lies a theoretical meaning and social consequence of classroom practice.

The identification of different emphases in classrooms in a sample of contrasting social class contexts implies that further research should be conducted in a large number of schools to investigate the types of work tasks and interactions in each to see if they differ in the ways discussed here and to see if similar potential relationships are uncovered. Such research could have as a product the further elucidation of complex but not readily apparent connections between everyday activity in schools and classrooms and the unequal structure of economic relationships in which we work and live.

Notes

1. S. Bowles and H. Gintis, *Schooling in Capitalist America: Educational Reform and the Contradictions of Economic Life* (New York: Basic Books, 1976).

2. B. Bernstein, *Class, Codes and Control, Vol.3. Towards a Theory of Educational Transmission*, 2d ed. (London: Routledge & Kegan Paul, 1977); P. Bourdieu and

J. Passeron, *Reproduction in Education, Society and Culture* (Beverly Hills, Calif.: Sage, 1977); M. W. Apple, *Ideology and Curriculum* (Boston: Routledge & Kegan Paul, 1979).

3. But see, in a related vein, M.W. Apple and N. King, "What Do Schools Teach?" *Curriculum Inquiry* 6 (1977): 34–58, R. C. Rist, *The Urban School: A Factory for Failure* (Cambridge, Mass.: MIT Press, 1973).

4. Ethnographical: based on an anthropological study of cultures or subcultures; the "cultures" in this case being the five schools observed.

5. The U.S. Bureau of the Census defines poverty for a nonfarm family of four as a yearly income of $6,191 a year or less, U.S. Bureau of the Census, Statistical Abstract of the United States: 1978 (Washington, D.C.: U.S. Government Printing Office, 1978), p.465, table 754.

6. U.S. Bureau of the Census, "Money Income in 1977 of Families and Persons in the United States," Current Population Reports Series P-60, no.118 (Washington, D.C.: U.S. Government Printing Office, 1979), p.2, table A.

7. Ibid.

8. This figure is an estimate. According to the Bureau of the Census, only 2.6 percent of families in the United States have money income of $50,000 or over. U.S. Bureau of the Census, Current Population Reports Series P-60. For figures on income at these higher levels, see I. D. Smith and S. Franklin, "The Concentration of Personal Wealth, 1922–1969," *American Economic Review, 64* (1974): 162–67.

9. Smith and Franklin, "The Concentration of Personal Wealth."

10. A dominant feeling, expressed directly and indirectly by teachers in this school, was boredom with their work. They did, however, in contrast to the working-class schools, almost always carry out lessons during class times.

11. Physical and symbolic capital: elsewhere Anyon defines capital as "property that is used to produce profit, interest, or rent"; she defines symbolic capital as the knowledge and skills that "may yield social and cultural power."

31

"Crossing Class Boundaries" (2000)

Gloria Watkins, who writes under the pen name bell hooks, is a feminist thinker whose writings cover a broad range of subjects on gender, race, popular culture, education, and social class. In the following piece drawn from her book *Where We Stand: Class Matters,* hooks talks about her experiences coming from a working-class, minority background to attending and working in elite colleges and universities.

As you read this selection, consider the following questions:

1. How does college and university education potentially contribute to class stratification?
2. What do individuals who cross class boundaries potentially gain and lose in their personal relationships?
3. Do working-class populations potentially lose their intellectuals and leaders as they are absorbed into the elite levels of the culture? If this is true, what implications does this have for working-class populations?

31

"Crossing Class Boundaries" (2000)

bell hooks

Most of my formative years were spent in segregated black communities where our immediate neighbors were from diverse class backgrounds. Some folks were poor—just barely getting by and making ends meet. They lived in tiny railroad shacks and kept them neat and tidy. Then there were the working-class families like ours, with lots of hungry mouths to feed, so that even if fathers had good jobs like working in the coal mines, it could still be hard sometimes to make ends meet. If the women in these families worked they did service jobs—housecleaning, cooking, or working now and then in the tobacco fields or on the loosening floor. The lovely freshly painted houses in our neighborhood usually belonged to middle-class folks and the rare person with lots of money. They were schoolteachers, doctors, lawyers, and undertakers.

If anyone suffered economic hardship in that world somebody knew and ways were found to share—to meet needs. In that small segregated world it was hard to keep secrets. At school teachers paid attention and they knew if a child was in need. At church everyone saw you. And if all else failed somebody would come by your house and see about you. Not all neighborhoods in the town were like ours; it was a place where folks knew each other's business and often did not hesitate to put their nose in it if need be.

Our family was big, six girls, one boy, mom, and dad. Dad worked various jobs but the one he held for most of his adult life was as a janitor at the local post office. He began working this job when racial discrimination was still the norm, and white folks thought they were doing no wrong when they paid white

Source: hooks, bell. 2000. "Crossing Class Boundaries." In *Where We Stand: Class Matters*, 142–164. New York: Routledge.

workers a fair wage and black workers far less for doing the same job. Laws forbidding unfair practices changed this practice for those employees who worked for the state but continued in all cases where there was no system of checks and balances.

Even though dad worked hard, in our household there was never enough money because there were so many of us. Yet we never lacked the basic necessities of life. Mama cooked delicious food. We always had clean clothes. And even though the old house we lived in was expensive to heat and often cold in winter, we had shelter. We did not think about class. We thought about race. The boundaries of class could be crossed. At times class-based conflict surfaced, often over the desires middle-class schoolteachers had for their working-class and poor students that differed from parental desires. No matter our class we all lived in the same segregated world. We knew each other and we tried to live in community.

When I chose to attend a "fancy" college rather than a state school close to home, I was compelled to confront class differences in new and different ways. Like many working-class parents, my folks were often wary of the new ideas I brought into their lives from ideas learned at school or from books. They were afraid these fancy ideas like the fancy schools I wanted to attend would ruin me for living in the real world. At the time I did not understand that they were also afraid of me becoming a different person—someone who did not speak their language, hold on to their beliefs and their ways. They were working people. To them a good life was one where you worked hard, created a family, worshiped God, had the occasional good time, and lived day to day.

Even though I wanted to attend fancy schools, like the working class and poor around me, I shared these beliefs. I was not afraid to work hard. I just wanted to work in the world of ideas. That was hard for working people to understand. To them it made sense if you wanted to be a teacher because schoolteachers earned a decent living and were respected. Beyond that they could see no practical use for the learning one would get in a fancy school.

I suppose the first major class conflict of my life was my decision about where to go to college. It would have been easier for my family had I chosen to go to a state college near home where I might be awarded a full scholarship, where dorms were cheap, and required books could be checked out of libraries. I wanted to go to a fancy private college. And since my folks did not talk openly about money matters or speak freely of their fears that I would leave home and become a stranger to the world of my growing, I did not realistically consider what it would be like to cross the boundaries of class, to be the working-class girl attending the rich school. No wonder my parents feared for me and my fate. They could see what I could not see.

Against the will of my parents I decided to attend a fancy college far away from home. To attend this school I needed scholarships and loans. I had to work to buy books and there would be no coming home for the holidays because it required excess money we did not have. I wanted to attend this school because I had been told by a favorite teacher that it was a place for serious thinkers, where ideas were taken seriously. This teacher, an anti-racist white liberal who came from an upper-class background, did not talk to me about the issue of class.

It did not take long for me to understand that crossing class boundaries was not easy. My class values were not the same as my college peers'. I resented their assumptions about the poor arid working class. I did not find black bourgeois elites to be any more aware of my world than their white counterparts. The few friends I made whether black or white usually came from a similar class background. Like me they worked; they had loans, scholarships. Publicly and at school I mingled with everybody, learning about different class values. Privately, in my home, whether dormitory room or cheap apartment, I nurtured the values I had been raised to believe in. I wanted to show my family and community of origin that I could go out into the world and be among more privileged class people without assimilating, without losing touch with the ground of my being.

Living among folks from more privileged classes, I learned more about class than I had ever learned in a small segregated neighborhood. Before living among upper-class and rich folks, I had never heard anyone speak contemptuously about poor and working-class people. Casual articulation of negative stereotypes stopped me in my tracks. Not only was I usually a dissenting voice about class, after a while it was just assumed that I would go my way. It was among privileged class folks that I developed both an awareness of the extent to which they are willing to go to protect their class interest and a disrespect for their class values.

Even though I was struggling to acquire an education that would enable me to leave the ranks of the poor and working class, I was more at home in that world than I was in the world I lived in. My political solidarity and allegiance was with working people. I created a lifestyle for myself that mixed aspects of my working-class background with new ideas and habits picked up in a world far removed from that world. I learned different ways to dress, different ways to eat, and new ways to talk and think. I took from those experiences what I wanted and linked them with my home training.

Confident that nothing could separate me from the world of my growing up, I crossed class boundaries with ease and grace. At home with my parents I spoke the language of our world and our ways. At school I learned to keep these ways to myself. I did not fit in, and I did want to fit in. At the same time I was coming to understand that this crossing of class boundaries had indeed given me a different sense of self. I could go home again. I could blend in, but the doors to that world threatened to close whenever I tried to bring new ideas there, to change things there.

Like much of the writing I have done on class, I began this essay by telling family stories again and again, often the same stories in different ways. My ongoing connection to the working-class world of my origin has consistently served as the site of challenge and interrogation for my class values and political allegiances. Affirming and sustaining direct connections to that world continually compels me to think critically about class dynamics in this society. In my twenties it seemed a simple matter to journey between varied class experiences. During those years the amount of money I made would have placed me among the ranks of the poor or bottom-level working class. But class is more than money. And the doctorate I was earning was preparation for entering the ranks of the upper-middle class.

My first full-time tenure track teaching job at a fancy school, Yale University, signaled a complete transition in class positionality. I was no longer in limbo, moving back and forth between the worlds of the haves and the have-nots. I was no longer officially a member of the working class. Like many folks from working-class and poor backgrounds, much of my salary went to the debts I had accumulated on the way. Raised by all the tenets of racial uplift to believe that it is the duty of those who get ahead to share their resources with others, especially those less fortunate, I committed myself to giving to the needy a fixed portion of my income.

Although I did not see myself as part of a talented tenth in the way Du Bois first used that term, I was among the first generation in my family to go to college and the only one of us then to finish a doctorate. It had been a journey full of personal hardship and struggle. And I knew that I would never have finished without the ongoing support of the working-class world I had come from. These connections were my strength. The values I had been raised to believe in sustained me when everything in the new worlds I entered invalidated me and the world I was coming from. I felt that I had both a debt and a responsibility to that world—to honor it and to remain in solidarity with it despite the change in my class position.

One way to honor this working-class world was to write about it in a way that would shed a more authentic light on our reality. I felt that writing about the constructive values and beliefs of that world would act as an intervention challenging stereotypes. Concurrently, I did not want to become one of those academics from a working-class background who nostalgically fetishized that experience, so I also wrote about the negative aspects of our life. My parents and other folks from that world refused to accept that it was important to write about negative experiences. They did not care how many positive comments were made, they felt betrayed whenever I focused on negative aspects of our lives. Not everyone felt this way, but it was still difficult to face that some of the folks I cared about the most felt I had become a traitorous outsider, looking in and down on the world I had most intimately known.

Ironically, the radical intellectual milieus I circulated in were ones where everyone talked about crossing class boundaries as though it was a simple matter. This was especially the case in feminist and cultural studies circles. To many of my peers from privileged class backgrounds, crossing boundaries often meant slumming or a willingness to go work in a poor community in an exotic foreign land. I was fascinated and oftentimes a bit envious when my white peers talked about their trips to Belize, El Salvador, New Guinea, Ecuador, all over Africa, India, China, and the Middle East; the list could go on. Sometimes these trips were about "eating the other," about privileged Westerners indulging in ethnic cultural cannibalism. At other times they were about individuals trying to learn about the experiences of people unlike themselves, trying to contribute.

Whatever the motivation, these experiences might someday serve as the cultural capital evoked to justify a lack of accountability toward the "different and disenfranchised" in one's own nation, town, community. Like a charity one has donated capital to and need never give again because the proof of generosity was already on record, their one-time contribution could take the place of any ongoing constructive confrontation with class politics in the United States. The starving in a foreign country are always more interesting than the starving who speak your language who might want to eat at your table, find shelter in your house, or share your job.

I found and find it difficult, though never impossible, to move back and forth among different classes. As I began to make more money and gain recognition as a feminist thinker and cultural critic, the money I earned became a source of conflict between me and members of my family and friends. Even though I had held different ideas from family and friends for years, when it came to making money, we were all struggling. By my mid-thirties, I was no longer struggling and my income was growing. The fact that I was single and had no children made it easier for me to pay debts and live cheaply in ways that family and friends could not. While I wanted to share economic resources with them, I also wanted to share knowledge, to share information about how we might all change our lives for the better.

Since I was not a flashy dresser or big spender in any highly visible way, less economically privileged peers often did not see me as a success. To them I was unconventional or weird. Once, my brother, who left the ranks of the middle class by overspending and substance abuse, came to visit me in my New York City flat and expressed shock that it was small and not very fancy. He shared: "I thought you had made it to the big time." And wanted to know: "Why are you living like this?" I explained that I lived a simple but to my way of thinking luxurious life so that I would have more to share with others. Still it was only when I concretely showed him the finances, how much I made, how it was spent (paying my expenses and helping others with rent, education, bills, etc.) that he began to realistically understand my perspective.

Like many lower-class and poor folk, he had an unrealistic sense of what one could actually do with money. This lack of awareness stems in part from the reality that credit and extended indebtedness allows so many people to consume beyond their means and create lifestyles that they cannot afford. I once did a workshop with a group of middle- and upper-middle-class professional black women on money and how we use it and was astonished to find that the vast majority of them were living so far beyond their means that they were just a pay check away from having nothing. Folks who do not have economic privilege and have never had it often assume that they can measure someone's economic worth by material objects. They do not see the indebtedness that may be bolstering what appears on the surface to be a lifestyle one could create only with class privilege and affluence.

Indeed, black folk with some degree of class privilege often create a lifestyle that has the appearance of prosperity (big house, new car, fancy clothes) though they may be suffering economic distress because of assuming responsibility for less-fortunate family members while still striving to appear on top of it all. Studies show that most middle-income black folks with a sizable income give a measure of that income to help extended family and kin. It is not the giving that undermines their finances but their desire to have an expensive lifestyle as well as excess funds to help others. Stress and conflict over money may undermine the relationships that they hope to maintain and strengthen by sharing resources.

The more money I made, the more needy individuals came seeking financial help. Difficulties began to arise when frustrations about having their material needs met and my response to those frustrations prevented us from attending to the overall emotional needs of any positive relationship. And it was evident that the politics of shame around being needy made it impossible for some individuals to not feel "looked down" upon for desiring assistance even if they were not actually being looked down upon.

Money is so often used as a way to coercively assert power over others that it can easily become an arena of conflict, setting up hierarchies that were not previously present. Like many folks in my position, I often confront needy individuals who see my willingness to share as a weakness and who become exploitative. And there are times when I am scammed and misused (for example, a student says that they need money to finish school—you give the money—and they drop out, pocketing the refund, etc.). Any effort to not ally oneself with the existing structure of class elitism, to share resources, will necessarily meet with conflicts and casualties because many underprivileged folks share the predatory capitalist values often associated solely with the affluent. Often consciousness-raising has to take place with those who lack material privilege so that old models of guilt-tripping and exploiting progressive individuals who are working to live differently are not deployed.

All too often the affluent want to share using the old models of philanthropy and patronage that support giving while protecting one's class interest. This kind of giving rarely intervenes on or challenges the structures of economic class exploitation. Concurrently, affluent individuals who care about those who suffer the brunt of an unjust economic system often lose heart if their efforts to share are misused. This response can be an act of sabotage and self-indulgence. Politically astute individuals with class privilege have to remain aware that we are working with inadequate models for communalism and social change so that there will necessarily be occasions when the best efforts fail to get the desired outcome.

When I have experienced a breakdown of communication and misuse, I use it as an occasion to invent methods of intervention that will work. When sharing resources does not work, it would be simple to refuse to identify with the class-based suffering of those in need and assume a protective stance that would indicate allegiance to privileged-class interests. However, I remain committed to an anti-class elitism vision of solidarity that sees working things out and processing issues in such a way that bonds across class are strengthened as part of resistance struggle. This has not been a straightforward or an easy task. There is little theoretical or practical work written about how we must behave and what we must do to maintain solidarity in the face of class difference.

The most difficult issues I have had to face in the struggle to help underprivileged comrades create better lives for themselves surface when I challenge the ways widespread acceptance of hedonistic consumerism and its concomitant insistence that one never delay gratification undermines the class power of poor and working-class citizens. Years ago my partner at the time, who was also from a working-class background, and I bought a house. For a year we were overextended financially. When we first moved in we did not have a refrigerator. We had decided we could afford to buy one with cash a few months later and thereby reduce our indebtedness. To many of our working-class friends and family this seemed like a hardship. They did not understand our wanting to stabilize our finances before making another big purchase. Similarly, both our families had difficulty accepting our commitment to driving the same car for years so as not to incur unnecessary indebtedness.

Crossing class boundaries, entering worlds of class privilege, was one way that I learned different attitudes toward money than the ones I was raised with. Among the privileged there was much more information available about how to manage money. Taking this knowledge and sharing with folks without class privilege can be a gesture that provides them with the means to assert more meaningful agency in their financial lives. Through reading self-help books about money I learned the importance of keeping accounts, of knowing how I spent money. When I first shared this with comrades who lacked material privilege they thought it did not pertain to their lives. One of my sisters, who was receiving welfare at the time, could not see the point in using this exercise. In her mind she had no money. I called attention to the fact that she smoked cigarettes, which cost money. The important point was to know how you spent your money whether or not you had ten, fifty, or five hundred dollars a month. Taking charge by knowing what we spend money on and budgeting our money no matter the amount empowers. It gives a sense of economic agency and lays the groundwork for economic self-sufficiency.

Like many individuals who have come from poor and working-class backgrounds into class privilege, I want to share my life with folks from diverse class backgrounds, and not simply my resources. Oftentimes it is easier to share resources than it is to bring diverse class experiences together. When we do cross the boundaries there is usually a clash in etiquette, values, the way we do things. Since I want my family to have a firsthand knowledge of the work I do, I often invite them to attend conferences where I am lecturing. At one conference I felt my youngest sister, who had joined me, was behaving disrespectfully toward me. A single parent who received state aid and who was aggressively seeking employment but finding it extremely difficult, she was depressed and fearful about her future. I confronted her about her behavior in front of another academic colleague and friend. This offended her. She felt that I had asserted class power to belittle her although she did not use those terms.

While I still felt my critique was justified, I did agree that I had not chosen an appropriate moment to lodge it. I acted from the assumption that we were all mature adults together who could cope with a moment of tension and conflict. I had not considered the dynamics from the perspective of class difference. Since I work hard to not develop ego-centered attachment to my class power and status it is often easy for me to forget that it can be intimidating to others. My brother and I have had the most productive personal class conflicts because he is totally candid about his own class frustrations. Previous states of indebtedness and unemployment have made it difficult for him to gain economic stability even though he works hard. He openly voices his resentment of my class position, and we are able to process together. To maintain our bond, our solidarity, is hard work. Friends from working-class backgrounds where siblings share similar income need not work as hard to maintain connection.

The fear of losing connection has led many an upwardly mobile individual from a poor or working-class background to cease their efforts to change their class status. Among people of color we see that decision to not go forward most intensely around the question of education. In the segregated schools of my growing up, to work hard at one's studies was a source of pride for the race and, though we did not understand it that way, for our class as well. That has now changed. At all educational levels students from working-class backgrounds fear losing touch with peers and family. And that fear often leads to self-sabotage. To intervene on this nonproductive pattern we do need more testimony both in oral traditions and in writing of how working-class and poor folk can remain connected to the communities of our origin even as we work to improve our economic lot. Hollywood dramatized these dimensions of class struggle in the hit movie *Good Will Hunting.* In the film, the working-class buddy persuades his blonde, blue-eyed "genius" friend to go forward and enter the corporate world and make big money even if he must leave his friends behind. Ironically, since he is supported by his poor and working-class peers there is no logical reason he must leave them behind. After showing audiences the pleasures that can be shared when people cross class boundaries (our poor boy hero has a lover girl from a rich background with a trust fund), the movie offers the age-old message that attaining money, status, and class privilege is the only thing that matters and not loyalty to friends and comrades.

Many intelligent, sometimes brilliant, young black males end up in prison precisely because they want to make the quick easy money rather than slowly with hard work and effort pull themselves up from the bottom. Their smarts are now being exploited by a booming industry that provides them jobs for little or no wages. They end up doing in prison what they were refusing to do on the outside without reaping minimal reward. In *The Seven Laws of Money,* Michael Phillips contends: "About ninety percent of all crimes are committed because of money . . . and about eighty percent of all people in jail are there because of money related crimes. . . . Money is a very significant reason for people being in jail. . . . Maybe one way of stating it is that their aspiration for money and their ability to accumulate it are radically different. People who commit a crime often reach a state where they want money so badly that they are willing to take a higher risk than most other people are." Of course Phillips, who worked hard to acquire wealth, makes this point using examples of working-class and poor men. However, he does not acknowledge that the values shaping their actions are those appropriated from more affluent individuals, usually white, from more privileged class backgrounds who have been able to make easy money. These attitudes trickle down to the masses through media. And whether true or false they are often passively appropriated.

Like many commentators who write about money, Phillips avoids the issue of economic injustice and makes it appear that anyone who works hard can easily earn money. Even though he acknowledges that the issue for most poor and working-class people is not that they do not make money but that their fantasies of what money can do far exceed reality. It is always troubling to me when I hear individuals with class privilege assert that the poor and working class are unwilling to work hard. I am enraged when I hear black elites talk about how the poor need to learn from those who have made it how to work hard. The truth is that the working class and working poor work hard but the money that they make is not enough to provide them with the means to attain economic self-sufficiency. One of the greatest threats to their economic well-being is the prevailing fantasy that if they work hard, they can attain all that they desire.

Crossing class boundaries I find that many of the working-class and poor people I know spend an inordinate amount of time fantasizing about the power of money, of what it can do. While this may hold true for middle-class people as well, the extent to which these fantasies negatively impact on those without privilege is more apparent. Obsessive fantasizing about money to buy things not only creates psychotic lust, it prevents individuals from realistically confronting their economic reality or using the time and energy to constructively respond to the world they live in. Poverty need not mean that people cannot have reading groups, study groups, consciousness-raising groups. Time spent fantasizing might be best spent buying a can of bright paint (if the funds are available) and painting old furniture or just cleaning up.

Using the example of two smart black men who were caught up in easy money fantasies, Phillip writes: "They were such bright and charming people that they could have had a high salary in almost any conventional business. At each point, though, they always wanted money instantly, not realizing they would always have gotten more money if they had just been able to wait a little. . . . The main lesson that I could draw from these two men, both skilled, charming, capable people, is that they have such a completely distorted view of what they 'need' that there is no way they can function in society. A minor adjustment in their sense of reality would have made them capable of functioning in a useful, viable way." Given racial discrimination in conventional business, it would no doubt not have been as simple for these two men to succeed as Phillips makes it seem, but they certainly did not need to turn to crime. The fantasy of easy money led them astray.

Sadly, no group should know better than the working class and poor that there is no easy money to be had in this society. And yet the fantasy of easy money coupled with hedonistic consumerism has distorted reality for many people. Dialoguing across class is one of the ways that we can share together a more realistic sense of the limitations of money—of what it can and cannot do. Like the struggle to attain money, to change one's class position, if you start on the bottom rung, these conversations require courage, a willingness to speak truthfully about class and money that is the first act of resistance challenging and changing class elitism.

PART VII

Technology and Education

The use of technology in education is most commonly associated with computers. In point of fact, "technologies" have been used in the schools as far back as Antiquity. In ancient Rome, for example, students inscribed their lessons on tablets covered with wax. This is where we got our modern term *tabula rasa*, or blank slate.

The most important technology affecting learning is the book. Moveable type is actually a relatively new invention dating from the late fifteenth century. Other educational technologies include the blackboard, record players, radio, motion pictures, filmstrips, video players, and, most recently, the computer.

Many educational technologies are ephemeral. Theorists such as Larry Cuban point to the fact that most educational technologies fail in the classroom because they do not sufficiently meet the needs of teachers. The blackboard has been popular because it is dependable and cheap. In contrast, elaborate multimedia systems, including computers, tend not to be used by many teachers if they are not easy to use and, most important, dependable.

Among the selections in this section are works that primarily address questions involving the use of computers. Limitations of space unfortunately prevented the inclusion of works such as B. F. Skinner's 1954 article "The Science of Learning and the Art of Teaching," in which he introduced his theories about behavioral reinforcement and the use of teaching machines, as well as Vannavar Bush's 1945 essay "As We May Think." This latter essay predicts many of the innovations in computing that were to emerge from the final decades of the twentieth century, and is widely available online.

The section begins with a brief selection from Douglas Engelbart on computers and the augmentation of intelligence, followed by an essay by C. A. Bowers, which examines what is gained and what is lost by using computers in the classroom. This section and the book conclude with a selection from Jean-François Lyotard's *La condition postmoderne*, discussing the computerization of society.

As you read the selections included in this section of the book, consider the following questions:

1. What does the use of technologies such as computers do to enhance what is learned in the classroom?
2. How do computers and their use potentially diminish what is learned in the classroom?
3. How do technologies like the computer affect older technologies such as the book?
4. How is traditional knowledge (oral traditions, folk traditions, etc.) affected by computers?
5. What is intelligence, and how is it redefined by augmented intelligence?

32

Augmenting Human Intellect (1962)

Douglas Engelbart (1925–), strongly influenced by the ideas of Vannevar Bush, developed such computing innovations as windows, the computer mouse, and icons. Like Bush, he believed that computers have the potential to augment the ability of men and women to think. His concept of augmenting an individual's functional intelligence by using a computer is outlined in this brief selection from his report, *Augmenting Human Intellect*.

As you read Engelbart's ideas, consider the following:

1. How does augmented intelligence potentially change how we instruct students in schools?
2. How important is it to have not only access to computing but also the appropriate or best means of using this technology?

32

Augmenting Human Intellect *(1962)*

Douglas Engelbart

By "augmenting human intellect" we mean increasing the capability of a man to approach a complex problem situation, to gain comprehension to suit his particular needs, and to derive solutions to problems. Increased capability in this respect is taken to mean a mixture of the following: more-rapid comprehension, better comprehension, the possibility of gaining a useful degree of comprehension in a situation that previously was too complex, speedier solutions, better solutions, and the possibility of finding solutions to problems that before seemed insoluble. And by "complex situations" we include the professional problems of diplomats, executives, social scientists, life scientists, physical scientists, attorneys, designers—whether the problem situation exists for twenty minutes or twenty years. We do not speak of isolated clever tricks that help in particular situations. We refer to a way of life in an integrated domain where hunches, cut-and-try, intangibles, and the human "feel for a situation" usefully co-exist with powerful concepts, streamlined terminology and notation, sophisticated methods, and high-powered electronic aids. . . .

Let us consider an augmented architect at work. He sits at a working station that has a visual display screen some three feet on a side; this is his working surface, and is controlled by a computer (his "clerk") with which he can communicate by means of a small keyboard and various other devices.

Source: Engelbart, Douglas C. (1962, Oct.). *Augmenting Human Intellect: A Conceptual Framework.* Summary Report AFOSR-3223 under Contract AF 49(638)-1024, SRI Project 3578 for Air Force Office of Scientific Research, Stanford Research Institute, Menlo Park, CA.

He is designing a building. He has already dreamed up several basic layouts and structural forms, and is trying them out on the screen. The surveying data for the layout he is working on now have already been entered, and he has just coaxed the clerk to show him a perspective view of the steep hillside building site with the roadway above, symbolic representations of the various trees that are to remain on the lot, and the service tie points for the different utilities. The view occupies the left two-thirds of the screen. With a "pointer," he indicates two points of interest, moves his left hand rapidly over the keyboard, and the distance and elevation between the points indicated appear on the right-hand third of the screen.

Now he enters a reference line with his pointer and the keyboard. Gradually the screen begins to show the work he is doing—a neat excavation appears in the hillside, revises itself slightly, and revises itself again. After a moment, the architect changes the scene on the screen to an overhead plan view of the site, still showing the excavation. A few minutes of study, and he enters on the keyboard a list of items, checking each one as it appears on the screen, to be studied later.

Ignoring the representation on the display, the architect next begins to enter a series of specifications and data—a six-inch slab floor, twelve-inch concrete walls eight feet high within the excavation, and so on. When he has finished, the revised scene appears on the screen. A structure is taking shape. He examines it, adjusts it, pauses long enough to ask for handbook or catalog information from the clerk at various points, and readjusts accordingly. He often recalls from the "clerk" his working lists of specifications and considerations to refer to them, modify them, or add to them. These lists grow into an evermore-detailed, interlinked structure, which represents the maturing thought behind the actual design.

Prescribing different planes here and there, curved surfaces occasionally, and moving the whole structure about five feet, he finally has the rough external form of the building balanced nicely with the setting, and he is assured that this form is basically compatible with the materials to be used as well as with the function of the building.

Now he begins to enter detailed information about the interior. Here the capability of the clerk to show him any view he wants to examine (a slice of the interior, or how the structure would look from the roadway above) is important. He enters particular fixture designs, and examines them in a particular room. He checks to make sure that sun glare from the windows will not blind a driver on the roadway, and the "clerk" computes the information that one window will reflect strongly onto the roadway between 6 and 6:30 on midsummer mornings.

Next he begins a functional analysis. He has a list of the people who will occupy this building, and the daily sequences of their activities. The "clerk" allows him to follow each in turn, examining how doors swing, where special lighting might be needed. Finally he has the "clerk" combine all of these sequences of activity to indicate spots where traffic is heavy in the building, or where congestion might occur, and to determine what the severest drain on the utilities is likely to be.

All of this information (the building design and its associated "thought structure") can be stored on a tape to represent the design manual for the building. Loading this tape into his own clerk, another architect, a builder, or the client can maneuver within this design manual to pursue whatever details or insights are of interest to him—and can append special notes that are integrated into the design manual for his own or someone else's later benefit.

In such a future working relationship between human problem-solver and computer "clerk," the capability of the computer for executing mathematical processes would be used whenever it was needed. However, the computer has many other capabilities for manipulating and displaying information that can be of significant benefit to the human in nonmathematical processes of planning, organizing, studying, etc. Every person who does his thinking with symbolized concepts (whether in the form of the English language, pictographs, formal logic, or mathematics) should be able to benefit significantly.

33

"How Computers Contribute to the Ecological Crisis" (1990)

C.A. Bowers has taught, in recent years, at the University of Oregon and Portland State University. His work on computing includes *The Cultural Dimensions of Educational Computing: Understanding the Non-Neutrality of Technology* (New York: Teachers College Press, 1988) and *Let Them Eat Data* (Athens: University of Georgia Press, 2000).

In the essay "How Computers Contribute to the Ecological Crisis," Bowers argues that computers contribute to the current ecological crisis by reinforcing the widely held assumption that the self is separated from the natural world. This Cartesian mindset is reinforced in models of computing that are increasingly in place in contemporary culture and schooling.

As you read this selection, consider the following questions:

1. What does Bowers mean when he says that computers contribute to the ecological crisis?
2. How do computers tend to reinforce certain ways of thinking and interpreting the world?

33

"How Computers Contribute to the Ecological Crisis" (1990)

C. A. Bowers

Recent reports on global changes in life-sustaining ecosystems, such as the annual *State of the World* published by the Worldwatch Institute and the special issue of *Scientific American* entitled "Managing Planet Earth," support the conventional thinking that computers are one of the most important technologies we have available for understanding the extent of the crisis and the steps that must be taken to mitigate it. Processing scientific data and modeling how natural systems will react to further changes caused by human activity suggest that the computer is essential to a data-based approach to understanding the dynamic and interactive nature of an ecology. Having recognized the genuine contributions that computers make to addressing the ecological crisis, I also want to argue that computers help reinforce the mindset that has contributed to the disproportionate impact that Western societies have had on degrading the habitat. Put simply, computers represent a Cartesian epistemology (an argument that has also been made by Hubert Dreyfus, Terry Winograd, and Theodore Roszak), and the use of this technology reinforces the Cartesian orientations of our culture—which includes the critically important aspect of consciousness, wherein the self is experienced as separate from the natural world.

This Cartesian way of thinking can be seen in how the lead article in *Scientific American,* "Managing Planet Earth," frames the nature of the ecological crisis as a problem of more rational management of the planet. As

Source: Bowers, C. A. (1990). "How Computers Contribute to the Ecological Crisis," *CPSR Newsletter* 8(3): 1, 6–8.

the author William C. Clark puts it, "Managing Planet Earth will require answers to two questions: What kind of planet do *we* want? What kind of planet can *we* get?" The italics were added here to bring out how a Cartesian way of thinking, with its emphasis on instrumental problem solving, also strengthens the cultural myth, which has roots much deeper in Western consciousness, of an anthropocentric universe (that is, "man" is the central figure and must treat the biosphere as a resource for achieving his purposes). The Cartesian mindset shows up in the special issue of *Scientific American* and the annual reports of the Worldwatch Institute in another way that is critically important to any discussion of how computers relate to the deepening ecological crisis. Although both publications provide a wealth of data which, according to one of the canons of the Cartesian position, is supposed to be the basis of rational thought, *they totally ignore that culture is part of the problem.* In fact, culture is not even mentioned in these data-based representations of the ecological crisis.

This is particularly surprising because culture, understood here as encompassing both the deep layers of a symbolic world and the whole range of human activities given distinctive form by the shared symbolic sense of order, is an aspect of every humanly caused change in the ecosystems now viewed as endangered. Beliefs, values, uses of technology, economic practices, political processes, and so forth, while varying from culture to culture, relate directly to population growth, loss of forest cover, destruction of habitats that threaten species with extinction, warming of the atmosphere, spread of toxic waste in water supplies and top soil, and so forth. The irony is that the researchers who provide useful data and computer simulations of how natural systems will react under further stress also contribute to putting out of focus the contributing role that cultural beliefs and practices play in the ecological crisis.

The Ecological/Cultural Crisis

The phrase "ecological crisis" should be represented as the "ecological/cultural crisis." When viewed in this way, we can then begin to consider more fully the cultural orientation that is reinforced not only by the epistemology embedded in the computer, but also by how the computer is represented to the public and to students. We can then also open up a discussion of whether it is possible, particularly in educational settings, to create software programs that take into account the deep levels of culture (including differences in cultures) which give form to human thought and behavior. This latter possibility, which may well be beyond the capacity of this Cartesian machine, is important to whether the computer can be used to help illuminate the cultural patterns that are degrading the habitat. But first we need to identify other aspects of the Cartesian cultural orientation reinforced by the computer—which has become the dominant icon for representing the authority of a particular form of knowledge.

The Cartesian mindset has distinctive characteristics that set it apart from other cultures that have, in a variety of ways, evolved along paths that have been more ecologically sustainable, some for many thousands of years. This is mentioned here not for the purpose of romanticizing these cultures but, instead, to bring out that one test of a viable culture is its ability to live in balance with its habitat. This test is perhaps too pragmatically simple for a culture where the abstract theories of philosophers have been given, in certain powerful circles, more legitimacy than the contextualized forms of knowledge that have evolved in habitats lacking a margin of surplus that allowed for experimentation with abstract ideas. But it is the test that all cultures must now meet as we recognize that our surplus is increasingly illusory.

The Cartesian mindset, in addition to ignoring the nature of culture (and its influence on thought) and furthering the view of an anthropocentric universe, has other distinctive elements reinforced through the use of computers. These include what has become in modern Western consciousness the basis for objectifying the world (that is, Descartes' distinction between *res extensa* and *res cogitans*—which also served to naturalize the Cosmos), a view of the rational process where data becomes the basis of procedural and constructionist thinking, and an instrumental and explicit problem-solving approach to a world that is posited as mechanistic in nature.

The dimensions of human life ignored by the Cartesian mindset correspond to the weakness in computers. Contrary to the myths constructed by Descartes, Bacon, Locke, and other thinkers of this period, a strong case can be made that most of our knowledge is *tacit* in nature, learned as analogues that serve as templates for future experiences, encoded in a metaphorical language that provides a shared schemata for thinking, and represents a collective interpretation framed by the epic narratives that constitute the basis of the culture's *episteme*. As we obtain better accounts of other world views—Hopi, Dogan, Koyukon, Confucian cultures in the Far East, and so forth—it becomes increasingly difficult to maintain the popularized rendering of Descartes' legacy: the image of a culture- and tradition-free individual, objective data, and a conduit view of language. The sociology of knowledge (within our own tradition) and cognitive anthropology point to the cultural basis of thought and behavioral patterns, and to the way in which each cultural group experiences these patterns as part of their national attitude—this also applies to the members of our Cartesian culture whose schemata cannot take into account tacit and culturally constituted knowledge.

Patterns That Connect the Individual

If we turn to the writings of Gregory Bateson, instead of the findings of cognitive anthropology, we find an account of human existence expressed in the language of science that challenges the conceptual foundations of the Cartesian mindset and, at the same time, points to the possibility that primary cultures (like the Hopi, Koyukon, aborigines of Australia, and so forth) may have taken developmental paths that are more ecologically sustainable. Unlike the modern Cartesian approach to viewing the rational process as something that occurs in the head of an autonomous, culture-free individual, Bateson emphasizes the patterns that connect, the information exchanges that constitute the life of an entire natural/social system of which the individual is a participating member, and the dangers facing humans when their conceptual mapping processes (what he calls "determinative memory") are unable to take into account the information exchanges that signal the condition of the ecology upon which they are dependent. As Bateson put it, "thus, in no system which shows mental characteristics can any part have unilateral control over the whole. In other words, the mental characteristics of system are immanent, not in some part, but in the system as a whole." (*Steps to an Ecology of Mind*, p. 316) His statement that "the unit of evolutionary survival turns out to be identical with the unit of mind," (p. 483) has a strong echo in the culture of primal peoples where human practices and the natural world are understood as morally interdependent.

Although it is tempting to dwell further on how a consideration of ecologically sustainable cultures enables us to recognize those aspects of our own belief system that are contributing to the destruction of our habitat, it is necessary to turn our attention more directly to the question of whether the use of computers is really helping us understand the ecological crisis in a way that does not perpetuate the very mindset that has been such an important contributing factor. At some point, accumulating more data on the extent of environmental damage and producing better computer models of changes in the ecosystems becomes a distraction from addressing the real challenge—which is to begin the exceedingly difficult task of changing the conceptual and moral foundations of our cultural practices. We already know that the trend line reflecting the demands of cultures on the habitat is upward, and that the trend line reflecting the sustaining capacity of natural systems is downward. More computer-processed data may enable us to predict with greater accuracy when we will cross certain irreversible thresholds. But that will be of little use if we cannot reverse the demands made by cultures whose belief systems represent the environment as a natural resource and human choices as limited only by a lack of data. The challenge now is to become aware of our own taken-for-granted culture, and to evolve *new narrative traditions* that represent humans as interdependent members of the larger information and food chains that make up the ecosystems.

Computers, the Environment, and Education

The use of computers in educational settings seems to be where the question of relevance can be most clearly raised. As educational software ranging from databases to simulation programs have been written by people who are embedded in the Cartesian/liberal mindset (objective data, autonomous individuals who construct their own ideas, progressive nature of rationally directed change and technological innovations, a conduit view of language), it may be premature to reach the conclusion that the educational uses of computers can only reinforce the Cartesian mindset that has helped, paradoxically, to create a form of technological empowerment that contributes to the possibility of our own extinction. As Theodore Roszak points out, the basic relationship in the educational use of computers involves the mind of the student meeting the mind of the person who wrote the program, and the mental processes that establishes what constitutes the "data." If the mind encountered by students, mediated of course by the amplification characteristics of computer technology, has never considered the aspects of human/culture experience ignored by Cartesianism, it would be impossible for the students to write a program that takes into account the deeper levels of culture. Or, for that matter, it would be impossible to frame the thought process in a way that enables students to recognize that language and thought are influenced by the *episteme* of a cultural group.

The close connection between computers and the form of consciousness associated with print technology make it impossible to represent the thought processes of other cultural groups in a way in which students could enter into its epistemic patterns at a taken-for-granted level. As Eric Havelock and Walter Ong argue, print makes what is represented appear as data—abstract, decontextualized, and rationally apprehended. But it should be possible to move some distance away from the more stultifying aspects of the Cartesian mindset reinforced through print-based discourse. Software programs that help illuminate the nature of culture would seem to be a step in the right direction, both in terms of understanding the symbolic foundations upon which thought and social practices rest, and in terms of recognizing that *culture is part of the ecological crisis.* One aspect of culture that needs to be illuminated, which would be a prelude to considering comparative belief and value systems, is the metaphorical nature of language. Particularly important would be understanding how the root metaphors of a cultural group (for us, a mechanistic image of Nature) influence the process of analogic thinking (i.e., choice of generative metaphors) and leads to the existence of iconic metaphors that encode the earlier process of analogic thinking. Iconic metaphors such as "data," "artificial intelligence," and "computer memory," are examples of this process of encoding earlier processes of analogic thinking, which in turn was influenced by the root metaphors taken for granted at that time. How the metaphorical nature of language provides the schemata for thinking becomes especially critical to the process of recognizing how current thinking about the ecological crisis largely is framed by the metaphors central to Cartesianism. Viewing language as encoding the process of analogic thinking also bring other aspects of culture into consideration: how people in our own past as well as members of other cultural groups have different views of reality, how the past can influence the present at a taken-for-granted level, and how the individual is, in actuality, giving individualized expression to shared cultural patterns. Becoming aware of culture, it should be kept in mind, is just the first step in a process that must eventually engage the more politically difficult problem of sorting out the cultural patterns that are ecologically sustainable over the long term.

There is another line of development in educational software that may be fruitful to explore. This could involve the use of problem-solving simulations framed in terms of the patterns of thinking of other cultural groups who have lived within the limits of their habitats (this would help students recognize the assumptions of our culture that ignore the problem of long term interdependency) and the use of simulations that consider the future ecological impact of our assumptions about human life, material and technological progress, and rational control of the environment.

The Moral Poverty of the Information Age

With the cultures of the world placing increasing demands on biosystems that are showing signs of disruption and decline, the most critical aspect of the problem—at least in terms of the human/cultural roots of the crisis—is to change the root metaphors that underlie the foundation of our Western value system. Serious consideration, for example, should be given to Aldo Leopold's argument that a land ethic should replace the anthropocentrism of the value orientation that now guides individual decisions—including our uses of technology. Very succinctly, he argues that an ethical consideration of our interdependency with the environment, if taken seriously, should lead to "a limitation on freedom of action in the struggle for existence." Restriction of self for the sake of others, where "others" is understood as including the entire "biotic community," now is paramount to human survival, given the size of the world's human population and the scale of its technological capacities.

What this will mean for how we use computers is not entirely clear at this time, but one point that now seems irrefutable is that the future has a moral dimension to it that is ignored by the image of an "Information Age." The moral dimensions of the ecological crisis bring us back to a central theme of this discussion: namely, that "data" and simulation models tend to hide the deeper levels of culture. The transmission of culture, which occurs whenever a language system is used as part of a computing process, points to a need to consider the cultural orientations that are being reinforced by this technology, and to asking whether it is part of the solution or part of the problem. The consequences of taking these concerns seriously are so important that they need to be given a more central place in future considerations of the educational use of computers and in understanding the influence of this technology on social change.

34

"The Field: Knowledge in Computerized Societies" (1979)

Jean-François Lyotard (1924–1998) is best known for his 1979 monograph *La Condition postmoderne,* which was translated into English in 1984 as *The Postmodern Condition.* In this work, Lyotard argued that Western culture has moved from a modern into a postmodern culture in which traditional modernist narratives and authority are challenged. Lyotard's work is important because it recognizes that a profound shift has taken place in society, beginning in the 1950s, as a result of new technologies, new systems of knowledge, and new social patterns and relationships.

Lyotard's ideas are important to the field of education because if what he wrote is accurate, the nature of knowledge, and in turn of learning, is profoundly redefined as a result of the introduction of technologies such as computers. In this context, consider how much the experience of college students has changed compared to thirty years ago, as a result of having access to personal computers and the Internet. Think, for example, about what it was like to produce a term paper without a computer (i.e., using a typewriter) or without having access to the Internet and online library resources.

Lyotard considered the organization and control of knowledge as radically redefined because of new technologies such as computers. The selection that follows is perhaps the most difficult piece in this book. It is also among the most important, because it directly addresses the origins of the world in which we currently live and must function.

As you read the following selection from Lyotard, the final reading in this book, think back to the essay by Vaclav Havel (Chapter 2). Havel's language is much more accessible, but he is, in fact, talking about many of the same issues. Each makes clear that it is impossible for educators and citizens to avoid the reality and complexities of postmodern culture.

As you read Lyotard, carefully consider the following questions. If you like, also consider them in the context of Havel's ideas.

1. How do postmodern phenomena potentially shape and redefine the work of teachers? (Consider factors such as the increase in the divorce rate in the United States in the past fifty years, large numbers of women entering the workforce, children's access to the Internet, etc.)
2. How do students learn differently than previous generations because of their access to screen-based media such as television and computers?
3. How is literacy potentially redefined in a postmodern culture?

34

"The Field: Knowledge in Computerized Societies" (1979)

Jean-François Lyotard

Our working hypothesis is that the status of knowledge is altered as societies enter what is known as the postindustrial age and cultures enter what is known as the postmodern age. This transition has been under way since at least the end of the 1950s, which for Europe marks the completion of reconstruction. The pace is faster or slower depending on the country, and within countries it varies according to the sector of activity: the general situation is one of temporal disjunction which makes sketching an overview difficult. A portion of the description would necessarily be conjectural. At any rate, we know that it is unwise to put too much faith in futurology.

Rather than painting a picture that would inevitably remain incomplete, I will take as my point of departure a single feature, one that immediately defines our object of study. Scientific knowledge is a kind of discourse. And it is fair to say that for the last forty years the "leading" sciences and technologies have had to do with language: phonology and theories of linguistics, problems of communication and cybernetics, modern theories of algebra and informatics, computers and their languages, problems of translation and the search for areas of compatibility among computer languages, problems of information storage and data banks, telematics and the perfection of intelligent terminals, to paradoxology. The facts speak for themselves (and this list is not exhaustive).

These technological transformations can be expected to have a considerable impact on knowledge. Its two principal functions—research and the transmission of acquired learning—are already feeling the effect, or will in the

---

Source: Lyotard, Jean-François. 1979/1984. In *The Postmodern Condition.* Manchester, U.K.: Manchester University Press.

future. With respect to the first function, genetics provides an example that is accessible to the layman: it owes its theoretical paradigm to cybernetics. Many other examples could be cited. As for the second function, it is common knowledge that the miniaturisation and commercialisation of machines is already changing the way in which learning is acquired, classified, made available, and exploited. It is reasonable to suppose that the proliferation of information-processing machines is having, and will continue to have, as much of an effect on the circulation of learning as did advancements in human circulation (transportation systems) and later, in the circulation of sounds and visual images (the media).

The nature of knowledge cannot survive unchanged within this context of general transformation. It can fit into the new channels, and become operational, only if learning is translated into quantities of information. We can predict that anything in the constituted body of knowledge that is not translatable in this way will be abandoned and that the direction of new research will be dictated by the possibility of its eventual results being translatable into computer language. The "producers" and users of knowledge must now, and will have to, possess the means of translating into these languages whatever they want to invent or learn. Research on translating machines is already well advanced. Along with the hegemony of computers comes a certain logic, and therefore a certain set of prescriptions determining which statements are accepted as "knowledge" statements.

We may thus expect a thorough exteriorisation of knowledge with respect to the "knower," at whatever point he or she may occupy in the knowledge process. The old principle that the acquisition of knowledge is indissociable from the training (*Bildung*) of minds, or even of individuals, is becoming obsolete and will become ever more so. The relationships of the suppliers and users of knowledge to the knowledge they supply and use is now tending, and will increasingly tend, to assume the form already taken by the relationship of commodity producers and consumers to the commodities they produce and consume—that is, the form of value. Knowledge is and will be produced in order to be sold, it is and will be consumed in order to be valorised in a new production: in both cases, the goal is exchange.

Knowledge ceases to be an end in itself; it loses its "use-value."

It is widely accepted that knowledge has become the principal force of production over the last few decades; this has already had a noticeable effect on the composition of the work force of the most highly developed countries and constitutes the major bottleneck for the developing countries. In the postindustrial and postmodern age, science will maintain and no doubt strengthen its preeminence in the arsenal of productive capacities of the nation-states. Indeed, this situation is one of the reasons leading to the conclusion that the gap between developed and developing countries will grow ever wider in the future.

But this aspect of the problem should not be allowed to overshadow the other, which is complementary to it. Knowledge in the form of an informational commodity indispensable to productive power is already, and will continue to be, a major—perhaps the major—stake in the worldwide competition for power. It is conceivable that the nation-states will one day fight for control of information, just as they battled in the past for control over territory, and afterwards for control of access to and exploitation of raw materials and cheap labor. A new field is opened for industrial and commercial strategies on the one hand, and political and military strategies on the other.

However, the perspective I have outlined above is not as simple as I have made it appear. For the merchantilisation of knowledge is bound to affect the privilege the nation-states have enjoyed, and still enjoy, with respect to the production and distribution of learning. The notion that learning falls within the purview of the State, as the brain or mind of society, will become more and more outdated with the increasing strength of the opposing principle, according to which society exists and progresses only if the messages circulating within it are rich in information and easy to decode. The ideology of communicational "transparency," which goes hand in hand with the commercialisation of knowledge, will begin to perceive the State as a factor of opacity and "noise." It is from this point of view that the problem of the relationship between economic and State powers threatens to arise with a new urgency.

Already in the last few decades, economic powers have reached the point of imperilling the stability of the state through new forms of the circulation of capital that go by the generic name of *multi-national corporations*. These new forms of circulation imply that investment decisions have, at least in part, passed beyond the control of the nation-states. The question threatens to become even more thorny with the development of computer technology and telematics. Suppose, for example, that a firm such as IBM is authorised to occupy a belt in the earth's orbital field and launch communications satellites or satellites housing data banks. Who will have access to them? Who will determine which channels or data are forbidden? The State? Or will the State simply be one user among others? New legal issues will be raised, and with them the question: "who will know?"

Transformation in the nature of knowledge, then, could well have repercussions on the existing public powers, forcing them to reconsider their relations (both *de jure* and *de facto*) with the large corporations and, more generally, with civil society. The reopening of the world market, a return to vigorous economic competition, the breakdown of the hegemony of American capitalism, the decline of the socialist alternative, a probable opening of the Chinese market, these and many other factors are already, at the end of the 1970s, preparing States for a serious reappraisal of the role they have been accustomed to playing since the 1930s: that of guiding, or even directing, investments. In this light, the new technologies can only increase the urgency of such a re-examination, since they make the information used in decision making (and therefore the means of control) even more mobile and subject to piracy.

It is not hard to visualise learning circulating along the same lines as money, instead of for its "educational" value or political (administrative, diplomatic, military) importance; the pertinent distinction would no longer be between knowledge and ignorance, but rather, as is the case with money, between "payment knowledge" and "investment knowledge"—in other words, between units of knowledge exchanged in a daily maintenance framework (the reconstitution of the work force, "survival") versus funds of knowledge dedicated to optimising the performance of a project.

If this were the case, communicational transparency would be similar to liberalism. Liberalism does not preclude an organisation of the flow of money in which some channels are used in decision making while others are only good for the payment of debts. One could similarly imagine flows of knowledge travelling along identical channels of identical nature, some of which would be reserved for the "decision makers," while the others would be used to repay each person's perpetual debt with respect to the social bond.

Author Index

Adams, M., 158
Alcoff, L., 216
Anthony, S. B., 142
Anyon, J., 254-269
Apple, M., 41-42, 154, 156
Apple, M. W., 269
Aristotle, 44-45
Arnot, 179
Aronowitz, S., 2n2, 156
Augustine (Saint), xivn6

Bailey, N. J., 235n10
Baldwin, J., 198-204
Banks, J. A., 228n1, 234n9, 241n16
Baron, G., 97
Barrett, M., 156, 156n2
Barton, L., 154, 156
Bateson, G., 293
Bernstein, B., Ch. 268
Bourdieu, P., Ch. 268
Bowers, C. A., 289-296
Bowles, S., 256n1
Bradford, W., 174-180
Bridenthal, R., 159
Brodkey, L., 211
Bruner, 251

Cairns, H., xiiin3
Callahan, R., 92
Cherryholmes, C., 211
Chodorow, N., 158
Clark, W. C., 291
Clarricoates, K., 154
Cochran-Smith, M., 231n5
Connell, R. W., 154, 156
Coser, R., 158
Cottell, P. H., Jr., 168-171
Counts, G. S., 7-10, 76-80
Coward, R., 156n2
Coward, R., 159

Dale, R., 156
Darling-Hammond, L., 161
de Beauvoir, S., 108n1
De Lauretis, T., 216, 217, 219
Deleuze, G., 213
Delphy, C., 157n5
Densmore, K., 157
Descartes, R., 99-101, 292
Dewey, J., 1n1, 22-30, 40, 42, 44, 238n13
Dinnerstein, D., 158
Dreeben, R., 161
Du Bois, W. E. B., 192-196

Eisenstein, Z., 155, 160
Ellsworth, E., 214, 222
Engelbart, D., 286-288
Epstein, 176

Ferguson, A., 159
Fine, M., 211, 221, 230n3
Flax, J., 156
Foucault, M., 210, 215
Franklin, S., 269
Freire, P., 106-117, 238n12, 242n17, 242n18
Fromm, E., 110n4-6

Gage, M. J., 142
Gardner, H., 43
Gardner, J., 40, 44
Gay, G., 242n19
Genovese, E., 161
Gilligan, C., 158
Gintis, H., 256n1
Giroux, H., 2n3, 159, 210-225, 211, 212, 216, 231n6
Giroux, H. A., 239n14
Goodman, P., 88-90
Grubb, W., 160
Grumet, M., 156
Guattari, E., 213

Habermas, J., 157
Haldane, E. S., 100
Hamilton, E., xiiin3
Hartmann, H., 156

Hartsock, N., 160
Haug, F., 221
Havel, V., 12-17
Havelock, E., 294
Heidegger, M., 96
Henry, J., 92-100
Hicks, E., 210
hooks, b., 272-281
Howe, F., 158
Husserl, E., 114n10

Illich, I., 120-133, 159

Jackson, D., 176
Jacobson, L., 248-251
Jaggar, A., 155, 159
JanMohamed, A., 217, 222, 223
Jefferson, T., 53-55
Johnson, L., 156

Kaplan, C., 213, 219
King, N., 269
Kozol, J., 230n4
Kramer, S. N., xiiin2
Kress, 177
Kuhn, A., 155, 159

Laclau, E., 214
Lather, P., 154-162, 156, 158n6
Lawrence, S. M., 232n8
Lazerson, M., 160
Leopold, A., 295
Lightfoot, S. L., 158, 161
Lloyd, D., 217, 222, 223
Loewen, J. W., 241n15
Lyotard, J-F., 299-302

Macdonald, M., 154
MacKinnon, C., 155, 160
Mahony, P., 155
Mann, H., 62-73
Marks, 157n5
Martin, J., 157
Martin, J. R., 41, 43
Mattingly, P., 158
Mazza, K., 155
McCall, A., 158n6
McCourt, F., 178
McLaren, P., 2n3
McRobbie, A., 154
Miller, J., 158
Mouffe, C., 214-215

Niebuhr, R., 111n7
Nieto, S., 228-244
Noble, C., 174-180
Noddings, N., 39-48, 40, 46

O'Brien, M., 154, 155, 156, 156n3, 159, 160
Ong, W., 294
Ortner, S., 154n1

Passeron, J., 268–269
Paul, A., 146
Phillips, M., 280-281
Pinar, W., 156
Plato, xiiin1
Pocock, 217
Pogrebin, L. C., 161
Pohan, C. A., 235n10

Quintilian, xivn5

Ramsey, P. G., 237n11
Rich, A., 161
Rist, R. C., 269
Rokoff, G., 158
Rosenthal, R., 248-251, 250, 251
Ross, A., 214
Ross, G. R. T., 100
Roszak, T., 294
Rousseau, J. J., 40-42
Rowbotham, S., 155, 156, 158
Rush, B., 58-60

Said, E., 211
Sargent, L., 155
Sartre, J-P., 110n2, 113n8114
Scholes, R., 211-212
Schubert, W., 156
Sears, J., 156, 157n4
Shor, I. 242n21
Simon, R., 211, 212
Singer, B. L., 169n1
Sleeter, C. E., 242n20
Smith, B. J., 216-217
Smith, D., 155
Smith, I. D., 269
Sokoloff, N., 156, 158, 161
Stanton, E. C., 142-144

Tabakin, G., 157
Tatum, B. D., 231n7, 232n8
Taubman, P., 156
Thomson, J. A. K., xiiin4

Walker, S., 154
Washington, B. T., 188-190
Weinberg, M., 229n2
Weis, L., 156
Whitehead, H., 154n1
Whitty, G., 160-161
Wollstonecraft, M., 138-140
Wolpe, A. M., 155, 159

Zaret, E., 159, 161

Subject Index

Active model of education, 105. *See also* Banking model of education
Adult education, banking model approach to, 109
Affluent professional school:
- classroom control, 264–265
- defined, 255–256
- independent creative activity, 262
- language arts, 263–264
- math, 262–263
- science, 264
- social studies, 263

Agrarianism, 66
AIDS/HIV, 171
Alabama, General Assembly of Commonwealth of, 185
"All children can learn," 40–41
American democracy, 36
American Historical Association, 9
American society, transition of, 7–10
Analytical intellectual power, developing, 265
"And women, of course" phenomenon, 155, 157
Anthropic Cosmological Principle, 16
Anthropocentrism, 15
Antidiscrimination, 229. *See also* Antiracist education
Anti-educationalism, 99
Antiracist education, 227–233
Anti-SWOT culture, 171–175, 179–180
Anyon, Jean, 253
Apology (Plato), xiii
Aquineas, Thomas, xiv
Aristotle, xiii-xiv
Art gallery, 55
Attendance, 84, 89. *See also* Compulsory education
Augmenting human intellect, defined, 288
Augustine (Saint), xiv
Authentic liberation, 111–112
Authentic thinking, 110

BAGLY. *See* Boston Alliance of Gay and Lesbian Youth (BAGLY)
Baldwin, James, 197
Banking model of education:
- approach to adult education, 109
- attitudes and practices, 107–108
- cognition and, 112–113
- consciousness, 109–110, 112–116
- defined, 106–107
- domination and, 111–112
- humanism and, 109
- oppression and, 108–111
- problem-posing education, 112–117
- students' creative power and, 108

Basic education, 227, 233–235
Behavior, differences between boys and girls, 178
Biased education, 235–236
Biophily, 110
Border pedagogy:
- as counter-memory, 213–218
- defined, 209–210
- educational theory and popular culture, 212
- politics of differences between societal groups and, 218–223
- role of teachers and, 220–223
- textual power and, 211–212

Boston Alliance of Gay and Lesbian Youth (BAGLY), 169
Boundaries, cross class, 271–281
Bowers, C. A., 284, 289
Boys:
- Anti-SWOT culture and, 174–175
- behavior of, 178
- underachievement of, 173–180

Brown, John, 230

Cambridge Rindge and Latin High School, 170
Canon, and multicultural education, 233–234

Capitalism, 155, 157–158
Caring, human, 43–46. *See also* Friendship
Castro, Fidel, 204
Catholic schools, 81
Certification, 124, 127, 132. *See also* Deschooling schooled society
Children:
- relations with intimate others, 43
- traditional male and female roles in care of, 42–43
- what we want for, 39–40
- *See also* Boys

Child's nature, 27–29
Cicero, 43
Citizenship, as education objective, 34–36
Civil rights, xiv
Class. *See* Social class
Class boundaries, crossing, 271–281
Classroom behaviors, rewards for, 254
Classroom control (management):
- in affluent professional school, 264–265
- in executive elite schools, 267–268
- in middle-class schools, 261–262
- in working-class schools, 259
- underachievement of boys and, 180

Class stratification, 271–281
Co-education, 137–140
Cognition, 112–113
Collectivism, 8–9
Colonial hegemony, 14
Common schools, 61–63, 71
Commonwealth of Virginia, General Assembly of, 185
Communication, 110. *See also* Technology
Communism, 14, 96–97, 99, 104
Community, duty of, in education, 29
Community life, 25
Competitiveness, national, 42
Compulsory education, 81–85
- alternatives to, 87–90
- attendance, 89
- children in marginal farms, 89–90
- decentralize urban school, 89
- dispense with school building, 89
- laws concerning, 81
- unlicensed adults as educators, 89

Computers:
- contribution to ecological crisis, 289–296
- environment and education, 294–295
- moral poverty of Information Age, 295–296
- weakness in, 292

Concealment, 93
Conceptual mapping processes, 293
Consciousness, 112–116
Constructive activities, 26
Costs of education, 139
Cottell, Paul H., Jr., 167
Counter-memory, 213–218
Counts, George S., 3, 5–6, 49, 75
Critical pedagogy, 227–229, 240–243
Cultural codes, 209–211
Cultural conflicts, 14–15
Cultural Dimensions of Educational Computing: Understanding the Non-Neutrality of Technology, The (Bowers), 289
Culture:
- anti-SWOT, 171–175, 179–180
- changes in, since 1980s, 3
- popular, 212
- *See also* Ecological/cultural crisis; Multicultural education

Curriculum, 26
- based on social class, 253–268
- centered on human caring, 43–46
- co-education and, 139–140
- multicultural, 229–231, 235–237
- popular culture in official, 212
- sanitizing, 230
- social rank and, 124–125
- standardization of, 40–42
- students invisible to, 235
- underachievement of boys and, 179
- *See also* Deschooling schooled society

Custom, 216–217
Cybernetics, 300

Declaration of Independence, 17, 141–142
Democracy, 15, 214–216. *See also* Social justice
Dependence, and vulnerability in education, 93–94
Descartes, Rene, 99–101
Deschooling schooled society:
- cost of teaching, 126
- defined, 120–121, 133
- educational "entitlements" and tuition grants, 127–128
- educational matchmaking, 129–132
- equal educational opportunity, 123–124
- institutionalization of values and, 120–121
- law forbidding discrimination, 124–125
- learning casually, 125
- modernization of poverty, 121–122
- skill learning, 126–128
- skill teachers, 126–127, 129
- teaching and planned programmed instruction, 125–126

Deschooling Society (Illich), 119–133
Determinative memory, 293
Dewey, John, xiv

Directions, following, 259–260
Discrimination:
based on sexual orientation, 167–171
classroom discussion about, 231–233
Equal Rights Amendment (ERA), 145–146
sexual, against students and school employees, 147–151
See also Gender; Race; Social class
Diversity:
inservice education and, 232
multicultural education and, 227
teaching, 231–233
"Domesticating education," 242
Domination, banking method of, 111–113
Douglas, William O., 122
Du Bois, W. E. B., 187

Ecological crisis, how computers contribute to, 289–296
Ecological/cultural crisis, 291–292
Economics, as education objective, 35
Education, aims of, 19–48
Education: Intellectual, Moral and Physical (Spencer), 19
Educational credit, 126
Educational "entitlements," 127–128
Educational equality. *See* Gender; Race; Sexuality and education; Social class
Educational matchmaking, 129–131
Educational passport ("edu-credit card"), 126
Educational process, 22–24, 28
Educational psychology, 33–36
Educational self-fulfilling prophecy, 249
Educational theory, 33–36, 212
Educational thought, xiii
Educational workers:
Equal Rights Amendment (ERA), 145–146
role of, in transition of American society, 8–9
underachievement of boys and, 179–180
Education and the Cult of Efficiency (Callahan), 92
Education for All Handicapped Children Act (Law 84–142), 181
Education for domestication, 242
Education for liberation, 242
Education of slaves, laws prohibiting, 183–185
"Edu-credit card," 126
Elementary education, *vs.* secondary education, 51, 53–55
Elementary Science Study (ESS), 264
Emotions, role of, in education, 29
Employment, changes in field of, 176–178, xiv
Engelbart, Douglas, xiv
Enlightenment Project, modernism as, 1
Environment, computers and, 294–295
Episcopal Church, 170
Equal educational opportunity, 123–124
Equalizer of classes, education as, 65–66
Equal Rights Amendment (ERA), 145–146
Equal schooling, 123–124
ERA. *See* Equal Rights Amendment (ERA)
Erasmus, Desiderius, xiv
ESS. *See* Elementary Science Study (ESS)
Ethical character, as education objective, 34, 36
Ethics, The (Aristotle), xiii
Examinations, 25
Executive elite school:
classroom control, 267–268
defined, 256
developing analytical powers, 265
language arts, 266–267
math, 265–266
social studies, 266

Families:
changes in, underachievement of boys and, 178
multicultural education and, 240
Farm-work, 89–90
Fear, 104
Fear of failure, 94–95
Fear of naming, 230
Feminism:
feminization of poverty, 160
relationship between, and Marxism, 155–157
women in public school teaching, 153–162
See also Gender
Ferreira, Al, 170
Fourteenth Amendment, 145
Franklin, Virginia, 96, 98–99
Freire, Paulo, 82, 105, 129
Friendship:
gender differences in, 46
love and, 43–46
moral requirement and, 45–46
Fundamental processes, command of, 34

Gaia Hypothesis, 16
Gay/Straight Alliance (GSA), 170
Gender:
interaction of, and class, 156–157
relationship between, and teaching profession, 153–162
role of, in shaping schools, 153–162
traditional roles of men and women, 42–43

See also Discrimination; Sexual orientation
Gender identity, 169. *See also* Sexual orientation
General Assembly of the Commonwealth of Alabama, 185
General Assembly of the Commonwealth of Virginia, 185
General Assembly of the State of North Carolina, 184–185
General Education Bills of 1779 and 1817, 51
General intelligence, 63–73
Genetic disposition, underachievement of boys and, 175–176
Geography, 35
Girls, behavior of, 178
Giroux, Henry, 209, 231
Goodman, Paul, 82, 87
Grading, 25
GSA. *See* Gay/Straight Alliance (GSA)
Guilt, antiracism and, 232–233

Hall, Stuart, 2
Handicapped children, 205–207
Harris, Barbara C. (Reverend), 170
Havel, Vaclav, 3, 11
Health, as education objective, 34
Heidegger, Martin, 96
Henry, Jules, 91
Herbart, Johann Freidrich, xiv
Heroes, "tailoring," 230
HEW pollution, 123
Hidden curriculum, 253–268
History, 35, xiii
Home-membership, as education objective, 34
hooks, bell, 271
Human caring, curriculum centered on, 43–44
Humanization, 111, 116

IDEA. *See* Individuals with Disabilities Education Act (IDEA)
Illich, Ivan, 82, 119
Image, role of, in education, 28
Individualism, 8–9
Individuals with Disabilities Education Act (IDEA), 205
"Industrial Education for the Negro," 187–190
Industry, education and, 34–35, 103–104
Inflated images, and vulnerability in education, 93–94
Information Age, moral poverty of, 295–296
Inservice education, and diversity, 232
Institutionalization of values, 120–121
Institutio oratoria, xiv
Interests, role of, in education, 28
Interpersonal self-fulfilling prophecies, 248

Jefferson, Thomas, 49, 51
Jencks, Christopher, 127

King, Martin Luther, Jr., 230
Kirkpatrick, William Heard, 5

Labels, 169–170
Laboratory School, 21
Language arts:
  in affluent professional school, 263–264
  in executive elite schools, 266–267
  in middle-class schools, 260
  in working-class schools, 258
Language study, 27
Let Them Eat Data (Bowers), 289
Liberal education, 41, 128
Liberalism, 302
Libertarian education, 17
Life cycles, 43
Lincoln, Abraham, 230
Literature, 26–27, 35
Love, friendship and, 43–46
Loyalty, 45
Lyotard, Jean-François, 3, 284, 297

"Managing Planet Earth," 290–291
Mann, Horace, 49, 61, xiv
Marx, Karl, 133
Marxism, relationship between feminism and, 155–157, 161–162
Massachusetts Compulsory School Law, 83–85
Matchmaking, educational, 129–131
Materialist-feminism, 157, 159, 162
Math:
  in affluent professional school, 262–263
  in executive elite schools, 265–266
  in middle-class schools, 260
  in working-class schools, 256–257
Memory. *See* Counter-memory
Memory-work, 221–222
Men, traditional roles of, 42–43. *See also* Patriarchal hegemony; Women
Middle-class schools:
  classroom control, 261–262
  defined, 255
  following directions, 259–260
  language arts, 260
  science, 261

social studies, 260–261
textbook, 260–261
Minorities, xiv
"Mirror images," critical pedagogy and multicultural education as, 242
Modern age, 12
Modernism, 1
Modernization of poverty, 121–122
Modern technological civilization, 13
Monocultural education, 234, 241. *See also* Multicultural education
Moral life, 47
Morris, Gerry, 127
Mott, Lucretia, 141
Multicultural education:
as basic education, 233–235
as critical pedagogy, 240–243
as education for social justice, 238–239
as process, 239–240
basic characteristics of, 228–243
curriculum, 229–231, 235–237
defined, 228–229
importance to all students, 235–239
inclusiveness of, 236
monocultural education as alternative to, 234
pervasiveness of, 237–238
Multicultural era, 13
Multiculturalism:
American culture and, 181
border pedagogy and, 209–223
Multicultural materials, 229
Multiple intelligences, 43–44

Narrative education, 106–107
National competitiveness, 42
National Education Association, education principles of, 31–36
Nature study, 26
Necrophily, 110–111
Negro. *See* Race
Negro Problem, The (Du Bois), 191
Nicomachean Ethics, 44
Nieto, Sonia, 227
Noddings, Nel, 37
North Carolina, General Assembly of the State of, 184–185

Official curriculum, 212
Oppression, banking model of education and, 108–111, 116. *See also* Feminism

Parents, as agents of vulnerability, 94
Passive model of education, 106. *See also* Banking model of education
Patriarchal hegemony, 156
Paul, Alice, 145
Pedagogy. *See* Critical pedagogy
Pedagogy of the Oppressed (Freire), 105
Philosophy of education, xiii
Pierce v. the Society of Sisters, 81
Plato, xiii
Political education, 67–73
Popular culture, 212
Positive alternative vision, 216
Post-fordism, 2–3
Postmodern Condition, The (Lyotard), 297
Postmodernism:
border pedagogy in a age of, 209–223
modernist and scientific assumptions *vs.*, 2–3
need for transcendence in, 11–17
Poverty:
feminization of, 160
intellectual education as means of removing, 63–67
modernization of, 121–122
Primary schools, increasing number of, 180
Problem-posing education, 112–117
Progressive education, 75–80
Project 10 East, 170
Psychological necessity, 23
Public education:
Thomas Jefferson's ideas on, 53–55
views of Horace Mann, 61–73
Public library, 55
Pygmalion Effect, 247–251

Quadrivium, xiv
Quintero, Angel, 127
Quintillian, xiv

Race:
American culture and, 181
"A Talk to Teachers," 197–204
"Industrial Education for the Negro," 187–190
laws prohibiting education of slaves, 183–185
"talented tenth," 191–196
See also Discrimination
Racism, 231. *See also* Multicultural education; Race
Radical democracy, language of, 216
Recess, 139
Recreational activities, as education objective, 36
Reductionism, 160–161
Relations with intimate others, 43–44
Religion, appropriateness of, in schools, 54

Remembrance, 216–218. *See also* Counter-memory
Report No. 12 of the Massachusetts School Board, 61–73
Republic, The (Plato), xiii
Reputation, 93
Role models, for boys, 178
Roles, traditional male and female, 42–43
Roman Catholic Church, 168–170
Rousseau, Jean-Jacques, xiv
Ruch, Benjamin, xiv, 49, 57

Sanitizing curriculum, 230
School administrators:
- underachievement of boys and, 179–180
- vulnerability of, 92
- *See also* Educational workers

"Schooled" society, financing, 122–123. *See also* Deschooling schooled society
School reform, multicultural education and, 227–243
Schools:
- affluent professional, 255–256, 262–265
- changes in population of, 33
- defined, 24–25
- discipline of, 25
- executive elite, 255, 265–268
- middle-class, 255, 259–262
- sexual discrimination in, 147–151
- social progress and, 29–30
- working-class, 255, 258–259

Science:
- Anthropic Cosmological Principle and, 16
- in affluent professional school, 264
- in middle-class schools, 261
- in working-class schools, 258
- nature study and, 26
- social life and, 27

Science Research Associates (SRA), 262
Scientific models of education, 1
Secondary education:
- cardinal principles of, 31–36
- changes in educational theory, 33–36
- changes in school population, 33
- changes in society, 32–33
- elementary education *vs.*, 51, 53–55

Secondary-school population, 33
Self-assertion, 95–96
Self-transcendence, 16–17
Separatism, 222
Sexual discrimination:
- against students and school employees, 147–151
- Equal Rights Amendment (ERA), 145–146

Sexual orientation, 135, 167–171
Skill learning, 126–128
Skill teachers, 126–127, 129
Skinner, B. F., 1, 283
Slaves:
- classroom discussion about, 233
- laws prohibiting education of, 183–185

Social changes and progress, 28–29, 39
Social class:
- co-education and, 139
- defined, 245
- education and, 245–281
- education as great equalizer, 65–66
- hidden curriculum and, 253–268
- interaction of gender and, 156–157
- *See also* Class boundaries, crossing

Social consciousness, 29
Social heritage, 26
Social justice, 227, 238–239
Social life, 26
Social rank, curriculum used to assign, 124–125
Social studies, 35
- in affluent professional school, 263
- in executive elite schools, 266
- in middle-class schools, 260–262
- in working-class schools, 258–259

Society, changes in, 32–33, 176–178
Sociological necessity, 23–24
Socrates, xiii
Socratic Method, xiii
Solidarity, 110
Souls of Black Folk, The (Du Bois), 191
Special needs, students with, 205–207
Spencer, Herbert, 19
SRA. *See* Science Research Associates (SRA)
Standardization of curriculum, 40–41
Stanton, Elizabeth Cady, 141
States, role of, in education of children, 62–73
Subject-matter, of education, 26–27
Symbols, role in education of, 28

"Tailoring," 230
Teachers:
- as agents of vulnerability, 94
- as social servants, 30
- border pedagogy and, 220–223
- expectations of pupils' intellectual competence, 249–251
- relationship between feminism and Marxism, 155–162
- skill, 126–127, 129
- social change and, 98–99
- teaching diversity and, 231–233
- vulnerability system and, 96–98

Teaching:
  cost of, 126
  from texts, 211–212
  gender and reshaping public school, 153–162
Technology, 283–309
  augmenting human intellect, 285–288
  changes in, xiv
  how computers contribute to ecological crisis, 289–296
  impact on knowledge, 297–302
  information, 2
  modern technological civilization, 13
  school responses to changes in, 39
  See also Communication
Text:
  in middle-class schools, 260–261
  teaching from, 211–212
Textuality, 211–212
Thorndike, Edward, 1
Title IX, 147–151
Transcendence, need for, in postmodern world, 12–17
Transition, of American society, 7–10
Trivium, xiv
Tuition grants, 127–128
Turner, Nat, 230
Tuskegee Institute, 189

Unconditional friendship, 45
Underachievement, of boys in schools, 173–180
Uniforms, 139
United States Constitution, 145
University of Virginia, 51
U.S. Foreign Service Institute (FSI) Spanish manual, 127

Vocation, as education objective, 34–35
Vulnerability system, 92–104

Wallace, George (Governor), 203
War, education and, 103–104
Washington, Booker T., 187, 191
William and Mary college, 51, 53
Wisconsin v. Yoder, 81
Wollstonecraft, Mary, 137
Women:
  extension of civil rights to, xiv
  in public school teaching, 153–162
  rights of, 138–140
  subordination to men, 155, 157–158, 161
  suffrage of, 142–144
  traditional roles of, 42–43
Women's suffrage, 142–144
Work ethics, underachievement of boys and, 177–178
Working-class schools:
  classroom control, 259
  defined, 255
  language arts, 258
  math, 257
  science, 258
  social studies, 258–259
Worldwatch Institute, 294–295
Worthy of home-membership, as education objective, 34
Worthy use of leisure, as education objective, 34, 36

About the Editor

Eugene F. Provenzo, Jr. is Professor in the School of Education at the University of Miami. The author of a wide range of books on education, culture, teaching, and technology, he is the editor of the Sage *Encyclopedia of the Social and Cultural Foundations of Education* (forthcoming) and the author of *Critical Literacy: What Every American Ought to Know* (2005). He lives in Staunton, Virginia, and Coral Gables, Florida.